Christianity and Animism in Taiwan

Chinese Materials and Research Aids Service Center, Inc.
Occasional Series No. 40

Christianity and Animism
in
Taiwan

Alan Frederick Gates

CHINESE MATERIALS CENTER
San Francisco
1979

ISBN 0-89644-573-9

PRINTED IN THE REPUBLIC OF CHINA

This book

is dedicated to

two special ladies

my wife

Sharon Lee Gates

and my mother

Hilda Maude Gates

Contents

Illustrations

Introduction

AIMS AND PURPOSES

THIS STUDY is an effort to develop a more adequate approach to Taiwanese animism as found within the folk religion of the people. It rests upon the assumption that animism in Taiwan has never been effectively encountered by Christianity and hence continues in its current virile form as a major roadblock to the growth of the Church.

The first five chapters constitute a functional-historical study of animism in China and Taiwan. Chapter 6 examines faulty missionary attitudes toward animism. The last two chapters attempt to set forth a *kerygma* drawn from Old and New Testaments. This *kerygma* is set within a theological framework of "the powers" as found in the writings of Paul. The purpose of the study is to define a more positive approach which missionaries and nationals might pursue in their evangelistic outreach among devotees of the folk religion.

I have chosen to examine animism in what appears to me as its four determinative periods in Chinese history and

1

culture. First, prehistory through Shang (to ca. 1123 B.C.); second, the Classical period (Chou through Early Han, 1123 B.C.-A.D. 9); third, the T'ang dynasty (A.D. 618-907); and fourth, contemporary Taiwan.*

The factors which have prompted the writing of this book are twofold: first, the realization that the Church in Taiwan is still a slow-growing, alien institution within Chinese society; second, the fact of the current resurgence of folk religion in Taiwan, especially during a time when the country is experiencing urbanization and technological development. These two phenomena suggest the possibility that slow church growth and the continuing presence of animism are related. I realize, of course, that the presence of animism, per se, does not necessarily constitute a barrier to church growth in every society of Asia. Indeed, animistic tribal peoples have often proven most receptive to the Gospel. The Bataks of Indonesia and the tribal peoples of Taiwan are two cases in point. However, Taiwanese animism, which includes a mixture of Confucianism, Buddhism and religious Taoism with its strongly developed polytheism, has proven to be a rather resistant opponent of Christianity. Obviously, I would not suggest that animism is the only factor that has impeded the growth of the Church in Taiwan. However, it appears to be a very potent element which most missionaries and scholars have tended to overlook. This omission has, as we shall see, been a factor of no small consequence for the Church.

My hope is that this study will stir up an awareness of the strong influence which animism continues to exert upon the lives and hearts of the Taiwanese, thus hindering their receptivity to the Gospel, at least in the form in which it has been traditionally presented.

*Dynasty dates unless otherwise indicated are taken from Thompson's *Chinese Religion: An Introduction* (1969).

I am hopeful, also, that this study may be used of God to bring more keenly to the awareness of national Christians and foreign missionaries the fact that animism comes within the circle of their biblical concern. In fact, animism seems to fall within the purview of all that the Bible has to say of "the powers." May God use this to cause one and all to take more seriously the words of Paul the Apostle in Ephesians 6:12: "For we wrestle not against flesh and blood but against principalities and powers. . . ."

I have been able to gather only a limited amount of data on current animism in urban areas. One is tempted to conclude that it must be a passing phenomenon unable to withstand the enlightening effects of scientific knowledge, and yet I seriously question this. Animism has long since demonstrated its tenacity in many cultures involved in rapid social change. Hence I feel any judgment that animism is a dying phenomenon in urbanizing societies is premature in the extreme. If the current mushrooming of occult movements in Southern California is any indication of the fruits of a secularized society, one should conclude that animism will be with us for many years to come. In any event, the comment of a Taiwanese national, an authority on Taiwanese folk religion, is most interesting. In a letter to the author he writes: "I don't think there are any differences in folk religion practices, whether ancestor worship, shamanism, home or temple worship, between rural and urban Taiwan" (Kuo, 1970b).

DATA SOURCES AND METHODOLOGY

This study is based largely upon library research. I have drawn most heavily upon sources available at the libraries of U.C.L.A., Fuller Theological Seminary, and to a lesser degree Claremont College. I have also utilized materials from the public library in Altadena. Other data are from Taiwan and include books, periodicals, correspondence, and personal observation.

Judging the relative value of materials used, I have given most weight to primary sources, especially those based upon personal research and observation. The studies done by Gallin, Diamond, and Ch'iu would represent this kind of data.

Secondary sources have been used in cases where primary data has not been available. I have sought to be as exhaustive as time has permitted in examining those writings of men of authority and experience which pertain to the subjects under consideration.

Wherever I have consulted Chinese historical documents, I have relied on recognized translations of their texts. Unfortunately, my ability in Chinese is limited to contemporary usage. In self defense, I can only plead that reading classical Chinese is a skill possessed by few foreigners and not many Chinese.

Concerning the use of the Chinese script, the reader will find the Chinese character written together with the romanization only at the first occurrence of that word in the text. Thereafter, I use only the romanized or English equivalents. For example, the term *wu* will be found in its first occurrence in the text accompanied by the character 巫. Thereafter, however, only the term *wu* or its English equivalent "medium" will be used.

Greek words have been romanized to facilitate reading by those who may be unfamiliar with the Greek script.

THEORETICAL FRAMEWORK

For a theoretical frame of reference from which to examine the historical dimension of animism in China, I have chosen what Nadel terms the "diachronic-synchronic" approach. Synchronic is from the Greek *sunchronos*, meaning "with time." According to Nadel, this approach would be "concerned with a (roughly) simultaneous as well as a continuous state of affairs assumed to be uniformly repetitive within an (undefined) time span" (1951:100): simply stated, a historical picture at a point in history. This could be illustrated with a bar graph representing the size and composition of a given religious denomination in 1970 but giving no indication as to trends such as growth or shrinkage. Diachronic, on the other hand, comes from the Greek *diachronos*, meaning "across" or "through time." Nadel defines diachronic as "concerned with broadly separated time phases." Again, using the graph as an illustration, we would find a diachronic picture in a line graph which plotted the growth of a given denomination, say from 1900 to 1950. To summarize: synchronic means viewing social and religious phenomena as though they were static; diachronic means looking at situations which offer evidence of change over long periods of time. In this study, we will look at animism in China and Taiwan both from the synchronic and diachronic points of view.

In order to discover and appreciate the importance of animism in Chinese society, I have used the functionalist approach as developed by Malinowsky and Radcliffe-Brown. The functionalist is interested in the function of cultural elements within society and operates on the premise that culture traits are related to each other as the members of a living body. Malinowsky and Radcliffe-Brown have developed the concept of function to include groupings of cultural elements into institutions, such as marriage, rites of passage, and ancestor worship. They liken them to configurations which not only manifest a structural identity but also tend to permeate the whole of a given society.

DEFINITIONS

Before proceeding further, it is necessary that certain important terms and concepts be defined, particularly since they will be used extensively throughout this study.

Animism. The term "animism" means the belief in spirit beings. This was the meaning given by Tylor. When he coined the term in 1873 it embraced primitive man's conviction that everything was endowed with "soul." According to Tylor, this universal belief accounted for most forms of "primitive" religion, including ancestor cults and the worship of various gods. A missionary anthropologist quotes Tylor's definition of animism: "He [Tylor] conceived the theory of animism as dividing into two great dogmas: 'first concerning souls of individual creatures capable of continued existence after the death or destruction of the body; second concerning other spirits, upward to the rank of powerful deities' " (Hackett 1969:432). Inherent within this and Morgan's subsequent use of the term was the idea that animism represented the most primitive form of religion, the lowest rung on the evolutionary ladder. Keesing's quotation from Tylor makes this clear: "[By] simply placing [the European] nations at one end of the social series and savage tribes at the other, ... ethnographers are able to set up at least a rough scale of civilization" (1958: 337). He thus conceived of animism as the first step in an ascending order of development leading through polydemonism, polytheism, and ultimately to monotheism. With subsequent development of anthropological studies,

scholarly reaction mounted against the evolutionary overtones connected with this term. This resulted in its gradual
disuse. It must be admitted, however, that no satisfactory
substitute has been found. I agree, therefore, with Keesing
that the term shorn of its "evolutionary mumbo jumbo"
can still be used as a broad classification of certain types
of beliefs and practices (1958:337).

J. Warneck so uses the term in his description of Batak
animism. Writes Warneck: "The realities of animistic heathenism today are polytheism and worship of spirits, together with the fear and magic which accompany them"
(1954:36).

W. Harris and E. Parrinder include polytheism under
the general umbrella word "animism" but suggest that
polytheism somehow represents a stage which is "beyond
simple animism" (1960:15). This will be a relevant question
for China and Taiwan, where polytheism is strong.

Harris and Parrinder further elucidate the concept of
animism: "From the beginning there is an attempt by man
to place himself in the right relationship to unseen powers,
to deprecate their hostility and to secure their good will.
With deliberate acts of worship, we come to a personal
approach to the spirits and often they are regarded as gods"
(1960:14).

Religion. The word "religion" in this dissertation will be
used as defined by Addison: "Religion at the animistic
level of the Chinese involves the basic beliefs in spirits
beyond the human control with whom men seek to establish
favorable relations" (1925:54). While this is a useful
definition, it needs improvement at one point: the words
"beyond human control" are misleading. It seems obvious
to me that in some sense the spirits are controlled by
various ritual techniques devised by the religious experts.
I would suggest then either the deletion of "beyond human

control" or the addition of "in some respects." Thus, the
phrase in question would read "Beliefs in spirits which in
some respects are beyond human control." This suggests
the idea that while the spirits do exist independent of
man and are generally superior in power, under certain
circumstances they can be influenced if not controlled by
man.

Another useful definition is given by C. K. Yang, who
describes religion as "Man's interrelations with the super-
human and supernatural powers" (1957:269).

Church Growth. A term which is used occasionally in
this study is "church growth." This expression has come to be
associated with the work of Donald A. McGavran and his
team of co-workers at the School of World Mission and
Institute of Church Growth of Fuller Theological Seminary.
Its basic elements are expounded in detail in such works
as *Bridges of God* (1955) and *How Churches Grow* (1957).
Theological and anthropological dimensions of "church
growth" will be found in Alan R. Tippett's work, *Verdict
Theology in Missionary Theory* (1969) and *Church Growth
and the Word of God* (1970).

Essentially the term includes three aspects: first, quantitative growth—that is, all forms of numerical increase
whether by transfer, conversion from the world or by
baptism of believing children of Christian parents; second,
qualitative growth in the sense of increasing maturity,
stability, and fruitfulness of individual believers; and, third,
organic growth in terms of organization and structure of
the local congregation in the face of changing needs.*

---

*The descriptive terms qualitative, quantitative and organic
were first used by A. Tippett, "Church Growth or Else," *World
Vision Magazine, February 1966.*

Folk Religion. My usage of the term "folk religion" fits well within the definition given by H. Y. Hsu: "Folk religion is to be defined as the religions practices and belief systems followed by the masses of the Chinese people without regard for the formal aspects of religion [such] as Buddhism, Taoism or the ethical system of Confucius" (1968:24).

World View. In the early part of this study we will be examining what might be called the "world view" of the Chinese people. By world view is meant the concept which a people have of the supernatural, of nature, of society, and of man, and the way in which these concepts form a system that gives meaning to life and motivation for individual or social behavior.

"World view," writes Redfield, "differs from culture ethos, mode of thought and national character." While "national character" refers to the way these people look to the outsider looking in on them, "world view" refers to "the way the world looks to that people looking out" (1962:270). Redfield, in his discussion of this subject, finds certain elements which are universal to all world views. First, he sees self as the "axis of world view," for all men are conscious of the self. Beyond this, he suggests the following as possible universals: not only a distinction of the self from the not-self, but parts of the self as distinguished from each other. That is to say, there is a part of me which is able to address another part. Another universal is the separation in some sense of the supernatural from nature, though this separation varies in many ways. Another universal would be the form of confrontation of man with that which is not self—that is, with other men, nature, and the supernatural. The attitude which man will take towards that which is confronted will, as Redfield points out, differ among peoples. Some people conceive of the universe as having a well-structured and defined order,

as do the Yucatan Maya. In contrast, the Arapesh regard
the universe as very loosely structured both in terms of time
and space.

Another universal element that grows out of one's
view of the universe is what Redfield designates as "the
obligation towards what is confronted" (1962:275). This
sense of obligation varies among different peoples. It is
usually expressed by verbs such as "accept, maintain, become
one with, yield to, obey, appropriate, transform" (p. 275).
Redfield illustrates the above with four societies: the
Arapesh, the Zuni, the ancient Mesopotamians, and the early
Americans. The first and last show a predominant emphasis
upon "maintaining it," the second upon "obeying it," and the
third "acting upon it" (p. 277). Redfield admits a problem
when seeking to describe the world views of societies which
existed long before written records. As a tentative solution,
he suggests that one's conclusions are largely inferred from
the world views of surviving primitive peoples today.*
He concludes his treatment of the primitive's world view
with three assertions. First, there is no clear distinction
between that which is confronted and that which does the
confronting—that is, man is in a sense already in nature.
Second, the attitude towards the world confronted is
primarily one of "participant maintenance"—that is, man
"works with the elements and not against them." Third,
the universe is "morally significant"—that is, there is one
moral order that binds together man, nature, and the
supernatural (1962:279). We will utilize these ideas as
a frame of reference and attempt to examine the Chinese
world view at several different periods in their history.

*In using Redfield's concepts, one must bear in mind the
evolutionary assumptions which underly his theory, assumptions with
which I am in disagreement.

Taiwanese. The term "Taiwanese" will be used to identify the dominant segment of the ethnic Chinese of Taiwan. Historical considerations press us to use this term. The ancestors of most long-term Chinese residents of Taiwan came to the island from Fukien Province as early as the seventeenth century. Thus, with three to four hundred years of residence in Taiwan, they have developed an island culture which in some respects is distinct from that of the Mainland. For these and other reasons, they will be referred to as Taiwanese, while those who evacuated from the Mainland following World War II and the Communist triumph of 1949 will be referred to as Mainlanders. The third and smallest segment of ethnic Chinese are the Hakka people from south China. While also of long-term residence and sharing much of the Taiwanese culture and religion, they will nonetheless not be considered within this study.

It should be noted that on Taiwan there are also many non-Chinese tribal peoples. Those who are interested in the animistic religions of these peoples will find no dearth of good material available. Actually, until recent years, far more anthropological and sociological studies have been done among these tribes than among the Taiwanese, Hakka, and Mainlanders combined. Fortunately, this emphasis is now shifting and social scientists are giving more attention to the problems of Taiwanese urbanization and related fields of current concern.

Mythology. Mythology provides us with a useful data source for the study of animism in China. The term "myth" is defined by Middleton as "a conceptual statement about man, his society and his universe" dealing with ultimate realities concerning spiritual powers, and supernatural events that took place in "primordial sacred" time (1967:10). Naturally, myths are vitally linked to a people's religious beliefs and practices. Malinowsky writes: "Myth fulfills in primitive culture an indispensable function: it expresses, enhances and codifies belief; it safeguards and enforces morality; it vouches for the efficiency of ritual and contains practical rules for the guidance of man" (1954:101).

To the ancients, the myth served as a vehicle for the communication of what to them was ultimate truth. Ideas about the cosmos, creation, the flood, and the problem of evil are often the themes within a people's mythology. Taken together, they give insight into the manner in which a people look upon the universe and upon life in general.

A people's mythology is also interrelated with their history. Indeed, the latter has left its imprint upon mythology. Some would even regard myth-making as a way of recording history by pre-literate peoples. Care must be taken, however, not to regard mythology as a mere chronicle of history. At best, the myth can only point to those past historical events and experienced realities which impinged upon a people's struggle to cope with their environment. Hence, it represents their verbalization of those elements which came to be embodied in their understanding of the mythic realm.

Shamanism. Since the subject of shamanism shall loom large in this study, we must define the term and define some of the concepts inherent to it. Eliade's important book *Shamanism* (1964) will serve as our chief source. He believes that the term "shaman" comes to us through Russian from the Tungusic word *saman*. The *locus classicus* for shamanism is the general region of Siberia and specifically Central Asia. For centuries it has dominated religion throughout this area. Shamanism means "a technique of ecstasy." Above all, the shaman is the "great master of ecstasy." By this is meant a trance-like state of mind into which the shaman enters while he is "controlling" the spirit of his patron god. During this time he is allegedly able to communicate with the supernatural, practice "magical flight," and reveal his "mastery over fire" and his power to heal. The range of the shaman's skills is considerable.

Our study will uncover the fact of a similar shamanic dominance of folk religion from time to time throughout China's long history. The link between Tibetan and Chinese Shamanism is suggested by de Groot in his study on *"wu*-ism": "The wu were nothing else than what we might call the Chinese ramification of a large class of priests of both sexes which is distributed over several parts of Asia under a variety of names, such as shaman in Siberian lands" (1892-1910:6:1190).

Eliade's basic definition of the shaman as one who deals in ecstacy seems to fit well with the data from ancient China and the so-called *wu*-ism described by de Groot, as well as the current *tang-ki* of Taiwan. Thus, when referring to the broad subject, I have used the term "shaman" and "shamanism". In describing the religious expert of ancient China, I have used *wu* (and related terms), as does de Groot. For current Taiwan I use the Amoy term *tang-ki*, "medium," with Jordan and others. I recognize that "possession" makes today's *tang-ki* an aberrant type of shaman according to Eliade's definition, and I, therefore, prefer the terms *tang-ki* or medium.

Culture. Who were the "Chinese" of early China? Did they comprise one distinct culture? These questions merit some attention since they bear upon any attempt to describe animism in early Chinese history. If the Chinese as an ethnic group can be traced to a single cultural origin, the problem is greatly simplified. All the evidence, however, indicates otherwise. From his important research on Asian cultures Eberhard concludes that "the area of modern China was the seat of more than ten sharply outlined cultures" (1968:15). If this is so, there must have been some period during which these multiple cultures merged to form what might be considered the first "Chinese" type culture. Eberhard concludes on the basis of ethnic and archeological data, that the first truly "Chinese" society did not emerge until as late as the Chou dynasty (1123-221 B.C.) and certainly not before the Shang (1751 B.C.?-1123 B.C.). On the other hand, Hsu identifies the "Chinese" as synonymous with the "Hsia" people of ancient Chinese history and folklore (1968:65). The term "Hsia" has also been used to designate a dynasty prior to Shang. According to the dating of Needham, this fell roughly within the period 2000-1520 B.C. (1956: 2:697).* Creel also sees the "Hsia" period as the beginning point for Chinese culture and looks to linguistic evidence to substantiate his view (1938:120). However, the arguments of both Hsu and Creel lack the force of Eberhard's, further details of which may be seen in Chapter.[1] With him, I will assume that the earliest manifestations of "Chinese" animism took place during the Shang period, with the understanding that full-orbed "Chinese" culture did not emerge until Chou times. While evidence for earlier religious rituals will be noted, they will be understood as belonging to the pre-Chinese period.

Ritual and Belief. It should be understood from the outset that Chinese animistic folk religion is not primarily concerned with a system of beliefs such as one often associates with Christianity. In fact, one can only arrive at the beliefs of the Chinese peasant through an observation of the religious rites and ceremonies which he practices. Radcliffe-Brown quoting Loisy writes: "In attempting to understand a religion it is on the rites rather than on the beliefs that we should first concentrate our attention. . . . Rites are in all religions the most stable and lasting element and consequently that in which we can best discover the spirit of ancient cults" (1952:155).

*Archeological evidence for the existence of the so-called Hsia dynasty is still lacking (Chang 1963:131).

RESEARCH PROBLEMS

Possibly the greatest single problem confronted in collecting data for this study has been the dearth of material descriptive of animistic folk religion at the peasant level, especially in early China. Although descriptions abound of the religious beliefs and practices in the courts of early China, it is not until well after the Classical period that one is able to gain a fairly clear picture of the religion of the peasants. For this reason, one is hard pressed to avoid a measure of speculation when he attempts to describe the precise nature of animism at the popular level before that time. Archeological findings have been of some help at this point. However, due to the tentative nature of their significance, calling for caution when tempted to hard and fast conclusions, I must conclude that I am not really sure of the precise forms of early folk religion. For this reason, I have at times been pressed to describe the religion of the elite cr of officialdom, from which one can at best only infer the general nature of folk religious practices of the masses. This is especially true for the so-called Classical period.

A second difficulty arises from the great variety in data descriptive of shaman-type religious experts throughout the history of China and Taiwan. Because I have failed to uncover one continuous stream of data descriptive of what would meet Eliade's minimal requirements constituting classical shamanism, I have chosen to research within the broader concept of what has been called *wu*-ism. This Chinese term embraces a wider corpus of religious experts that includes a fairly continuous manifestation of the shaman type, complete with ecstatic trances and spirit possession. Actually, further research is needed in this area, especially to determine the historical relationships existing between the shamanistic medium and the Taoist priest of Taiwan.

A third difficulty arises from the fact that a quantity of valuable material is said to exist in certain European languages not known to this writer. I am, therefore, forced to depend on indirect sources for this material where it is available.

A fourth difficulty was encountered when I sought to decide which were the four most appropriate periods in China's long history in which to examine Chinese animism. The Shang, Classical, and T'ang periods of China and contemporary Taiwan were natural selections. My reason for choosing the Classical period arises out of observations made by Eberhard and Yang.

Eberhard contends that a clear-cut break in folk religion occurred in the popular religion somewhere between 100 B.C. and A.D. 200. He correlates this with the rise of the gentry class around 200 B.C. triumphing over the remnants of feudal society and introducing bureaucratic government. This new class of administrators left a mark so profound that even the popular gods began to appear as officials of the celestial realm (Eberhard 1952:21-23).

Yang, in his excellent study on Chinese religion, includes the Early Han as part of the Classical period (1961:106). I have chosen to do the same.

SEQUENCE OF DEVELOPMENT

The following is a brief summary of the way in which the contents of this study are developed.

Chapter 2 is a description of animism in earliest times up through the Shang era. Animism makes its appearance in the burial practices, worship of nature deities, fertility cult, and activities of the shaman. An attempt will be made to reconstruct in rough outline what may have been the world view of these early ancestors of China.

Chapter 3 is a description of animism in the Classical period. Developments and changes from Shang and earlier times will be noted. The influence of Confucian philosophy upon peasant beliefs and practices will be discussed. Special attention will also be given to the ancestor cult and shamanistic practices, since they represent the mainstream of animistic belief. I will trace the emergence of animism in the courts of Chinese emperors, a development resulting from the presence of the shaman and the practice of divination. In conclusion, a brief reconstruction of the world view of this period will be suggested.

Chapter 4 is a description of animism in the T'ang period. I will trace the three streams of Confucian, Buddhist, and Taoist influence as they began to exercise a major influence upon animistic belief and practice. I will observe the process by which Buddhism and Taoism, through interaction with and accommodation to existing folk religion, gradually evolved new, popular cults. The altered world view of the Chinese during this period will conclude the chapter.

Chapter 5 will describe animism in the modern era, especially in Amoy and Taiwan. Attention will focus on the animistic forms of east China as exported to Taiwan. Once again we shall find evidence of change, both development and decline, in the key areas of ancestor worship and shamanism. As far as possible, a fairly full account will be given of the contemporary picture of Taiwan. An effort will be made to detect aspects of Taiwanese folk religion in which animistic activities are either increasing or abating. Due to the apparent resurgence of temple building in many areas of Taiwan, we must ponder the present-day function of temple cults in the life of the Taiwanese people. I will conclude with a brief outline of their current world view. Obviously, it needs to be remembered that the world view in each period represents the popular conceptions of the common people. I shall not explore the world views held by the elite.

Chapter 6 attempts to trace missionary attitudes toward the folk religion of Taiwan during three consecutive periods. The purpose is to discover whether or not missionaries attempted to understand Taiwanese animism and the influence which such insights may or may not have had upon missionary strategy.

Chapter 7 sets forth a theology of "the powers." Taking biblical data mainly from the epistles of Paul, I develop a theological approach to the Taiwanese folk religion based upon Paul's concept of "the powers."

In Chapter 8, I have developed what Bavinck calls a "kerygmatic approach." Utilizing data from Old and New Testaments plus insights from Chapter 7, I emphasize those aspects of the biblical *kerygma* which are most meaningful to a people of animistic orientation. I conclude the chapter with an expansion of Paul's sermon on Mars' Hill, adapted in this case to Taiwan.

PERSONAL NOTE

I am only too conscious of the vastness of this subject. In addition, most studies of primitive religion are philosophical and speculative in character, armchair research,'" rather than practically phenomenological based on face-to-face encounter. Data of the latter sort is more likely to be found in, say, the missionary experience than in library research. This study attempts to relate my theological training to an anthropological approach to primitive religion in the ultimate interests of the Christian mission. In this respect, I hope this is an original contribution to missiology.

1

Animism in Early China

INTRODUCTION

T HE PURPOSE of this chapter is to examine the animistic religion of the ancestors of today's Chinese, to ascertain, where possible, the function which it fulfilled in society, and finally to reconstruct a simple world view at about the time of the late Shang period.

Chinese Culture or Local Cultures?

As indicated in the introduction, problems arise when one uses the terms "Chinese" or "Chinese culture" in describing people and cultures much earlier than the Chou (ca. 1123-221 B.C.) or Shang (ca. 1751?-1123 B.C.) periods. In his learned work on early Chinese culture, Eberhard writes: "Whether or not one should call the pre-Shang societies 'Chinese' is a question which I would answer in the negative" (1968:28). The basis for his judgment rests upon a detailed study of several "local cultures" which occupied much of the area of today's China and which predated the presence of any cultural development that could be called "Chinese."* According to Eberhard, the subsequent Chinese societies were a gradual outgrowth of the commingling of these ten or more local cultures. This included a stratification process during which other local cultures of Turco-Mongolian, Tungus, and Tibetan elements arose and spread southward and eastward into the area of the local cultures of south and east China.** This coalescing and stratification of cultural movements eventually gave rise to the Yang-shao culture of north China about the end of the third millenium B.C. Subsequent development of the Yang-shao resulted in the Hsia culture centering around southwest Shansi.*** By this time, village life was well developed. Following the Hsia, there emerged the Lung-shan culture in which genuine towns began to replace earlier villages. Partly based upon the Lung-shan culture but located to the north, there arose around 1500 B.C. the Shang culture. Meanwhile, the Chou, an erstwhile shepherd-nomadic type people which was developing to the west, continued to spread largely into the southeast where it encountered the T'ai and Yüeh local cultures and eventually the Shang culture to the north. After a period of cultural struggle, the Shang was defeated and the Chou state was formed. This became the first great political power on East Asian soil. It is here then that we must look for the first manifestation of a "high-Chinese culture" complete with its "Son of Heaven" and "claim to domination of the world" (Eberhard 1968:29). The approximate locations of

*Most of these local cultures are found as early as the turn of the third millenium B.C. (Eberhard 1968:24).

**By "stratification" I understand Eberhard to mean the overlaying of one culture tradition upon another.

***Conclusive archeological evidence for the existence of the Hsia culture is still lacking. However, it is still a convenient term for designating what appears to be a distinct period before the Shang.

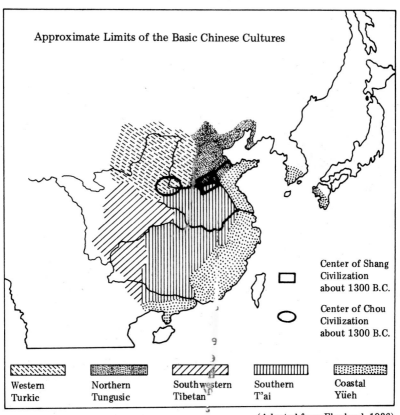

Approximate Limits of the Basic Chinese Cultures

Center of Shang
Civilization
about 1300 B.C.

Center of Chou
Civilization
about 1300 B.C.

| Western Turkic | Northern Tungusic | Southwestern Tibetan | Southern T'ai | Coastal Yüeh |

(Adapted from Eberhard, 1936)

Fig. 1

the Shang and Chou civilizations in the midst of the "local cultures" about the year 1300 B.C. is seen in Figure 1.

Problems of Available Documents

A second problem arises pertaining to source materials on animism within the folk religion of these ancestors of the Chinese. While literary Chinese documents date well back into the Chou dynasty (1123-221 B.C.) and tell us something of the religion of the elite of that time and earlier periods, yet it is unfortunately true that "We have . . . few documents which deal with religion and practically none with the popular beliefs" (Eberhard 1968:23). It seems that the lords and philosophers were little interested in the animistic religion of the common people. The only literary sources that shed light upon the early religious life of the people are a few songs in the *Shih-ching*, or *Book of Songs* (ca. 1000 B.C.), which describe the early festivals. These simple love songs were subsequently reinterpreted by Chinese scholars, who found in them "deep political meaning" changing the lover into a faithful minister and the beloved into a king or lord (Eberhard 1952:124).*

Archeological and Ethnological Materials

Turning to the data available from archeology, linguistics, ethnology, and mythology, we are on somewhat better ground. I will draw upon a few of these data to outline animism in its broader dimensions.

It is impossible to describe the early forms of animism even in the Shang period with anything approaching completeness. At best, one can only attempt to sketch in what appear to be the primary dimensions of animistic activities,

---

*The whole problem of textual criticism cannot even be touched upon here. Suffice it to say that textual corruption of early classical works has complicated the task for the scholar who works directly from the literary Chinese.

namely the ancestor and fertility cults, festivals, and activities of the shaman-type religious expert. Since my approach is primarily ritual-orientated, statements concerning beliefs, world view, and functional values will be drawn from these data. Less will be said concerning animism among the nomadic peoples of pre-Neolithic times since data is less dependable.

TIME CHART

Date	Period	Archeological Horizon	Cultural Development
500,000 to 25,000 B.C.	Middle Pleistocene to Upper Paleolithic	Loess	Discovery of *Sinanthropus pekinensis* (500,000 B.C.) and Homo sapiens (25,000 B.C.) at Chou-kou-tien
25,000 to 4000 B.C.	Mesolithic to Early Neolithic	P'an Chiao	Hunter-fishers, simple tools, beginnings of plant cultivation and animal domestication, village life
4000 to 1900 B.C.	Early to Late Neolithic	Yang-shao	Proto-Chinese, village farmers, elegant painted "Yang-shao" ware
1900 to 1751 B.C.	Hsia	Lung-shan	Expansion of village farming, elegant black polished "Lung-shan" ware
1751 to 1123 B.C.	Shang	High Bronze	Elegant white "shang" ware, beginning of Chinese high civilization, first cities

In order to facilitate understanding of the time periods which will be used below, I have constructed the above chart from data in Chang's work, *The Archeology of Ancient China* (1963:304-305) and Campbell's *The Masks of God* (1962:2:372-373). There is a lack of consensus as to the usefulness of such terms as Neolithic, Mesolithic, and Paleolithic in describing the prehistory of East Asia, but better terms are still wanting. Dating of all periods prior to the Shang is still a matter of much speculation. These given in the chart above should be taken as tentative.

ANIMISM IN PRE-HISTORIC CHINA

The most abundant and useful data for probing questions of culture and religion in pre-historic China comes to us from archeological findings. Hsü Hsin-yi, commenting on the folk religion of China, says: "The material culture remains from archeological excavations are still the most reliable data for reconstructing prehistory" (1968:77). He warns us, however, against the conclusion that the non-material culture can easily be understood from material artifacts. H. Wales combines the data from archeology (especially art) and comparative ethnology in his attempt to reconstruct the culture and religion of pre-history of this area (1957). His views are somewhat tentative and open to further study.

The first inferential evidence of the human species known as *Sinanthropus pekinensis* has been found at Chou-kou-tien (near Peking) and dates back to the Middle Pleistocene period perhaps some 500,000 years ago (Chang 1963:29).* Peking Man, according to Chang, was one who could light

*The Pleistocene Period is estimated to have been close to one million years in duration. For a discussion on the geological and paleontological background of China, see pp. 25-34 of Chang's *Archeology of Ancient China*.

fires and who lived by hunting and nut collecting. Quite possibly he was cannibalistic.* Similar species of Paleolithic datings have been found in south China. If these are indeed species of Homo sapiens, then it is obvious that we are dealing with a people of remarkable antiquity who lived through many millenia before simple agricultural forms of life began to emerge in the Mesolithic period.

In dealing with the question of animism in pre-historic China, I am making two assumptions: one, that these pre-agricultural peoples were given to a certain religious inclination, a sense of existence of and dependence upon a supernatural power outside of themselves.** Second, I am assuming with Hsü that there are factors outside of man which also operate in the formation of animistic-type beliefs and practices among primitive societies. These he calls "physiological-psychological processes" and "cultural-ecological processes" (1968:242). An excellent demonstration of this is given by Hsü in which he traces in recent times the birth and growth of several locust cults in China. Hsü is able with carefully researched data to correlate growth areas of the locust cults with the areas affected by locust plagues (p. 193-214). He terms this a manifestation of man's "coping method" to adjust to his environment. If these are valid assumptions, then one may give some credence to Wales, who sees pre-historic religion developing primarily in terms of stimulus and response and judges the first religious response to have been to "the Power that seemed most immediately connected with the game and with fruit supply" (Wales 1957:15). Subsequent to this, man's

*While using the word "human" here, I am aware of the controversy which has surrounded efforts to identify the Peking Man with Homo sapiens. Many would identify him as Homo erectus.
**I realize that the religious interpretation of the way of early man is considered speculative, but I see no better interpretation.

attraction was to the sky and the earth, though the latter
meant much more to later agriculturists than these nomadic
hunter fishers. I would only add to this the likelihood that
with the passage of time there was almost certain to have
developed varying forms of animism. Reichelt, author of
Religion in a Chinese Garment, describes some possibilities
at this point (Reichelt 1951:9-10):

> Conditions were specially favourable in prehistoric
> China for the development of animism. There may
> have been in the first place a long period of nomadism,
> when they journeyed steadily eastward through the
> vast mountain and desert regions of Central Asia. Here,
> as never before, they encountered the mighty powers
> of nature, and nature's terrors. They had immense
> mountain ranges and endless deserts to cross. Great
> snow expanses and glaciers, swift rivers and gloomy
> forests were obstacles in the way of both travel and
> though. Wild beasts filled the nomad with fear, and
> some species now extinct, which in strength and
> ferocity surpassed anything which they had yet seen,
> agitated the mind and stimulated the imagination. Add
> to these things the many bloody encounters after their
> arrival in Chinese territory, and the continual attacks
> of the natives, and one need not wonder that the army
> of spirits as first described is chiefly a cruel, revengeful
> host of demons. It was not till later, when the possibly
> previously nomadic Chinese had arrived at settled life
> amid the smiling landscapes of Shansi, that the idea of
> beneficent spirits and their influence gained any prom-
> inence.*

*Whereas we would challenge Reichelt's evolutionary view that
the nomad had no evidence of beneficent spirits, we would underscore
his emphasis on animism as a reality to the nomad.

If it is true that these pre-agricultural peoples moved continually from place to place, I assume that they seldom lived in close proximity to the remains of their dead for any length of time. I also conclude that the ancestor cult was largely absent from their society: "The dead though early recognized as heirs to an after life were too soon left behind and forgotten to be endowed with major cults." (Wales 1957:9)

With the emergence of the Mesolithic period, dwellers of north China, especially in the Yellow River valley, give first evidence of a cultural transformation from "forest hunting-fishing into . . . full-fledged village farming communities" (Chang 1963:52).

It is from this nuclear area of the Yellow River in north China that the Neolithic culture first arose, subsequently extending both east and west, a development which Chang refers to as "a few millenia B.C." (p. 52). It is from this period that archeology begins to provide us with data helpful in the reconstruction of animistic beliefs and practices of the time. We also get the first glimpses of the shaman-type religious expert active among the common people, as well as a fairly well-developed ancestor cult and various forms of divination.

During the Neolithic period, animism may be examined in two stages: the Yang-shao and the Lung-shan. Archeologist Chang Kwang-chih describes the Yang-shao society as groups of shifting cultivators who lived in small self-contained and autonomous villages in which the unilinear kin group was already of significance in community structure. The presence of a fertility cult is indicated by designs of the female vagina on ceramic decoration as well as painted designs suggesting the head of a shaman who was in charge of the fishing ritual (1963:66).* There is also evidence of a cult

*Harvey cites a reference from Shu-ching, (Book of History) which speaks of shamanic activities about 3000 B.C. (1933:139).

of the soil.   As for the ancestor, Chang finds little or no
evidence of an institutionalized ancestor cult at this early
period. He does suggest the probability, however, that while
the cult was not yet institutionalized, it did exist in some
form by this time (p. 65).

In the more recent Lung-shan period, Chang finds
"definite evidence of an institutionalized ancestor worship"
(p. 95). This appears among a farming people in which there
is a sharply differentiated status-and-role based on a kinship
structure which stressed the coherence of the linear group.
Evidence further indicates that the cult centered around the
more privileged of the village dwellers and involved phallic
images, ceremonial vessels, and oracle bones.   Importance
hitherto given to the fertility cults which were performed for
the community now appear to be overshadowed by the
ancestor cult. Chang suggests that this is possibly a reflection
of change in the total "cultural-social configuration" (p. 270).
Wales's description corroborates the above (1957:17):

> One may suppose that the productivity of earth
> coupled with the ... importance ... accorded to the
> sky ... led to the recognition of an animistic Mother
> Earth, Father Sky couplet.   At the same time, the
> sedentary way of life of the agriculturists would have
> endowed many striking features of the environment, the
> stream, the mountain, the big rock each with their
> spirits requiring propitiation. But perhaps none received
> a greater accretion of reverance than the ancestors,
> in a settled existence where their remains lay buried
> close at hand and their continuing influence was felt
> to the full.   So it would appear that the early agri-
> culturists primarily sought the fertility of the earth
> through the cooperation of the ancestors in cults which
> had a phallic aspect.*

*Wales speculates on the possibility that the ancestor cult
originated in a Father Sky phallic cult (1957:36).

Granet points out that in the early family organization a relationship of the sexes evolved which had some analogy to the matriarchate, and he adds: "Ancestor worship when it was combined with the worship of the soil was the worship of the maternal ancestors" (1958:154).

As to the origins of the various elements of the above religion, one can only speculate. It would be interesting to know for example whether one developed out of the other, that is, ancestor worship from nature worship, or whether one was imposed upon the other by outside influence.

ANIMISM IN THE SHANG DYNASTY

Social Structure

The next cultural horizon is that of the Shang, considered by many scholars to be the beginning of Chinese civilization.* It becomes possible at this point to determine chronology with some accuracy. Tradition has placed the founding of the Shang at about 1766 B.C. (Chang 1963:133), a period about 1500 years behind the beginning of civilization in the Near East. Discoveries at An-yang in the late nineteenth century began the uncovering of a wealth of material objects of Shang civilization. This, together with written history, provides the main data for examining animism during this period.

According to Chang, Shang society was characterized by a complex of urban-peasant culture in which individual villages were organized into "inter-village networks in economy, administration and religion" (p.166). Society was made up of three social strata, "the aristocracy, the crafts-

*Ancient Chinese history refers to a Hsia dynasty (ca. 2000-1520 B.C.) prior to the Shang, but no archeological evidence has as yet been found to confirm this tradition (Chang 1963:134).

man and the farmers" (p. 166). The religious system of the
time divided naturally into two parts, official worship and
popular worship. I find animism at both levels.

The Shang Ancestor Cult

At the level of the royal house, Chang describes highly
organized ceremonial patterns which carried on much of
what was common to Neolithic times, that is, institutionalized
ancestor worship, scapulimancy, and the use of ceremonial
vessels.* By late Shang times, certain forms of animistic
ritual were very much tied up with the aristocracy. Priests
divined and foretold the future. Elaborate ceremonial
bronze vessels were used in performing "rituals of ancestor
worship" together with "large scale human and animal
sacrifice" (p. 169). Here Chang sees the ancestor cult functioning to reaffirm and enforce rules of inheritance and
lines of kinship. In all of these ceremonies, the king as
"supreme ruler" was the "focus of attention for all rituals"
(p. 170).

The rest of Shang society was made up of craftsmen
and farmers. Economically and religiously these groups had
much in common. The dwellings of the craftsmen were
distributed among the farming villages. Historical evidence
indicates handicraft as "possibly a kin group affair" (p. 171).
This foreshadows the later guilds of China. Bone oracles
indicate that farmers planted millet, rice, and wheat (two
crops a year) and supplemented their living by hunting
and fishing. Hsu, drawing from the works of Needham
(1955), Ch'ü Wan-li (1951), de Bary (1960), and Eberhard
(1960), describes the popular religion. First, it centered in
the ancestor cult. To the ancestors, prayers were made
for rain, health, good harvest, and many children. Also of

---

*Scapulimancy was a form of divination using the shoulder
blades of animals.

prominence among the masses was worship related to the nature and fertility cults. The popular pantheon included gods of the mountains, rivers, earth, four directions, and deities of fertility. Above all was Shang-ti (上帝), the high god, thought by some to have derived from the ancestor cult, possibly a deified ancestor of the ruling family (Hsü 1968:98). Hsü notes also that sacrifices made to the local deities often became popular festivals and so these gods or their successors were saved from oblivion.

Further light is shed upon the Shang ancestor cult by Creel who uses linguistic evidence to show that the living regarded their dead with a mixture of fear and devotion as well as genuine grief at the time of their death. Three Shang characters used of the dead are interesting:

1. a man with a large head of fearful aspect, used to mean ghost.

2 a ghost holding a rod symbolizing his power to chastise the living, and used to express the idea of fear or respect.

3. possibly symbolic of forces streaming down from heaven to man below, used with the meaning of "spirit" (Creel 1937:178).

Creel in a more speculative vein adds, "The ancestor's real power began when he died. For then he was transformed into a spirit of power undefined but vast. . . . They were not, it seems, either omnipotent or omniscient yet in practice they were very nearly so" (p. 175). Creel sees evidence to indicate that Shang people called upon their ancestors and sacrificed more to them than all the other deities put together.

Shang Shamanism

Data for shamanism in the Shang period may be gleaned largely from two sources: art and literature. Evidence of the first is given by Campbell, who writes: "Shamanism is an extremely prominent feature of Chinese and Tibetan religious life; and a sign of its force already in the Shang period may be seen in the demonic animal which appears prominently on the bronzes" (1962:399). The reader may not appreciate the significance of the animal unless he is aware of the vital part which animal symbolism played in early shamanism. For insight, we turn to Eliade. He points out that the early shaman often identified himself with the spirit of an animal such as the bear for the purposes of rituals such as those which ensured an "abundance of game and good luck for the hunters" (1964:459). The animal with which the shaman identified himself was itself charged with mythological meaning and looked upon as the "Ancestor or the Demiurge" (p. 460).* Through identification with the animal, the shaman thus became something greater than himself and entered into communion with cosmic life. Through dance and imitation of the animal, the shaman's soul "came out of itself" and was thus freed for ascent or descent into the world beyond (p. 461).

One of the earliest historical references to shamanism in China is found in the Shu-ching (Book of History), in which a minister criticizes the drunkenness and dancing among government authorities and castigates it as being "wu fashion" (de Groot,1892-1910:6:1187). This is one of the first appearances of the term wu (巫) which subsequently becomes the primary term for the shaman-type priest of China. Another quotation from the Kuo-yü (Chou dynasty), which seems to be describing earlier shamanism, possibly during the Shang, differentiates between the male shaman shih (覡巫) and the female shaman wu. These were both possessed by "intelligent shen" (神, gods) which descended into them in consequence of their ability to "concentrate all their feelings of reverence," thus enabling them to "clearly

*Eliade becomes somewhat speculative at this point.

observe things in the distant future and explain them"
(p. 1192). De Groot suggests that the character for the male
shaman *shih* suggests special powers of sight for the male,
that is, *chien* (見, see). This is not strange for a people
who associated the *yang* (陽) principle of light and brightness
with the male sex. However, subsequent use of *wu* has come
to include both female and male.*

 Concerning the place of the *wu* in early Chinese
religion, Eliade writes: "Chinese animism appears to have
dominated the religious life prior to the preeminence of
Confucius and of the state religion" (1964:454). He also
points out that the spirits with whom the *wu* had communion
were primarily those of the ancestors. Eliade makes the
important observation that with the incarnating of the
ancestral spirits "possession" proper begins. Since "possession" is not a mark of true shamanism, he concludes that
the *wu* was an aberrant form of true shamanism. The
real shaman, says Eliade, is one who controls the spirits, not
one who is possessed by the spirits. I recognize that this
view is currently under fire by certain Russian scholars, but
my own observations in Taiwan lead me to stand with
Eliade on this controversial issue.

 One other aspect of Chinese shamanism calls for our
attention. That is the matter of contact between Chinese
shamanic tradition and that of neighboring tribes. Harvey
observes that "the *Book of History (Shu-ching)* repeatedly
refers to malpractices on the part of the priest among the
Chinese from neighboring . . . tribes." He goes on to
point out that "Shamans from Siberia and Mongolia were
employed by the ancient monarchs of China for divining
and prognostication" (1933:126). The abundance of similar

 *Eliade and others find evidence for dating the female shaman
before the male and indicate that the possession of magic, up to a
certain date, lay with women (1964:448).

evidence of infusions of shamanic influence from non-Chinese sources during subsequent periods of Chinese history impress upon us the fact that elements of Chinese animism as we know it today may often be of foreign origin.

Shang Festivals

The picture of animistic religion of the Shang would not be complete without some reference to the great festivals of the lunar year. Doubtless these predated the Shang period. Unfortunately, little pre-Shang data of dependable nature is available. Granet in his two works, *Chinese Civilization* (1958) and *Festivals and Songs of Ancient China* (1932), attempts a reconstruction of the earliest festivals largely on the basis of records such as the *Shih-ching* (*Book of Songs*), archeology, and mythology. Of these early fetes, Granet writes in a somewhat speculative vein (1958:152):

> The Chinese peasants lived a hard and monotonous life from day to day, but at set times great fetes occurred to awake in them the joy of living. . . . These fetes date back to an immemorial past, and the general conditions of rustic life suffice to explain them.

Granet finds two major festivals in earliest times. one marking the beginning of spring and the other of autumn. These festivals were made up of "communions, orgies and games" and were expressions of the oneness of man with the rhythmic changes of nature. Covenants which bound men "group to group and all to nature" were renewed at the great festivals (Granet 1958:161,173). In all the festivals, activities centered around the holy places which in the minds of the people were associated with fertility and long life. Festive rites in the spring season involved the crossing of rivers by women, half naked, who felt themselves "pene-

trated ... with floating souls" (171). From the renewal of
spring waters flowing from the earth came the idea of
"souls of the dead seeking new life ... escaped ... from a
deep hiding place where death had shut them in," a place
which came to be known as the "Yellow Springs" (171).
By these acts, the Chinese celebrated the deliverance of souls
and called down upon their land the fertile rains and upon
themselves the fertility of spring. Eventually, the idea arose
that water was possessed of a female nature and that woman
alone possessed the virtue necessary for invoking the rain
spirits. Possibly, this relates to the subsequent development
of the dualistic yin-yang (陰陽) theory in which the female
element is identified with yin or that which is damp and
dark. It also suggests one reason why the female shaman
was so popular in early China with its agricultural societies
so dependent upon rain.*

Social Function of Shang Animism

Approaching the religion of the Shang from the
functional point of view, it would not be an overstatement
to say that even at this early period the animistic folk
religion of the people was the integrating factor of society.
As we have seen, most aspects of life, whether social,
economic, or political, were bound up with animistic ritual
and beliefs, all of which served as means by which man
regulated his relationships with the living, the dead, and with
his environment.

In terms of the dead, the early Chinese found in the
ancestor cult a means whereby they could cope with the
"emotionally shattering and socially disintegrating event of
death" (Yang 1961:29). The sense of fear and mystery
surrounding death was lessened by regular communion with

*Other writers on primitive religion have identified rain with the
male element of the cosmos.

the departed; indeed, death served only to remove the physical presence of the ancestor, while in a more powerful spirit form he continued as a living force within the clan, influencing its members for good or for evil.

Of lesser influence yet of great importance was the ritual worship of the gods, especially those of the earth and grain. The earth god from earliest times served as a focal point of village life and his shrine as a holy place where important events took place. Here was the continual reminder of man's dependence upon the soil for his food and a place where feelings of gratitude for plenty or petitions in time of famine could be expressed in ritual activities. For occasions of special needs, the charismatic service of the shaman was available to the whole community. Through him it was possible to inquire concerning future events, commune with the departed dead, and receive assurance that evil spirits had been routed. The shaman's ability to dislodge his soul from his body and ascend or descend into the spirit world provided a bridge between the known and the unknown and into his care were committed all problems touching the soul of his fellow man. While there is evidence to indicate activities of a deceptive nature on the part of some shamans, there is no good reason to doubt that in general his was a sought-after service in the rough and tumble life of early China. In many respects he was the psycho-therapist of Shang society.

World View of the Shang Period

One could wish that the ancients had written more concerning the beliefs of the common man, that is, his feelings about the universe, nature, the supernatural, and his place in the midst of it all. Any attempt to reconstruct what might be called a world view for the Shang period is certainly open to the danger of speculation and the reading back into history of data from later periods. If, however, we take our cue from Radcliffe-Brown and work back from ritual to belief, it may be possible to sketch in outline form a few of the ways in which these early Chinese looked at their world (1952:155). Some directives in determining the possible nature of the Shang world view will be taken from Redfield's material which was presented in the introduction.

Assuming the self to be the axis of primitive man's world view, we may begin by examining the way in which the early Shang peasant viewed himself. Evidence is not lacking that would indicate the peasant recognized in himself the "other self," which he may possibly have related to his breath or shadow but which he believed continued to exist after death. From earlier evidence of stress upon lineage and kinship with relationship to the ancestor cult, one might infer that the Shang peasant saw himself primarily in terms of his relationship to a group the members of which he was dependent upon, especially for his security.

It would seem from the data examined above that the Shang peasant tended to look upon nature and the supernatural as less than distinct entities. While he may have been more conscious of the presence of his ancestors, he was also aware, at times distressingly so, of the spirits which incarnated themselves in the wind, the sun, the moon, and the earth. Evidence from the ceremonial bronzes points, moreover, to an awareness that many spirit powers were malevolent and therefore demanded propitiation. The supernatural elements in nature were in a sense localized in certain areas which the Shang villagers regarded as holy places. This sense of "the holy" possibly pervaded much of their thinking as they considered the way in which the spirit world tended to be concretized in certain aspects of nature.

The rhythmical changes of nature made a deep impression upon the early Chinese, especially since the fertility of the land was so vitally affected. It appears that much ritual, especially in the spring and autumn festivals, was related to the maintenance of the status quo in terms of the cycles of change within nature. Increasingly by the Shang period man had come to see his place in nature as one of harmonious cooperation, one in which he worked with and not against the elements.

This brings us to a consideration of the peasant's view of his universe. What attitude and feelings of obligation did he sense as he confronted his universe? At this point, I am tempted to read back into the peasant's mind much of the philosophy of the Classical period. However, I may be justified in looking in Shang times for some of the germinal ideas which by Chou times had blossomed into a full-orbed dualistic cosmology known as the system of the *yin* and the *yang*. Thompson writes concerning the *yin-yang* theory, "This principle had suggested itself, perhaps as early as 1000-500 B.C." (Thompson 1969:3) If this is the case, then though the articulation of the idea was primarily the work of the scholar class, there is good reason to believe that concepts basic to the theory had arisen from the masses in the first place. Redfield articulates this idea as a general principle and illustrates from India (1960:2:54):

> ... The little traditions of the folk exercise their influence on the authors of the Hindu great tradition who take up some element of belief or practice and by incorporating it into their reflective statement of Hindu orthodoxy, universalize that element for all who thereafter come under the influence of their teaching.

From earliest times, the ancestors of the Chinese have been impressed with the phenomenon of opposites in nature: light and dark, life and death, spring and fall, male and female, good and evil, etc. It seems very possible that the

Shang peasant was already accustomed to considering his universe with the dualistic framework of good and evil forces. Even the spirit world partook of the dualistic nature. Spirits were either beneficent *shen* (gods) or malevolent *kuei* (鬼, demons) (Creel 1937:178).* It must be remembered, however, that the peasants of Shang time were very much aware of a supreme being whom they called Shang-ti or "Lord-on-High," one who presided over all things, rewarding good and punishing evil. As with many other primitive societies, however, he was *deus remotus*, far removed from the everyday things of life. Nonetheless, his existence made for a moral order in the universe and doubtless contributed to the moral and ethical foundation of the Chinese folk religion, which according to Hsu existed prior to the Shang period (1968:104).

It is questionable whether or not the Shang peasant looked at the life of the ancestors as do present-day Chinese. Burial sites even in late Neolithic societies indicate the sacrifice of humans who were buried with kings and other people of nobility. This suggests that the early Chinese envisioned a life to come which was similar in many ways to their earthly existance. Thus, a king in the next world would still have need of servants and food. Beyond the idea of the Yellow Springs—the underground place where winter held imprisoned the spirits of the dead—there is little evidence to indicate concepts of purgatory and punishment such as flourished with Buddhism in later times. This, then, is what the world view in Shang times may have been—basically one in which man found his chief task to be that of maintaining the status quo in his struggle to sustain harmonious relationships with his fellow man, nature, and the spirit world.

*Thompson would seem to disagree at this point (1969:4).

2

Animism in the Classical Period

INTRODUCTION

THIS CHAPTER will examine animism as embodied in
the fully developed folk religion of the Classical periods
of Chou (1123-221 B.C.) and early Han (206 B.C.-A.D. 9).
The limits of this period are defined on the basis of C. K.
Yang's statement: "The original indigenous religion of China
. . . attained full development in the Classical periods of Chou
. . . and early Han before the foreign influence of Buddhism
and the rise of Taoism as a religion" (1961:23).

Historical Background

First, a brief review of the cultural developments at-
tending the fall of the Shang and rise of the Chou and Han
dynasties. It is necessary to reconstruct this as a background
against which to appreciate popular animism. I note in
passing that it was the religion of the Chou court which
marked the emergence of the remarkable Cult of Heaven.
Later, I will trace the influence upon animistic folk religion
arising from the philosophy of Confucius.

Little is known of the Chou peoples prior to their invasion of the Shang civilization around 1123 B.C. Most likely they were animal-tending nomads dependent upon their herds for food and clothing. Apparently, they were of the same Neolithic stock from which the Shang peoples emerged. Prior to this conquest, their tribes lived in and around the Wei basin, the heart of present-day Shensi.

As the Chou attained political and military prowess, continued conquests brought them to the margins of the Shang world. At this point a remarkable idea emerged within the leadership of Chou armies, an idea subsequently referred to as the "Decree of Heaven." The theory behind this idea is simple yet profound (Creel 1937:367):

> It holds that the ruler is appointed by Heaven . . . for the purpose of ruling the world so as to bring about the welfare of men. . . .The moment he ceases to bring about the welfare of the people, it is the right and duty of another to revolt and displace him taking over the appointment of Heaven and administering the government for the public good.

Armed with this sacralizing ideology, the Chou monarch led his people from victory to victory. History indicates that this new concept of the Chou greatly aided in the task of changing the Shang peoples from conquered enemies into loyal subjects. Somehow they convinced the masses that insubordination on their part was akin to revolting against Heaven.

Together with the idea of "Heaven's Decree" working through one man, the Heaven-ordained ruler, there also arose the concept of the central state, Chung-kuo 中國 surrounded by barbarian peoples. Thus, the theory of the supremacy of the Chinese culture was born.

The Chou dynasty historically can be divided into the two periods that saw the emergence of the Western and Eastern Chou.* The Western period continued very much in the cultural tradition of the Shang. On the political scene intermittent wars were fought with surrounding barbarian peoples who were gradually incorporated into the emerging unified Chinese civilization. As the "Decree of Heaven" became more widely accepted, the emerging dynasty congealed into a unified whole. The kingdom of Chou, united under the "Son of Heaven," was the first full manifestation of the culture, ideas, and institutions subsequently considered as truly "Chinese."

The Western Chou period ended in 771 B.C. The corrupt leadership of King Yu together with his weakened administration was no longer able to withstand the attacks of neighboring peoples.** Following the total collapse of their empire, the Chou capital removed to Loyang—a royal domain of greatly reduced size and power. From this point on, the Chou kings functioned as puppets in the hands of powerful nobles. Before long, the four strong states of Ch'i, Chia, Ch'u, and Ch'in emerged occupying much of what is north China today.

The transition period from the Eastern or Late Chou to the first unification achieved by Ch'in Shih-huang-ti is known as the Ch'un-ch'iu 春秋 (Spring and Autumn) and Chan-kuo 戰國 (Warring States) periods (722-221 B.C.). This era was one of relentless strife and warfare as may be seen in the following statistics. From 722 to 464 B.C. only thirty-eight years passed without some form of war. During the Chan-kuo period of 242 years, only eighty-nine years saw any measure of internal peace (Hsü 1968:128).

*The Eastern or Later Chou period also divides into two sub-periods, the Spring and Autumn period (722-414 B.C.) and the Warring States period (464-221 B.C.).

**King Yu of the Chou dynasty was on of the last to bear the name "Son of Heaven."

The rise of the Han dynasty marks the last stage of the classical period of Chinese religious, ethical, and philosophical thought. The short-lived Ch'in dynasty (221-206 B.C.) torn by internal strife ended in large-scale revolts and bloodshed. The power-wielding families which had controlled the many warring states were decimated and no longer capable of wielding further political control. Thus, when order was restored under the unifying powers of the Han dynasty, a long period of war and bloodshed ended. The potential strength of the nation was released once more to weld together the divided kingdoms into a mighty empire. In ture, this developed a culture that surpassed all that had gone before.

Post-Chou Social Structure

Ch'ü T'ung-tsu gives the following picture of social structure following the collapse of Chou feudalism. China's class structure in post-Chou times was modified by historical changes in those factors which determined one's class and status in society. One of these changes was the result of Confucius' extension of education to members of the lower classes. This meant that commoners potentially could become candidates for official careers. By the same token, these offices were no longer filled on the basis of inheritance but rather according to merit. Vertical mobility was greatly enhanced. Class structure, even after the Chou period, was still determined by the ancient concept of the "ruling" and the "ruled." The ruling class were those who did mental labor and the ruled were those who did physical labor. The ruling class of officialdom comprised the superior people. Those ruled were the "common" people and the "mean" people. Both were considered as inferior. The "common" and the "mean" peoples subdivided into further groups according to occupation, but the two groups were separated one from the other, very much as were castes in India.

Social mobility was limited to the commoner, while the "mean" person had little hope of bettering his lot (Ch'ü 1957:235-50).

ANIMISM IN THE COURTS OF CLASSICAL CHINA

The religion of Chinese officialdom during the feudalistic periods of Chou, Ch'in, and early Han has been described as having four leading elements: "ancestor worship, the worship of Heaven and its subordinate system of naturalistic deities, divination and sacrifice" (Yang 1967:106).

Artifacts pertaining to burial rites during the Chou period indicate a continuity of belief and practice from Shang times. Even the sceptics, the kings and nobles, continued to give evidence of a deep belief in the life of the afterworld. Changes are largely of a material nature and involve only the size and construction of the tomb, the use of bricks, burial mound, and posture of the dead (Chang 1963:217).

Ritual practice surrounding the ancestor cult of Classical China was complex and played an important role in political activities as well as the religious life of officialdom. Sacrifices to the dead were frequent immediately following death but slowly diminished thereafter as it was thought that the dead required less nourishment with the passage of time. A tiny portion of every meal eaten was shared with the spirits.

One innovation in the ancestor cult of the Classical age was the "personator." This was a living descendant considered to embody the spirit of the ancestor to whom sacrifice was being offered. Subsequent use of the ancestral tablet was in some respects a functional substitute for the personator.

This age also produced the ancestral temple. At the nuclear family level it became the center around which the main events of family life revolved. The ancestral temple also had a function at the state level. The underlying thesis was that no important event, whether of the family or of the state, should be celebrated without reference to the ancestor and the blessing which he might confer. At the highest level, the ancestral temple of the king was the center for all affairs within the kingdom. Every important decision ranging from the installation of officers to the planning of military expeditions was made here. In fact, from this time on, nothing of any consequence was done without reference to these powerful spirit-protectors of the state.

With the establishment of the ancestral temple, it was but a short additional step to conceive of the spirits of the dead as living in the heavens. They were reached through the medium of ceremonies at the ancestral temples. Belief in the power of the ancestors is well illustrated in the following account. In 660 B.C., Ti barbarians defeated the armies of the state of Wei (in Shansi) and were moving to take the capital. They captured two officials of Wei who said: "We have charge of the sacrifices of the state; if you do not allow us to precede you, it will be impossible for you to take the city" (Creel 1937:339). Without further ado, they were released and returned ahead of the invaders to warn the city.

Another aspect of the ancestor cult comes into view at this time, namely, a preoccupation with the spirits of neglected ancestors. This development did not pass unnoticed by officialdom. Evidently the fear of the neglected dead or the fear of becoming one of the neglected dead through an untimely death created a powerful moral force to deter rebellion among the subjects, for failure in rebellion always posed the threat of one's being killed and left without the necessary sacrifices (p. 341).

Official worship was offered not only to the spirits of the ancestors. Offerings were also made to the spirit of the Yellow River and many other lesser deities. Above all was the more remote, though all powerful, Shang-ti 上帝 (Ruler on High), better known during Chou times as T'ien 天 (Heaven), apparently a high-god concept introduced by the Chou peoples (Creel 1937:342).

Divination already noted from the oracle bones and bronzes of the Shang continued to play an increasingly important role in Classical times. Among the kings and nobles of the times divination was performed by means of the tortoise shell and the *I-ching* (*Book of Changes*) (Creel 1937:334).* The practice of divination was, during both Shang and Chou periods, in the hands of official priests and nobles and was used for the purpose of social control. It served as a link between the world of men and the world of gods. By divination men looked into the future. By monopolizing the right of divination, political leadership was able to impart to itself a sacred character, thus facilitating popular acceptance of the decisions it made. In short, through divination "political decisions became commands of the gods" (Yang 1961:107).

The depths to which animism had penetrated official circles by the early Han may be seen in the following statistics dating to 31 B.C. In that year a census revealed a total of 683 temples under imperial patronage. The gods worshipped were primarily "tribal and nature deities" taken over from the peoples conquered in outlying districts of the empire (Hughes 1950:52).

It is difficult to assess the function of animistic practices among the privileged classes of this period. Judging from contemporary China, much of officialdom differed but

*One of the earliest classics of Chinese literature, the *Book of Changes* was valued primarily for its method of divining the future.

little from those of the masses of whom I will speak in the next section. The rest, including the scholar class, were of a more philosophical mind and outlook. And yet it is clear that they also believed in spirit powers. Hsü's following extract from Hsün-tzu's commentary on the *Li-chi* (*Book of Rites*)* gives some idea of the social function of religion among this class of people (1968:105):

> In general, rites begin with primitive practices, attain cultured forms, and finally achieve beauty and felicity. When rites are at their best, men's emotions and sense of beauty are both fully expressed. When they are at the next level, either the emotion or the sense of beauty oversteps the other. When they are at still the next level, emotion reverts to the state of primitivity. . . .

> Funeral rites are those by which the living adorn the dead. The dead are accorded a send-off as though they were living. In this way the dead are served like the living, the absent like the present. Equal attention is thus paid to the end as well as to the beginning of life. . . .

> Sacrifice is to express a person's feeling of remembrance and longing, for grief and affliction cannot be kept out of one's consciousness all the time. When men are enjoying the pleasure of good company, a loyal minister or a filial son may feel grief and affliction. Once such feelings are not given proper expression, then his emotions and memories are disappointed and not satisfied, and the appropriate rite is lacking. Thereupon the ancient kings instituted rites, and henceforth the principle of expressing honor to the honored and love to

Records of Ritual and Protocol, compiled about 100 B.C.

the beloved is fully realized. Hence I say: Sacrifice is to express a person's feeling of remembrance and longing. As to the fullness of the sense of loyalty and affection, the richness of ritual and beauty—these none but the sage can understand. Sacrifice is something that the sage clearly understands, the scholar-gentlemen contentedly perform, the officials consider as a duty, and the common people regard as established custom. Among gentlemen it is considered the way of man; among the common people it is considered as having to do with the spirits.

CONFUCIAN TEACHING AND THE POPULAR RELIGION

My task now is to define those areas in the life of the common people in which the teachings of Confucius were influential. C. K. Yang suggests that this interaction occurred chiefly among the concepts of Heaven, predetermination, *yin-yang*, the practice of divination, sacrifice, and ancestor worship (Yang 1957:271).

There is general agreement among scholars that Heaven during the pre-Confucian period was considered to be a "personified supreme force, dictating the events of nature and man [and] wielding the power of reward and punishment" (p. 273). However, with the intellectual trend towards secularism during the Ch'un-chiu and Warring States periods, the tendency was to look upon Heaven as an impersonal natural force. This naturalism, however, was confined to only a few advanced groups and was not representative of the masses. Moreover, the inclusion of the Five Classics within the Confucian canon was tantamount to a Confucian endorsement of supernaturalism. This brought to all levels of society the belief in Heaven as a personal and beneficent ruler.

The same may be said of the idea of predetermination of fate (*ming* 命). This is a very vital part of Chinese religious thought and is prominent in the Confucian doctrines. A representative statement from the *Analects* runs: "Death and life have their determined appointment: riches and honor depend upon Heaven" (Yang 1957:273).

The practice of divination also found ample support from Confucian teachings at the officials' level. Once one has assumed that all events are predetermined, it is but a short step to desire beforehand the knowledge of that which was foreordained. Indeed, the possession of this would guarantee to man assured success and avoidance of failure. Confucius himself was concerned with "knowing fate." Perhaps this accounts for his great interest in the *I-ching* (*Book of Changes*), a manual on divination which became very popular among early Confucianists.

There is no need to review the *yin-yang* theory which developed during the Classical and later Han periods into a full-orbed philosophical system of thought. This development would have been unthinkable had Confucian teaching been hostile to its basic concept of "interaction between Heaven and man" (*t'ien-jen hsiang-ying* 天人相應). Yang summarizes (1957:276):

Man's deeds may anger or please Heaven and Heaven metes out punishment or reward accordingly. By assigning moral significance to each of the factors of Yin and Yang and the Five Elements, it was possible to work up a frame of reference by which to interpret the intentions behind the phenomena of the supernatural forces in the sky, the earth, the seasons, the crops, the governing of the state, the rise and fall of a dynasty, life and death, health and sickness, poverty and prosperity, divination, palm reading, physiognomy, astrology, chronomancy and geomancy.

The *yin-yang* theory was capable of wide application, ranging from the interpretation of the movements of the heavenly bodies to the private activities of the individual. Little wonder that this simple principle of the uniting of opposites became popular both among the common people and the Confucian gentry. Indeed, they were but the logical extensions of the concepts of Heaven and fate. From them the peasant derived his cosomology and his religious thought and practice. Preoccupation with this theory during the Classical period is indicated, says Yang, by the fact that approximately one-third of all the books listed in the bibliography section of the *History of the Former Han Dynasty* (*I-wen chih* 藝文志) are devoted largely to the *yin-yang* theory. Moreover, by the third and second centuries B.C., this theory together with that of the Five Elements became prominent as a means of divining the future.* The great Confucianist Tung Chung-shu later made extensive use of these theories in his campaign to establish Confucianism as the orthodoxy of the state (Yang 1957-275). All subsequent Confucianists were influenced by these philosophies in their writings. It is evident then that while Confucius himself should not be directly credited with propagating the theories of *yin-yang* and the Five Elements, those of his apostolic succession maintained his interest in divination, and thus helped to crystallize the official acceptance of this tradition.

Sacrifice, long a stable element in Chinese culture, finds ample support in the Confucian canon. Yang defines sacrifice as "a form of man's ritualistic behaviour toward the gods and spirits for the purpose of inducing their protection and

*For a full development of the *yin-yang* and Five Element theories, the reader may refer to Fung Yu-lan's work.

blessing" (p. 276). Sacrifice must have been common both among the masses and the privileged. At any event, this is the impression that comes through from his writings. Confucius looked upon sacrifice as a means for controlling and regulating the conduct of all classes of society. A clear endorsement of sacrifice is the gist of the following words attributed to him: "The sages devised guidance in the name of the gods and [the people of] the land became obedient" (p. 277).

When I examine the Confucian tradition touching the rite of sacrifice more closely, I discern a dual principle: one for the superior man and one for common man. Sacrifice for the former is considered only to be a "human practice," while for the common man it is a "serving of spirits" (p. 277). But did this dual principle mean a double standard? Hardly. Passages from *Li-chi* give strong evidence of animistic experience even for the superior man: "On the day of sacrifice, when he enters the apartment [of the temple] he will seem to see [the deceased] in the place [where the spirit table is] . . . and in his dreamy state of mind seeks to communicate with the dead in their spiritual state" (1957.278).

It is evident from the Chinese rites of sacrifice that the idea of the efficacy of ritual had been deeply ingrained among the ruling class, if not among the common people as well. The following myth suggests one of the sources from which this idea emerged. In it I find that the Chinese have created a virgin birth narrative strikingly similar at points to the biblical account of Jesus' birth. The point to note, however, is the stress placed upon the "pure offering and sacrifice" made by the virgin Chiang Yüan, wife of a celebrated ancestor and founder of the Chou line (Harvey 1933:240):

The first birth of our people was from Chiang Yüan. How did she give birth to our people? She had pre-sented a pure offering and sacrifice, that her childlessness might be taken away. Then she trod in the toe-print of Shangti, and was moved. In the large place where she rested, she became pregnant; she dwelt retired; she gave birth to, and nourished a son, who was Hao Chi. When she had fulfilled her months, her first born son came forth like a lamb. There was no bursting, rending, no injury, no hurt; showing how wonderful he would be. Did not Shangti give her the comfort? Had he not accepted her pure offering and sacrifice? So that thus easily she brought forth her son?

When I recall that mythological stories among ancient peoples were regarded as authoritative accounts of the activites of gods and men in primordial time, I can easily understand that myth also served as an authority by which the Chinese lived and believed. Chiang Yüan succeeded in communicating with Shang-ti because her ritual was effective, and her ritual was effective because it was correct. With the example and authority of these great ancestors behind them, it was natural for Chinese to believe and act accordingly. Confucius himself was but one of many who on the basis of myth tended to canonize the concept of ritual efficacy. He did this by his personal example and then followed with a formal exposition of its significance.

Furthermore, the concept of ritual efficacy reveals one specific attitude which the Chinese bore towards all spirit beings. While the spirits were usually reckoned as more powerful than man, there was a sense in which they were obligated to respond to sacrifices properly offered, especially when made by virtuous rulers. It was written of King Wu, founder of the Chou dynasty, that "he contained in himself . . . hundreds of *shen* [gods] and . . . bent them to his will" (de Groot 1892-1910: 6:1155).

The ancestor cult held a central position within the Confucian scheme of social organization. On one hand it functioned to cultivate kinship values of filial piety, family loyalty, and the obligation to continue the family lineage. For the common man, however, the supernatural dimension loomed large. It was this later aspect that made ancestor worship an integral part of his life. His hope for supernatural blessing and his fear of supernatural punishment motivated him to perform the proper sacrifices and rituals for the departed. In turn, these activities served as stabilizing influences in the relation between the kinship system and the cyclical, recurring rhythm of agricultural life. This animistic cult was in many ways confirmed and strengthened by Confucian thought.

Thus, Confucianism served to impose upon the people of China, rich and poor alike, an ethical superstructure which buttressed popular religion at most of its focal points. The picture which emerges is not so much a distinctively different group of Confucians standing apart from the superstitious masses. Rather, the impression is one of a "general pattern of Chinese life with only relative differences due to . . . social and economic differences" (Yang 1967:277).

POPULAR ANIMISM OF THE CLASSICAL PERIOD

I will now deal with those developments of animism at the popular level which apparently emerged within the Classical period. Unfortunately, data touching on the ancestor cult and temple worship is scarce. The primary focus, therefore, will be upon the well-documented shamanism and the way in which shamanic activities influenced the entire spectrum of social life during this period.

I have outlined the social and political background against which animism developed during the Classical period. It was characterized by prolonged periods of war, famines, and poverty. Particularly, during the time of Ch'un-ch'iu and Chan-kuo the people were reduced to unspeakable suffering and insecurity. In retrospect, I can easily see how the form of animistic folk religion which developed during this period was in large measure a product of the times and was primarily an expression of the peasant struggle to find personal meaning and security through the manipulation of spirit power.

Shamanism

Throughout this period, shamanism was well documented in Chinese historical records. De Groot has uncovered a rich body of data on the shaman in the third section of the *Chou-li* (*Rituals of Chou*). This describes in detail the nature and influences of the shaman within the ruling class. What his influence was upon the animism of the masses can only be inferred from these data (de Groot 1892-1910:6:1187-211).

Who was the shaman? What was his role in the animistic practices of Classical China? De Groot considers the shaman as the original priest of China, the natural product of a primitive animism and unbroken tradition that reaches to the Chinese of modern times. He likens them to an official priesthood. In time, shamanism found a place in the Confucian system under the rubric of Ministries of Rites and Ceremonies. As religious "officials" they were responsible for the administration of the state religion. De Groot warns, however, that the shamanic priesthood should not be regarded as a creation of the state. Although they often exercised official responsibilities, they were more a spontaneous product of the folk religion itself.

The shamanic priesthood of Chou and early Han times was made up largely of women, both married and single, who possessed the ability to "invoke and employ" spirits.* They were identified with the *yin* or female part of the

*Female dominance of the shamanic art continued until recent times in parts of mainland China (de Groot 1892-1910:6:1211).

universal order and had a dominant role in rites pertaining to fertility. They also operated within the sphere of the *kuei* (demon) powers.

In contrast, the male *wu* were usually young men, identified with the *yang* or masculine principle of the universe. Since they were animated by the benevolent *shen* (gods), they were a complementary power to the female *wu*. As the ancestor cult gained in prominence, we are not surprised to learn that the *shen* and *kuei* employed by the priesthood in the animistic rituals, were for the most part conceived to be the spirits of the dead.* "Among men, the dead speak through living persons whom they throw into a trance, and the *wu* . . . call down souls of the dead which then speak through the mouths of the *wu*" (p. 1211).

I must link a third class with the male and female *wu* called *chu* 祝, variously translated as "invokers" or "conjurers." These worked together with the *wu*. The *chu* were evidently above the *wu* in rank and participated with them in religious functions. From the Han dynasty onwards, however, the expression *wu-chu* 巫祝 appears frequently in literature. It usually denoted but one person. It seems, then, that these two functions must have come together at a later date, possibly reflecting the desire of the *wu* for a title of higher social status in Chinese society (p. 1192).

The work of the shaman covered the broad areas of exorcism, sorcery, healing, prediction of future events, and the manipulation of the powers of nature. His power as exorcist lay in the belief that the *shen* were mighty in opposing, expelling, and destroying the *kuei*. The art of sorcery is attributed to the *wu*. Evidently, it became a source of much persecution. In the year 91 B.C. the emperor employed

---

*According to Eliade's view, this involvement with ancestral spirits would indicate something of a departure from the classical form of shamanism (1964:454).

wu from Hunnish tribes to the west to assist him in the discovery and persecution of sorcerers (p. 1201).

The shaman's role as healer derived from the universal belief that illness resulted from possession by *kuei*. The expulsion of these evil *kuei* occupied a major part of his activities. The medical role of the *wu* is evidenced by the word's subsequent use in the Chinese character denoting the medical art (often written 醫). Some hold that the *wu* 巫 radical in the lower part of this character indicates the influence of the *wu* in Chinese medical history.

The *wu* also figured prominently in Classical times as prophets in the foretelling sense. As such, they were often found in the courts of the king. They explained ominous dreams and warned of dire events. If the records we have are dependable, these predictions were often fulfilled with amazing accuracy. The role of the *shen* and *kuei* in the natural phenomena (floods and droughts, earthquakes and eclipses) again involved the *wu*. This fact would appear to be confirmed by the following words from the *Chou-li* as quoted by de Groot: "at every great calamity in the kingdom, they entreat the gods or spirits, chanting and wailing" (p. 1189). In all the activities of the *wu*, the ever present phenomena of dance and ecstasy seem to mark them as a part of a larger shamanic tradition extending from Siberia to Borneo.

From the above survey of the shaman's role and function, I conclude that he had an influence, which he was not reluctant to exercise, especially among the ruling classes. The following account indicates the powerful image which the *wu* had created among the masses. It deals with human sacrifices to a river god, a common theme in this period. Apparently it had become an annual custom in the kingom of Wei for the *wu* of a certain area to sacrifice a beautiful maiden to the god of the river. This ritual demanded that large sums of money be collected from the people. As a

consequence, the ritual had the dual effect of impover-
ishing the people and creating a state of depopulation as
multitudes fled the area, fearful of losing their daughters
to the cult of the river god. In one particular case, the ruling
monarch put a stop to the cult and killed the *wu* involved
(p. 1196-99). It is not surprising that the *wu* were often
in conflict with the ruling class. The paradox is that in
many cases the very rulers who had attacked the *wu* movement were often found shortly thereafter invoking *wu*
assistance once again, even worshipping the gods employed
by them.

The above data appears to be sufficient to establish the
thesis that in the Chou and early Han periods, the *wu* priesthood was the priesthood proper of China. Its influence for
good or evil was felt thoughout the empire and influenced
the life of both peasant and king. During this period,
shamanism experienced little opposition from the Confucian
state religion, the one power which would later become its
greatest rival. De Groot concludes: "The power of the Wu-ist
priesthood to have intercourse with ancestors . . . and to
reveal their will, was the great source of the influence of that
priesthood among every class, upon human conduct of every
kind" (p. 1208-9).

As I leave the subject of shamanism in the Classical
period, it should be pointed out that this flourished particularly in the southern regions of China. In the records of that
era one comes upon many references to the people of Yüeh,
among whom the *wu* were most numerous. This would
seem to explain why we have a vivid tradition of shamanism
marking the culture of Fukien and eventually spilling over
into Taiwan.

Festivals

In the previous chapter, we looked briefly at the animistic religion of the peasant in the festivals of the Shang

period. From earliest times, these festivals were related to
the seasonal rhythm of peasant life and were held most often
in spring and fall seasons when peasants were changing from
one manner of life to another. Originally, they were quite
possibly linked to the ritual of marriage.

The term *pa-cha* 八蜡 is found frequently in the ancient
writings of this period. It points to a festival which in some
form possibly lasted until the second century B.C. (Hsü 1968:
212). A brief study of Granet's views on the *pa-cha* sheds
considerable light upon the animistic practices of the early
Chou period, and reflects the *pa-cha* festival very much as it
probably was during the Shang.* We also note that various
changes in these practices occurred with the rise of feudalism
and the village nobility.

The *Shih-ching* (*Book of Poetry*) assigns the *pa-cha*
festival to the tenth month, just following harvest (Granet
1932:169). The celebration had all the characteristics of
an orgy in which people ate and drank to the full. Sexual
rites were a feature in earlier times. Great numbers of people
turned out for the occasion and joined the dances, masquer-
ading as cats and leopards and shooting at targets of animals.

It was by nature a festival of thanksgiving. Ceremonies
included prayers for the harvest year to come and the offering of sacrificial victims to the god of the public fields, as well
as the sacrifice of venison at the gates of the villages and
towns to the "ancestors and the fire spirits of the house"
(p. 171). Actually, the term *pa-cha* may connote eight sacrifices which were thanksgiving offerings to "all classes of beings,
animate and inanimate, imaginary and real, in groups and
separated" (p. 172). Prominent among the objects of thanks-

---

*Data on the *pa-cha* festival is taken largely from an ancient docu-
ment called the *Yüeh-ling*. It was analyzed by Granet in his work
Festivals and Songs of Ancient China (1932). I am indebted to this
work for the following picture of the early festival. Although speculative at points, his reconstruction is generally credible.

giving were Shen Nung 神農 and Hou Chi 后稷, agriculture
divinities of great antiquity. Another feature of the festival
was the search for all *kuei* (demons) and *shen* (gods) to
whom sacrifice was also made.

According to custom, every one contributed to the
sacrifices and all took part in the rituals. Granet describes
the sending of gifts and participation according to social
rank (Granet 1932:172-73):

> The people of the whole state gave in proportion to the
> yield of the harvest; the vassals sent their gifts to the
> emperor by envoys. The envoys took part in the cere-
> monies; the sovereign prepared a grand drinking bout
> for his adherents, the flesh of the sacrificial victims
> being set out on tables. . . . The heads of districts col-
> lected all the people in the arena. All the basic rules
> of the social order were displayed during the ceremony:
> filial piety, respect for elders, respect for rank, a spirit
> of deference, a desire for purity, feelings of reverence.
> Those present were divided into two groups: one group
> taking the side of the Master of the Ceremony, the other
> that of the guests. The position of the guests was fixed
> by an orientation whose influence, it was believed, con-
> nected each group with the opposing forces of the
> universe—heaven and earth, sun and moon, *yang* and
> *yin*—which decide the rotation and the opposition of
> the seasons. The leaders of the two groups and their
> assistants offered goblets to one another in turn. Two
> companies of musicians played one after the other and
> then together. The effect of this festival was general
> harmony.

This thanksgiving festival served to stress the unity of
the world of matter with the world of men. This unity was
recognized by a formal apposition of all components, arranged in opposites. All things were used in the sacrifice

and sacrifices were made to all things. Even those taking part in the sacrifices were divided into two groups according to the belief that all nature could be divided in two equal and opposite categories.

The *pa-cha*, according to Granet, was the concluding festival of the agricultural year. Since it marked the close of the aging and dying year, mourning garb was worn. With this ceremony its end was finalized. Naturally, as would be expected, it was an occasion when the old were reverenced, and both man and earth prepared for the winter rest. In a very real sense, then, the festival served to manifest the universal harmony of the nature cycle. It ushered in the dead season when nature rests and the social covenants of life are renewed. In every way, the rhythm of human life was made to reflect the larger rhythm of nature. The prevailing view seems to have been that as the human order of things is made to pattern itself after the cycle of nature, so the re-enactment of this human pattern by the festival ritual was also a means of preserving in desirable balance the course of human affairs and the well-being of nature.

With the coming of feudalism (ca. 800 B.C.) to China, towns emerged and people for the first time began to live in permanent agglomerations. Social activity became a part of everyday life. The festival, which formerly served to renew the benefits of social relationships, was no longer regarded as sufficient to maintain order. The need for social control led inevitably to the development of the coercive aspects of government. In the nature of things this meant the acceptance of "the lord," the local leader. In turn, he became the principle of the social order and functioned as a substitute for the festival, since he tended to bear the same august authority. "All the hallowed powers once set free in the festivals now seemed to be concentrated in the virtue of the Lord" (Granet 1932:232). The virtue and holiness of this new leader radiated to all around him,

conferring especially upon those in closer contact with him
an endorsement of his fitness to exercise governing authority.
Thus was created a body of nobility, who in turn became
his officials. Holiness extended to the residence of the lord.
Temples were built nearby, and markets were set up. This
produced a new center for community activities. True,
religious ceremonies were still periodic in nature, but in time
all institutions were modified by the civil presence.

With the emergence of government, the role of women
in public life was abruptly terminated. Hereafter, the difference between sexes became a difference in value. Henceforth the only participation of woman in worship was her
semi-private worship of the ancestors. Marriage was no
longer a solemn ceremony under the control of the whole
community. It was now contracted at the behest of political expediency.

In time, all the mysterious power attributed to the
festival and its holy place was transferred to the lord. All
the blessings of community security, fruitful harvests, prosperity, and peace seemed to emanate from his tutelary power.
In fact, these men were believed to be directly descended
from mythic, benevolent ancestors and their homage was
directed to the holy places identified with their origin.

Eventually, however, the religious quest led to further
innovation. Man came to feel the need for a more direct
cult related to everyday life. Somehow, the periodical festival of mountain and stream seemed increasingly remote.
"Specialized in religious practices and surrounded by a body
of specialists, they ended up by setting up distinctions in
the all-inclusive activities of the earlier ages" (Granet 1932:
235). Thus, the original festival cults were broken up and
reorganized around the temples. This meant that they could
now go to them for a new sense of contact with the powers
of the unseen world. The original holy places faded in importance and either became places of pilgrimage or slowly

lost their importance altogether.

Before long, every town had its lord, its market, its ancestral temple, and its god of the soil. The ancestors were now regarded as the guardians of the social order. Their mandate was sought for every important official decision. They looked to the god of the soil, the heir to the holy place, to guarantee the regular alternation of the seasons. Gradually, this all-inclusive religious activity was dissociated from the dimensions of time and space. It was taken from the collective possession of all and given to a particular group. In turn, they developed and dominated all the new ritual techniques.

"The ancient festivals were thus reduced to a clutter of rites which the different systems of religious thought distributed up and down the calendar" (Granet 1932:237). With this was begun the long process by which the folk religion of the people was increasingly influenced and controlled by the powers of the state. This development continued throughout the remainder of the Chou and subsequent dynasties.

SOCIAL FUNCTION OF CLASSICAL ANIMISM

Because of the scarcity of data descriptive of the religious life of the peasantry during the Classical period, I cannot give anything like a comprehensive statement on the social function of the animistic practices of that time. It seems apparent also that such description as could be given would differ according to whether the religion described was that of the early Chou or the former Han periods. For purposes of contrast, I have chosen the latter part of the Classical period for our focus of attention. By this time, especially in the former Han, the gentry class had arisen and the Confucian state religion was in process of formation.

Thus, great changes were underway marking the times as distinct from the feudalism of the early Chou dynasty.

Concerning the Confucian rites pertaining to burial, the social functions seem quite clear. Radcliffe-Brown describes them as they obtained among the upper class: "The rites gave regulated expression to certain human feelings and sentiments and so kept these sentiments alive and active. In turn, it was these sentiments which, by their control of or influence on the conduct of individuals, made possible the existence and continuance of an orderly social life" (1952:160).

I assume that by this time a certain amount of Confucian teachings about the funeral rites had percolated down to the peasants' level, a process which Redfield terms "parochialization" (1960:47). In the process, there was likely a certain amount of adaptation and change. If so, the animistic orientation of the ancestor cult doubtless influenced the way in which Confucian burial rites were regarded by the peasant.

The shaman found an exceedingly prominent role during this period. His influence at the levels of both state and the peasantry can best be ascribed to the fact that he functioned as an intermediary between the supernatural and man: "Against magical evil powers, whether in animate or inanimate bodies, there was no more certain antidote than the artifices of the medicine man, for he himself was intimate with and partook of the very nature of the spiritual influences he sought to counteract for his clients" (Harvey 1933:150-51).

How deeply the philosophical ideas of the *yin-yang* and the Five Element concepts had permeated the masses by this time is uncertain. It seems very possible that the dualistic ideas of the *shen* and the *kuei* long since present among all Chinese may have been developed and strengthened following the great influence of Confucius and his disciples.

Finally, we may note Granet's speculation concerning

the genesis of temple building and temple worship early in the Chou dynasty. Certainly by the former Han the religious practices centered in the temple must have played an important part in the life of the people. Given sufficient data along these lines, I am confident that we would find that animistic folk religion, centered as it was in the ancestor cult and shamanism and manifested in home, temple, and festival occasions, functioned as the integrating factor of peasant life.

WORLD VIEW

It is also difficult to state with any confidence what may have been the prevailing world view of the Chinese peasant during the former Han. As the empire continued to expand during Han times, the social and natural factors of the environment in which people lived were increasingly diverse. It is doubtful, therefore, that there was anything that approximated one world view common to all. At best, I can only suggest several elements which may have been widespread in the religious thinking of the peasantry. Some of these I will compare and contrast with those views suggested for the Shang period.

If I may begin with man's view of the universe and the supernatural, it is very possible that by this time the peasant had come to see all supernatural beings, whether *shen* or *kuei*, in terms of a fairly fixed ascending and descending hierarchy. At the top, he would have placed T'ien, the high god of Heaven. If anything, T'ien was even further removed from the people of the Han than was Shang-ti from the people of the Shang. Beginning with Confucius and his disciples, there had arisen a distinct tendency to depersonalize T'ien, thus leaving him more of an absolute impersonal cosmic force resident in the heavens. Whether or not the peasant regarded T'ien in this impersonal way is another question. Below T'ien and arranged according to descending rank were the major and minor deities and demons. Evidence is adduced by Eberhard which would indicate that the emergence of the gentry and Chinese bureaucracy somewhere around 200 B.C. had such an impact upon the thinking of the masses that before long even the gods were conceived of as major and minor officials of Heaven (1952:25). Thus both the nature of the gods and their interrelationships was seen to mirror the earthly monarchy. This would account for the removal of the high god one step farther from the ordinary man. Like the emperor, the high god was no longer accessible to man. He could only be approached through his intermediaries and that only if accompanied by the performance of correct ritual and sacrifice by the suppliant.

Man's concept of nature around him most likely changed but little from Shang times. While the evils of feudalism had largely passed, calamities of drought, disease, flood, and earthquake were constant reminders to the peasant of his need to control the forces of nature. For this reason, he doubtless continued to see spirit intelligences at work in all dimensions of nature and the universe. Needs like these made him a ready patient for the "spiritual ministries" of the shaman.

As for himself, man continued to view himself somewhat as a microcosm struggling for harmony with all the forces of the macrocosm. This integration with the universe and the forces of natures, especially those which regulated seasonal change and the fertility of the land, continued to be one of his major concerns in life. This included a constant battle with the spirit forces and constant employment of magical ritual to expel the *kuei* and coercive manipulation to harness the *shen*.

As for the peasant's view of the afterlife, the continuing presence of the ancestor cult bears witness to his belief in

life after death.   The unanswered question, however, is
whether or not there was developed by this time some
concept of a place of judgment to which the dead must go.
Data touching on this subject is provided by the great sino-
logist A. Waley, who quotes from Chuang-tzu concerning
the death of his wife: "For not nature only but man's being
has its seasons, its sequence of spring and autumn, summer
and winter. . . . She whom I have lost has lain down to sleep
for awhile in the Great Inner Room. To break in upon her
rest with noise of lamentation would but show that I knew
nothing of nature's Sovereign Law" (Campbell 1962:427).
Waley reckons the above to be "but part of a general attitude" of that time towards the universal laws of nature.
I question, however, whether the peasantry held such philosophic views of death. I submit that their concept of the
place of the departed was at least as clear cut as the Shang
view of the Yellow Springs. More likely it had advanced
far beyond this by Han times. Possibly they conceived of
furture retribution somewhat in terms of discipline ad-
ministered in the name of the emperor.

3

Animism in the T'ang Period

INTRODUCTION

BY THE TIME of the T'ang dynasty, three major religious forces had appeared within Chinese culture: the state religion of Confucianism, Buddhism, and religious Taoism. My objective in this chapter will be to discover the way in which these three religious movements influenced animism. The main focus will be upon the religion of the masses, but I will also note changes at the level of the ruling class as well.

Historical Background

The intervening centuries from the latter Han to the T'ang dynasties were marked by many cultural-historic events. These helped to mold the changing forms which animistic religion manifested in each dynasty. A brief sketch of this period will provide a background against which animism of the T'ang period may be better understood. Hu Chang-tu's summary includes the following high points (1960:16-18). During the Han (206 B.C.-A.D. 220), which of course was one of the great dynasties of Chinese history, Confucian

67

scholars were reinstated after the Ch'in persecution and the bureaucratic system of government with its hierarchy of officials was born. The gentry class also arose at this time. The empire expanded north into Korea and west into central Asia even to the borders of the Roman orient. The expanded empire brought new burdens upon the people in taxation and inflation. Peasant uprisings eventually began to undermine the authority of the ruling house. The capital then moved to Lo-yang in Honan, but palace intrigues, weak emperors, internal unrest, and external pressure brought the dynasty to an end in A.D. 220.

The Collapse of Han was followed by three and a half centuries of division and chaos. The country was first divided into the Three Kingdoms. Chinese remember this unsettled period because it is celebrated for romanticism, chivalry, and valor in a flood of poems, short stories, and novels of later periods.

The Chin dynasty (265-420), which for a while presented a semblance of unity, was too weak to stem the tide of barbarian advance. In 317, the Chin court was driven south of the Yangtze River where it re-established its capital at the present site of Nanking. Meanwhile, the barbarians drove south as far as the Fei River where they were defeated in 383. For the next 206 years the barbarians ruled north China. In the south four successive native dynasties struggled to stabilize the countryside and preserve Chinese culture. This was a period of increased contact from abroad. Foreign philosophies and religious ideas found entrance into China, acquired Chinese garb, and became part of the Chinese life and culture.

In 589 the empire was united once more under the short-lived Sui dynasty (589-618). The capital was moved back to Ch'ang-an and Lo-yang. This period saw renewed efforts to develop industry and transportation. Chinese forces sallied forth against neighboring states, checked the rising power of the Turks, invaded the Liu-ch'iu islands, and struck north into Korea and south into Annam. But expansion brought crushing taxes, and the peasants revolted.

Ensuing events witnessed the fall of the Sui and the rise of the T'ang dynasty. The T'ang, inaugurated by Emperor T'ai-tsung, lasted from 618 to 906. Chinese look to this period of history as their Golden Age.

The T'ang period was marked by much stimuli from outside cultural influences. The civil service examination system and bureaucratic form of government were perfected. T'ang government and law codes became models for neighboring countries. Literature flourished in the patriotic lines of Tu Fu (712-770), the haunting poetry of Li Po (701-762), and the stirring essays of Han Yü (768-824). Art, sculpture, and education attracted devotees from many lands to the cosmopolitan city of Ch'ang-an. This was an age of missionaries— Nestorian, Persian, and Muslim— each finding a tolerant atmosphere in the high T'ang world.

The empire of the T'ang was larger even than that of Han. Military expeditions pushed China's frontiers west into Turkestan and north into Korea. They vanquished sea and land forces of Japan and penetrated even into India. And yet the days of T'ang were numbered.

By the middle of the eighth century, T'ang power had declined. Turkestan was lost to Islam, and parts of southwest China fell to the Thais. Uigurs and Tibetans sacked the T'ang capital, peasants revolted against misrule and economic exploitation, and the empire crumbled in 906.*

Social Structure

Hu Chang-tu states that "the positive and fundamentally idealistic social system developed by the Chinese from

_____

*The Uigurs were tribal peoples from the northwest often included among the Hsiung-nu.

Confucian teachings remained basically unchanged for over two thousand years." (1960:141). The Confucian concept of society grew out of the belief that the perfect society was that in which all segments lived in harmony. This in turn could be realized only as each member recognized and accepted his role in relation to other members, performed his duties, and behaved according to a set code of ethics. The ruler was expected to be "tolerant, benevolent and restrained in his exercise of power; commoners were to be respectful, industrious and obedient" (p. 140).

The Confucian scheme of social structure always necessitated a hierarchy of classes. The authoritarian character of the system was counter-balanced by the ideal of moral rectitude cultivated through education and balanced with a knowledge of etiquette and music. The stress on ethics made for a basically humanistic outlook and provided for some vertical mobility among the commoners. As a whole, the ruling class was able to transform this social system into a powerful apparatus for perpetuating its power.

Despite the successive changes in dynasties from the Han to T'ang times, the basic social structure of the ruling class and the ruled remained intact. This was due to the basic economy which was always agrarian. With little incentive to commerce and manufacture, no middle class emerged.

Four factors determined social status: moral character, political position, wealth, and education. These also distinguished the rulers from the ruled. The latter divided into four groups, scholars, farmers, artisans, and merchants, of which only the scholars belonged to the ruling class. Official exams provided the bridge by which one theoretically might elevate his position from the ruled to ruling class and attain a gentry status next only to the nobility. The other part of the lower class were those who by virtue of their "occupational meanness" were excluded from officialdom.

Functionally, they were a caste. At the base of the social
pyramid was the slave class, distinguished either as domestic
or productive. The latter worked in the trades, in mining,
and in farming. At no time was the institution of slavery so
broad as to effect the basic economic structure of society.

Gentry status implied leadership in the community
whether as a government official or as landowner. The
gentry were responsible to represent the people before higher
officials in matters of taxation, education, and important
local affairs. They were exempt from labor conscription and
could often evade tax payment. Opportunities for illegal
economic gain often led to their corruption and to exploitation of the peasantry.

While class distinction minimized inter-class social relationships, some social contact did occur, but this was
mainly within the clan. Thus, all children of the same clan
regardless of social class attended the same school. The
clan had other social and economic functions, such as holding
clan property which was farmed for the benefit of needy
members, temple upkeep, and the like.

Another social organization of similar function was the
"provincial club" located in national and provincial centers.
These were mutual aid societies for out-of-towners who had
come from the same district to do business or take the civil
examinations. Functions of the club included provision for
burial, legal aid, and social activities.

The other group of considerable social import was the
secret society. These were usually of a political or religious
nature, although the latter predominated in the north while
those of a primarily political interest were more numerous in
the south. Secret societies very often became activated in
times of social stress and functioned to provide for local
interest. During periods of corrupt government, they openly
opposed the ruling class. Within these societies, there was
scope for religious expression often marked by a measure

of individualism. The secret society was one of the few
places where those without clan and family could find some
sense of social acceptance.

THE RISE OF BUDDHISM, RELIGIOUS
TAOISM, AND THE CONFUCIAN STATE CULT

Introduction

An important development in post-Han religious life
was the rise of what Yang calls "voluntary religion" (1961.
110). Before this time religious expression among the masses
and the classes was of a communal nature (p. 111):

> The worship of Heaven and the sacrifices to the an-
> cestors and other deities were conducted by officials
> and civic leaders for the well being of all the people in
> the state or community and the great ideal was to enlist
> the help of Heaven and the spirits to build a kingdom
> on earth after the pattern of the celestial order.

Within this system, every individual was a believer by
virtue of his birth into the society, clan, and family group.
For the individual there was no choice in religious beliefs.
Religious values were imbedded in the traditional order of
things; religion was an integral part of all activities, insepar-
able from one's existence.

The rise of Buddhism and of Taoism as a religion
changed the communal pattern of religion. For the first
time in history membership in "consciously organized religion" was based not upon one's inherited position in society
but rather upon voluntary choice, what might be called
"conversion." It was the introduction of religious Taoism
and Buddhism which first gave rise to those systems of

voluntary religion (Yang 1961:112). Hitherto, religion in its communal and classical forms was unquestioned in its supportive role of the political status quo.* Now, however, voluntary religion offered a channel for deviation and the development of opposition to the political machine.

Another factor which played a part in the successful rise of the new religions was the decline of the central government during the second century A.D. The Confucian idealogy, which had been the guiding doctrine for the sociopolitical hierarchy of the Han period, was by this time losing its hold, even among the intellectual elite. Clearly it had failed to offer convincing explanations and cures for the accelerating disintegration of Han society. Nor did Confucian ideology satisfy the longing of the masses for a knowledge of the supernatural, life after death, and the possibility of immortality. As has often been the case in China's history, when suffering became widespread through famine, drought, and ruinous taxation, the emergence of a new religion offered hope of recovering order out of chaos. Into this moral and political vacuum poured the ideas and beliefs later to be developed into the Chinese religions of Taoism and Buddhism.

Although Taoism antedates Buddhism and is indigenous to China, it did not mature in its popular religious form until after the introduction of Buddhism. For this reason, I will examine Buddhism first.

Chinese Buddhism

Early in the first century A.D., Indian forms of Buddhism entered China along the silk roads which led east from Asia. In a surprisingly short time the new religion had reached even to the emperor's court. A memorial presented to Emperor Huan in A.D. 161 refers to a sacrifice made to

*The activities of the shaman often posed an exception to this rule.

Buddha by the emperor. In A.D. 166, Buddha is mentioned as a palace god along with the Yellow Emperor (Yang 1961: 117).

Several factors led to the early establishment of Buddhism in China. One of these was the Buddhist emphasis upon magical functions in religion. Another was the energetic activities of Indian monks who settled down to life-long service in China. Through their labors of translation and teaching, Buddhism was able to take root and become part of the culture of the people. There is also some evidence that several of the emperors of the Later Han period were willing to extend patronage to one or two of the Buddhist monasteries near the capital (Hughes 1950:68).

More important than these were the social disorders which marked the day. People were ready for any new teaching which offered deliverance from the evils of the age. In this sense, Buddhism had come in the "fullness of time."

As we pursue the rapid development of Buddhism from the Han to the T'ang dynasties, two factors loom large: one as noted above was the almost unbroken chain of natural and social calamities which immersed the masses in long periods of unspeakable suffering.* The other was the sporadic invasion of barbarians. During the fourth and fifth centuries, the entire Yellow River basin, the home of Chinese civilization, was overrun by invading hordes of Hun, Mongol, Tungusic, and Turkic tribes. Thus, for long periods of time war decimated the land and a suffering humanity eagerly reached out for anything which offered hope for physical and spiritual salvation.

In its early phase of development, Buddhism was largely a magical cult. Claim for magical power for Buddhist deities

---

*In the two centuries from 220 to 420, the histories record 304 calamities, and between 420 to 589, a period of 109 years, 315 calamities in each of which tens of thousands perished (Yang 1961:116).

attracted devotees both among rich and poor. In an age
when it seemed as if the old gods had lost their power, new
gods were received and the belief spread rapidly that these
gods would provide protection both for the state and the
individual worshipper. In fact, it was through this belief in
the magical efficacy of Buddhism and its power to ward off
demonic influences that the new faith continued to spread
and maintain its influence (Yang 1961:118).

The form of Buddhism which took root and spread
throughout China was known as Mahayana, or the Greater
Vehicle. It is to be contrasted with Hinayana, the Lesser
Vehicle, which spread from India to Ceylon, Burma, and
other areas of French Indochina. While the Hinayana school
emphasized the salvation of the individual, Mahayana Buddhism advocated pity for all creatures and salvation for all
humanity. This salvation was made possible for the masses
by the merits of Buddhas and Bodhisattvas, the latter being
saints who, having merited nirvana, yet vowed to devote all
their religious power to helping others along the way. Both
Buddhas and Bodhisattvas were approachable by the peasantry. This new emphasis tended to lift the movement above
the individual and magical levels so characteristic of Hinayana
Buddhism. Peoples of all social classes were attracted to
the new religion with its metaphysical dimensions, universalist
teachings, and many moral precepts which at points bore a
resemblance to Confucian ideology.

The subsequent spread of Chinese Buddhism is closely
linked with the rise of a number of prophetic leaders as well
as a vigorous period of translation and dissemination of
Buddhist teachings. Of particular importance was the translation of the *Fa-hua ching* (*Lotus Sutra*). This monumental
work teaches a world of fantasy in which numberless gods
and demons are dramatized. The doctrine of salvation
involves the awakening and enlightenment of the Buddha
nature which is latent in every man. This universalized faith

together with karma, the "endless revolution of the wheel of causal retribution," and the concommitant belief in reincarnation had a natural appeal during the four centuries of disunion in China (Yang 1961:120). It was easy for the people to see in the protracted struggles with barbarian devils, a mirror of demonic wars in the Buddhist scriptures. Nor was it difficult during these chaotic periods to accept the teaching that life was illusory and transitory; neither dynastic fortune nor personal life and property were enduring.

From the third to fifth centuries, Mahayana Buddhism found increasing favor among intellectuals, officials, kings, and emperors. By the fifth century it was a common saying, though doubtless exaggerated, that "nine out of ten families worshipped the Buddha in the northern capital of Chang-an" (p. 120). The growth of monastic orders, especially in the fourth and fifth centuries, was doubtless given added impetus by the multitudes seeking refuge from the fierce struggles of the time. For both rich and poor, life in the Buddhist priesthood was at once a spiritual consolation, a magical protection, and a material relief. Burdens of taxation and threats of conscription were thus removed, and the possibility of a peaceful and ordered life was once again realized.

The expansion of such a movement could not but come into eventual conflict with the secular and political powers. By the early sixth century the Buddhist movement had become a state within a state. A tract of the times describes the situation (Yang 1961:122):

> Over a hundred thousand monks and nuns possess vast wealth and property.... Nearly one half the population in the whole empire is lost to them. I fear that every building will turn into a monastery and the people in every family will be ordained into the priesthood

and not one foot of soil will remain to the state.*

Between 477 and 535 there were eight attempts at armed rebellion by Buddhists in the Northern Wei area. Even in the politically unified period of T'ang, Buddhist encroachment upon state prerogatives of taxation and conscription was such as to provoke the famed memorial of Han Yü: "Restore its people to human living! Burn its books! And convert its buildings to human dwellings" (p. 122). These events lie behind the four great persecutions of Buddhism which occurred in 446, 574, 845, and 955. From this period on Buddhism became acculturated to the Chinese social milieu both in its theology and organization. The forces of secular and political power won out in the long struggle to bring the new religion into a place of conformity with and support of the status quo.** The continued expansion of Buddhism during the T'ang dynasty was doubtless related to the continued cosmopolitan character of the current policy which was generally favorable to foreign influence.***

Among the common people, many basic Buddhist beliefs had by this time become firmly imbedded. Possibly the most potent of these was the belief in transmigration of the soul and causal retribution. This doctrine was two-pronged

---

*Early in the fifth century, it was estimated that in the northern capital of Lo-yang with a population of about half a million, there were 1,367 temples. The famous Buddhist cave temples of Yün-kang were also begun at this time (Smith 1968:120).

**Resurgence of Chinese national culture and classical Confucian ideology did not occur until the end of the T'ang period.

***It is beyond the scope of this study to deal with the various Buddhist sects which began to arise around the fifth century and flowered during the T'ang period.

in function. On the one hand it served to elaborate the
concept of the soul and of life after death; it also functioned
to enforce socio-ethical mores. It provided a powerful support for the political order as well as giving a system of
belief about the afterlife. Many deities were also added to
the existing pantheon. By 845, Buddhist temples numbered
4,600 and shrines 40,000 (Yang 1961:123).

The services of Buddhist monks found an important
and permanent place in the ancestor cult, especially in the
funeral rites. It was probably at this point touching the
rites of death and burial that Buddhist theology made its
greatest impact. Until the third century A.D., popular belief
concerning the soul lacked any developed idea of a hell or
purgatory. It is paradoxical that Buddhism in its Hinayana
and Mahayana forms, both of which were based upon the
non-existence of the ego, should have introduced into Chinese
religion the concept of the soul going through trial and
punishment in a purgatory and then being reborn according
to the laws of karma (Thompson 1969:11). I see here a
remarkable cross-fertilization taking place between concepts
basically Buddhist and Chinese. Having incorporated the
idea of the soul from Chinese religion, the Buddhists pro-
ceeded to attach to it ideas of retribution and suffering. Not
only this, the Buddhist monk then came to function as a
priest saying "masses" to alleviate the sufferings of the soul
in purgatory!* The end result at the level of animistic folk
religion was a "purgatorial system organized along Confucian
bureaucratic lines with a well-organized program of karmic
bookkeeping, trials in courts, and . . . punishments in various
hells where the tortures meted out exactly fitted the crimes
of the guilty soul" (Thompson 1969:11-12).

---

*Some writers see in this aspect of Buddhism the possible in-
fluence of a decadent Nestorianism.

Thus, there came to be two concepts of the soul, one based upon the *yin/kuei, yang/shen* system of native tradition and the other based upon Indian belief in karmic process. The first is bound up with family religion and the ancestor cult and the second is strong especially in the funeral rites.

Religious Taoism

The term "religious Taoism" is used to distinguish the popular animistic forms of Taoist religion from its philosophic superstructure. We will see that these are two distinct developments not to be confused.

The origins of philosophic Taoism are lost in the mists of antiquity. In the latter half of the Chou period, Taoism in its philosophic dimensions developed alongside Confucianism to form one of the main streams of philosophic thought (Smith 1968:69). It was not until the early centuries of the Christian era that Taoism took on the form of an organized religion claiming, like Buddhism, the loyalties of millions of the common people. It is this religious dimension which concerns me in this study, for it was from this source that a new stream of animistic belief began to flow as a tributary feeding back into the main artery of the folk religion.

The primary source for the study of religious Taoism is the *Tao Tsang* or Taoist Canon. This work comprises at least 1,120 volumes compiled like the Bible over some 1,500 years (Welch 1957:88). Most of these are without date and name of author. Many are written in esoteric language known only to the initiates. Some books claim to be divine revelation made to Taoist adepts during trance (Smith 1968: 98). Few of these materials have been translated to date, so the essential nature and development of early religious Taoism is at best imperfectly understood even among scholars.

The leading doctrines of religious Taoism at first were distinct from those of Buddhism. Buddhism looked upon life as suffering. Suffering, they said, arises from passion, which in turn results from the erroneous conviction that the ego exists. The religious quest, then, was for enlightenment and a deadness to the things of the world.

Taoism, on the other hand, held that life was good and to be enjoyed. The individual, with all of nature, is a product of the *yang* and *yin* as operational processes of *tao* 道. Both the ego and the world are real, not illusory, as in Buddhism. The religious quest is for "liberation of the spiritual elements of the ego from physical limitations, so that it may enjoy immortality or at least longevity" (Thompson 1969:89). This could also be viewed as triumph of the *yang* (good) over *yin* (evil). While the connection between these concepts and the classic Taoist texts attributed to Lao-tzu and Chuang-tzu is not readily discernable, there are numerous passages in these classics which lend themselves readily to mystic and esoteric interpretation.

It is impossible to discuss the spread of religious Taoism without referring to the different schools or branches of which it was composed. Holmes Welch sums these up: "The science of alchemy, maritime expeditions in search of the Isles of the Blest,* and indigenous form of Chinese *yoga*; a cult of wine and poetry; collective sexual orgies; church armies defending a theocratic state; revolutionary secret societies; and the philosophy of Lao-tzu" (1957:88).

Broadly speaking, four main streams converged to form religious Taoism in about the fourth century. These were philosophical Taoism, a "hygiene school," a school which searched for the elixir of life, and a movement of expeditions from the northeast coasts of China in search of the Isles of

*The elixir of life was thought to be found in the mythical religion known as the Isles of the Blest.

the Blest. These various strands were brought together.

It was during the third and fourth centuries B.C. that the names of Lao-tzu, Chuang-tzu, and Lieh-tzu became associated with what we call philosophical Taoism. Their writings in turn refer to a "hygiene school" which practised breathing exercises and gymnastics with a view to longevity. The same period witnessed the writings of Tsou Yen on the Five Elements. His disciples began research on the elixir of life to be followed shortly with expeditions seeking the Isles of the Blest. In the development of these several streams, it is likely that the shaman with his dance and ecstasy, the mediums, and the diviners all played a part. By the last century B.C., these four streams (all but the first of which were united in their search for long life) were united into one broad river by the *fang-shih* 方師 , magicians from northeast China (Welch 1958:98). These men were to have great influence upon emperors such as Shih-huang-ti of the Ch'in dynasty, persuading them to send out extensive voyages in search for the mushroom which would prevent death.*

Experiments in alchemy and hygiene were begun as early as 133 B.C. by the *fang-shih* Li Shao-chun, who hoped to turn cinnabar into gold. This experiment was begun with a sacrifice to the God of the Stove (Tsao-chün), later to become a leading divinity of Taoism (Welch 1957:100).

The next period in religious Taoism covers the first to fourth centuries A.D., called by Welch the period of the "Interior Gods Hygiene School" (105). Basic to the thought of this school was the idea that every man has three vital centers to his body, one in the head, one in the chest, and one in the abdomen. They are called the Fields of Cinnabar (*tan t'ien* 丹田). The body is inhabited by 36,000 gods,

---

*This mushroom was thought to grow on P'eng-lai, the Isles of the Blest.

the same as those, the celestial bureaucrats, that rule heaven and govern the universe. Thus, the human body becomes a microcosm of the universe. Without going into the complexity of Taoist beliefs, it is sufficient to note that maintaining life, to the Taoist, consisted in keeping the "interior gods" at their posts: "When the gods depart, the adept dies" (p. 108). This was accomplished by trance, controlled diet, gymnastics, and controlled breathing. Doing good works to accumulate merit was an idea introduced by this school.

In time the quest for physical immortality gave way to mere longevity. Eventually, the ideas of paradise, purgatory, and the immortality of the soul were taken in from Buddhism, and the quest for immortality was limited to life in the paradise to come.

Welch speaks of a Taoist "church" movement which arose in the second or third century. Thompson challenges the use of the word "church," pointing out that these Taoist institutions were like Buddhist temples in that they lacked any overall organization and functioned as independent units (Thompson 1969:97). There is evidence, however, pointing to the existence of northern and southern schools of Taoism. These arose during the disintegration of the Han in response to the widespread misery and suffering of the peasants. Here was the fertile field waiting only for the rise of a prophet with the vision to preach the coming of a millenium and the apocalyptic establishment of a new era of peace through supernatural intervention.*

In the case of China, Taoist prophets arose and mighty movements were born, not the least of which was the Yellow Turban sect claiming upwards of three hundred followers (Welch 1957:105). Often these sects took on revolutionary

*Similar nativistic messianic movements are found in the history of every nation and are well documented in works such as A. R. Tippett's *Solomon Island Christianity* (1969).

overtones, overturned dynasties, and functioned to check excess corruption in government circles. Largely as a result of these movements, Taoism became a popular religion highly organized among the masses.

At the popular level, Taoism came to be loosely organized into districts presided over by priests or *tao-shih* 道士. These were often itinerant, but by the fifth century monastic life began to appear, and by the sixth it was the pattern. Priests could marry and have children. The office became hereditary and passed from father to son. Small groups of "elders" assisted the priest in performing ceremonies and collecting dues. Support for the Taoist priest came from the people whom he served at such occasions as birth and death.

In the sixth century, Taoism adopted celibacy for all priests living in monasteries, and nunneries were established for women. Certificates issued to priests allowed exemption from military service and taxation.

By the time of the T'ang dynasty, Taoism had gained a measure of imperial favor. Hsüan-tsung (712-756), one of the several T'ang emperors to follow Taoism, ordered that a Taoist temple should be built in every city and that every noble family should possess a copy of the *Tao-te ching* (Welch 1957:109)*. The Taoist religion was by this time well established and few fundamental changes were to be made during the next few centuries.

The development of the Taoist pantheon suggests the influence which religious Taoism exerted upon the masses. The earliest gods were personifications of natural forces and of metaphysical concepts (p. 135). Around these there arose a multitude of *hsien* 仙 (immortals) who were human beings who had won divinity through hygienic ritual. With the competition of Buddhism, the Taoist felt the need for gods

---

*The Chinese classic alleged to be written by Lao-tzu and claimed by the Taoist movement as their main scripture.

who would answer the prayers of the masses for protection and success in troubled times. The Celestial Lords (*T'ien-chün*) were thus introduced as the gods who are constantly occupied with the salvation of all men. Eventually, the Jade Emperor (*Yü-huang*) became the supreme deity, doubtless from a belief in his greater power and efficacy (138).

Other gods included *Ch'eng huang* 城隍 (God of Moats and Walls) and *Tsao wang* 竈王 (God of the Hearth). The latter is possibly the oldest of the pantheon and served as a recorder of all deeds, good and bad, which he observed within each family.

These and a multitude of other gods inhabited heaven and hell, each holding a position within a bureaucratic hierarchy and all responsible to the Jade Emperor, to whom they reported once a year for promotion or demotion.

State Cult of Confucianism

It was not until the early days of the Han dynasty that the elaborate system which has been called the state cult became firmly grounded in the doctrines of Confucius and his disciples. By the time of Han Wu-ti (141-87 B.C.), Confucius and his disciples were deemed worthy of sacrifical honors not only by their own descendants but also by the emperor and his officials (Smith 1968:140).

In A.D. 57, it was decreed that sacrifices should be made to Confucius in the imperial college and in all the principle colleges of the empire (Harvey 1933:261). By the early T'ang dynasty separate temples were assigned to both Confucius and the Duke of Chou, but by 628 they were all given over to Confucius in connection with the colleges and examination halls, a custom which remained until the turn of the twentieth century.

Prayers to Confucius offered by the emperor included such phrases as "the ancient Teacher, the perfect Sage, . . . in virtue equal to Heaven and Earth" (p. 262). Offerings of fruit and vegetables were also made to his spirit. Thus, by T'ang times the Master was by slow degrees exhalted to a position of divinity and made a "pillar of support" for the imperial power (Thompson 1969:66).

The state cult of Confucius was but one part of the state religion. In fact, much of what made up the state religion far antedated Confucius. Archeological evidence dating back to the late Shang (ca. 1300-1100 B.C.) lists the following deities which were worshipped in addition to the all-important ancestors: the Supreme God Shang-ti, the God of Wind, the God of Clouds, gods of the Sun and Moon, gods of the mountains and Yellow River, and gods of the four directions and different localities (Thompson 1969: 69). By the time of the Ch'ing dynasty (1644-1911), the bulk of these divinities were still being worshipped in official ceremonies.

The point at which state religion touched upon animism among the masses was through the state cults maintained in each local area by appointed magistrates (Thompson 1969: 72):

> The moral influence of the magistrate was reflected not only in his own behavior but even in the reactions of nature. The magistrate as deputy of the emperor, played the same role of intermediary between human and natural forces in the small territory under his control.

The local people looked to the magistrate as representative of the powers that be to use his authority to intercede with the appropriate spiritual powers in times of flood, drought, or pestilence. To facilitate these religious services, the state provided each local capital with memorial halls, altars, and official cult temples.

Among the gods worshipped in the official cult, the local earth god was most important. As in ancient times, the shrines of earth gods were found in every village and in every government office. Since they were so close to the lives of the people, the officials dared not leave him out.

Thus, the state religion functioned to preserve, strengthen, and control the animistic beliefs and practices of the masses. This was done, as we have seen, through inclusion of the most revered divinities of the people in the official religion and their manipulation so as to give divine authority to the bureaucratic system as a whole. It must be remembered, however, that the entire Confucian system was relatively weak during the early T'ang period. Not until the late T'ang and early Sung (960-1126) did the neo-Confucian movement lift the state religion once more to a place of great influence throughout the empire.

T'ANG SHAMANISM

Shamanism during the T'ang continued to have much the same influence as in former times. Data from de Groot's study indicate that the influence of the shaman touched the religious life of society from peasant to emperor. In 472 a decree from Emperor Wen decreed that "female *wu* and sorcerer *shih*" should forever be excluded from the Canon of Sacrificial Worship of the Confucian state religion (de Groot 1892-1910:6:1234). This did not, however, exclude the *wu* as exorcists and destroyers of evil, and, as before, emperors continued to employ them for sacrifices to state gods to avert dangers for the realm and the throne. In the eighth century we read of a prefect enlisting the help of female shamans during a great drought to offer "prayers against calamity . . . for more than twenty days" (p. 1236).

It is interesting to note that by the time of the T'ang Taoist priests have taken over many of the characteristics of the shaman. De Groot writes (p. 1254):

> Actually . . . the *tao shih* became a priesthood working
> for the same great object for which *Wu*-ism had existed
> since the night of time: moreover, *Wu*-ism properly
> considered was Taoism because the spirits which it
> exploited or exorcised for the promotion of human
> happiness were Taoist gods and spectres, that is to say
> the same parts of the dual Universal Soul, *Yang* and
> *Yin*, which compose the Tao. It is accordingly quite
> natural, that as soon as the *tao shih* made themselves
> priests of Universal Animism, their assimilation with
> the *wu* was imminent.

Evidently, the Taoist priesthood learned the ancient art of
exorcism from the shaman and wove it into the sacrificial
worship of the gods. When the older philosophical function
of the *tao-shih* was discarded, namely, his assimilation with
the *tao* by mental and bodily discipline, any basic differences
between the *tao-shih* and the *wu* were erased. This process
was likely linked with Buddhist monasticism, chief competitor
of religious Taoism. The conclusion suggested is that the
Taoist priesthood gradually assimilated and supplanted the
shamanic priesthood in Chinese religious life, so that even
in places like Amoy, where shamanism has thrived down
to the present century, the term *wu* has apparently disappeared from the vernacular language.

The role played by magic throughout the tradition of
religious Taoism, especially in its shamanic aspects, is of great
importance. Data on this subject presents a kaleidoscopic
system of Chinese belief and ritual of the most complex
nature. Taoist books abound with magical charms and
incantations useful for every conceivable problem in which
there is need for the expulsion of demonic powers. The
magic rope, the exorcising sword, and noise-making instruments are but a few of the paraphernalia which date back
to antiquity and survive even today in Taoist circles.

We may safely conclude that the animistic ritual and belief of the T'ang period was very much influenced by the Taoist shaman. More than anyone else, the shaman was the great expert in dealing with spirit powers. His presence and activities among the masses was a continual reminder to them that all kinds of sickness and calamity were the result of evil spirits. The shaman was living testimony to the efficacy of magic and correct ritual for the expulsion of spirits powers. And yet the peasant was never freed from the anxious fear that, while one spirit had been expelled, there was always a host of other spectres and demons waiting to invade his life.

BARBARIAN INFLUENCE

Animistic influence entering China via contacts with barbarian peoples prior to and during the T'ang period must have been considerable. Without going deeply into this complex problem, one illustration can be given which points to the introduction of fire worship into China via the Manicheism of the Persians.

As early as 631, record is made of temples being erected by the emperor in which ritual was performed to the fire spirit (Parker 1905:110). In 677 another Persian temple was erected in Ch'ang-an and in 694 Persian holy books were introduced. These were works elaborating dualistic principles similar to those of Chinese *yin-yang* dualism.

Persian religious thought did not effectively penetrate Chinese society until the coming of a northern tribe of Turks known as the Uigurs. These tribesmen had been allies with the Chinese in resisting Tibetan invaders (A.D. 763-777). Subsequent to this, many of the Uigur settled in north China and took the Manichean religion under their official protection, thus extending its influence into the south of

China. Subsequent edicts against Manicheanism and ban-
ishment of the Uigurs doubtless removed much of the
Manichean religious influence from China. It is highly
probable, however, that a residue of animistic beliefs was
successfully implanted in Chinese minds. One is tempted to
speculate that Chinese religious feelings towards fire were
somewhat affected, possibly resulting in the survival of
Persian-type fire cults.

SOCIAL FUNCTION OF T'ANG ANIMISM

The social function of animism is not easy to delineate
during T'ang times. The indigenous mainstream of animistic
shamanism, ancestor worship, and the religious rites clustering
around ancient temple deities had by T'ang times been
thoroughly imbued with Taoist and Buddhist metaphysical
concepts. If I may assume the popular religion of the time
to be a rather thorough mixture of all these elements, as
it has been in recent times, then I am safe in seeing certain
functions which the popular animistic religion fulfilled within
peasant society.

The services of the shaman together with the protector
deities doubtless provided a sense of security for life and
property. Other gods, largely the earth tutelaries under
the suzerainty of Ch'eng-huang, provided for the peasant
a sense of adjustment to the earth and environment. Provision for peace and harmony in the home was the concern
of the ancestors and of other deities, such as the kitchen god.
A prosperous livelihood was assured by the correct ritual
offerings to the patron gods of farmers, artisans and those
of the professions. Particularly related to the teachings of
Buddhism and Taoism and Buddhist monks whose "mass-
like" prayers combined with the efforts of King Ti-ts'ang for
the release of suffering souls from the Buddhist and Taoist

forms of purgatory. The objective of many was, of course, not mere deliverance from torment but the attainment of some form of reward in heaven. To this end the Buddhist and Taoist "savior" deities were ready to lend assistance.

I have found little data on the festivals of the T'ang period. However, I am doubtless not far from the truth in assuming that the festival continued to play an important role in Chinese society. There can be little question, for example, that the Festival of Hungry Spirits was by T'ang times a prominent communal activity in many areas of China (Day 1969:126).

WORLD VIEW OF THE T'ANG

The way in which T'ang peasantry looked upon the world, the supernatural, and man may have varied from place to place. The age was hardly characterized by a simple homogeneous folk religion. Kitagawa reminds us that while various forms of Buddhism held first place in the lives of the people, Taoism was also strong. Moreover, this period witnessed the introduction of Muslim, Persian, Manichean, and Nestorian forms of religion, while Confucianism continued to be the guiding principle of state (Kitagawa 1960: 65). It is not likely that the newer religions influenced the thinking of great numbers. The formative religious forces almost certainly continued to derive from the ancient forms of animism together with certain innovations adopted from Buddhism and religious Taoism.

Perhaps the most significant development in the peasant world view was the concept of purgatory introduced through Buddhism and largely taken over by Taoism as well. By T'ang times the concept of the soul passing through various forms of torment in purgatory was familiar to all. The idea of prayers for the dead became widespread and must have reinforced the peasant's firm belief that the state of the departed was dependent upon the fulfillment of filial obligations on the part of the living.

Further development in the popular pantheon is traceable to T'ang times. The "Pearly Emperor on High" (Jade Emperor) consolidated his place of supremacy in the Taoist temples while Kuan-yin became the female partner to Buddha. The idea of the compassionate "Mother of Heaven" found ready acceptance by a suffering humanity (Hughes 1950:80).

Under the dual influence of a growing Buddhism and a progressively corrupted Confucianism, many a peasant came to see the good life as that lived in the monastery. There, within the quiet and protection of monastic life, the peasant believed he would find peace of soul and eventual access to the "heavens beyond heavens of purity and brightness and infinite compassion" (Hughes 1950:82).

T'ang man continued to look upon nature as under the influence of the *yin* and *yang* powers. The beneficent earth bountiful in its harvest for man today might be the scene of raging floods or rending earthquakes tomorrow. These uncertainties of life pressed the peasantry to call hard and often upon the services of shaman, ancestor, and deity. Life was essentially under the powers of the spirit world, and the fear of death was only heightened by visions of torment in purgatory.

In the latter part of the T'ang, state persecution of Buddhism became widespread. Under the Taoist Emperor Wu-tsung, a systematic attack was launched to purge Buddhism from the empire. The result was the demolition of 4,600 monasteries and shrines and the forced repatriation of 260,000 priests and nuns into secular lay life (Kitagawa 1960:66). I wonder what effect such an attack on a popular aspect of religion may have had upon the world view of the peasant.

4

Animism in Modern Taiwan

INTRODUCTION

WHAT IS THE current manifestation of animism in the folk religion of Taiwan today? To what degree does it represent a continuation of the animistic religion of T'ang and earlier times? In what way has Taiwanese animism responded in recent years to the secular forces of education and technology? The answer to these questions will take up the major part of this chapter. But first I will reconstruct the historical background. Without it I cannot develop balanced and adequate answers to these questions.

Historical Background
    The following thumbnail sketch of Chinese history from the rise of the Five Dynasties (907-960) to present-day Taiwan is intended to serve as an historical and cultural bridge to link the present with the past.*

    *I have not attempted to fill in the development of Chinese social structures for this long period.

The T'ang dynasty collapsed as a result of misrule, economic exploitation, popular revolt, and foreign invasion by northern barbarians. This ushered in the period of the Five Dynasties. For more than half a century, military chieftains ruled the empire. Five ephemeral dynasties rose and fell in quick succession. None was able to exercise rule over all of China proper. One result of this internal weakness and subsequent break-up of the empire was that North China once again fell victim to Tartar invaders.

The Sung dynasty (960-1279) succeeded in uniting most of the fragments of the empire which had emerged as separate states during the confusion of the Five Dynasties. However, there remained large areas in the north and northwest which border peoples occupied throughout the Sung period.*

In 1127, one of these peoples, the Jurchens, invaded China proper and annexed a large area, roughly designated as North China. The Sung court fled to Hangchow. This signaled the abandonment of interior provinces in favor of coastal regions.

In some respects the Sung period was the beginning of modernity in China, not only in government and social organization, but also in culture and economy. Civil authority of regional military governors was curbed. Stated objectives of the new regime were "government efficiency, prosperity and a strong army" (Hu 1960:19). However, disagreement over methods of reaching socio-political-economic goals soon divided the Sung court between reformers and conservatives. With the help of the gentry class, the conservative faction won out. Nonetheless many gains were realized by the end of the Sung period. Social mobility increased. A new influential class of wealthy businessmen

*These peoples included the Khitan, Tangut, and Jurchen.

emerged with the growth of cash economy. Invention of the compass spurred development of shipping and navigation.

Meanwhile, continued pressure year after year from barbarian invaders on the northern frontiers had an unsettling effect on the people. Although at first they were able again and again to drive them off, a war-weariness settled on the land. All longed for peace and order. Almost unconsciously, they turned to those reformers who called for a return to Confucian ideas and metaphysical solutions. They began to seek a new cosmic order and moral philosophy around which to build a more stable society. Out of this was born Neo-Confucianism, the system of thought which was to dominate the minds of Chinese leaders down to the nineteenth century.

Despite Sung China's cultural achievements, she was unable to stand against the increasing strength of the barbarians. Weakened by Khitan and Jurchen attacks, China eventually was unable to cope with the Mongol invaders who suddenly emerged from the north. By 1260, Kublai Khan (1214-94) had captured North and South China and inaugurated the Yüan dynasty (1280-1368). This was the first non-Chinese regime to rule all of China.

Anti-foreignism was strong during this period. The Mongolian rulers were too hungry for further spoil to be content with China. They began to mobilize Chinese manpower and resources for expeditions against Japan, Annam, and Java. While they brought a measure of economic improvement to China, the price was a deliberate policy of exploitation and discrimination against the Chinese people.

Rebellion finally erupted in the Yangtze region. The Chinese cut off the flow of supplies to the Mongol leaders, and the beleaguered Mongol court was finally ousted in 1368. With the end of the Yüan period, the Chinese regained their independence under the new Ming dynasty (1368-1644).

Like many earlier dynasties, the Ming was born out of the aspirations of great men for governmental reform and social uplift. Emphasis was placed upon farming. The attention of the masses was once again turned to constructive pursuits. The first Ming emperor reached for absolute control. He gained this only after arresting and executing hundreds of gentry scholars. This meant the shifting of political power from trained bureaucrats to a group of untutored eunuchs and palace attendants. Strange as it may seem, for a time all went well.

The zenith of Ming civilization witnessed territorial expansion into Annam and the successful checking of Mongol invaders. Maritime expeditions ranged as far as India and eastern Africa. They brought back tribute from many lands.

But the Ming ascendancy over East Asia was transient. Its earlier vigor gave way to political languor under a new but conservative bureaucracy. It was the old story of a weak emperor surrounded by unscrupulous eunuchs bringing China to economic and social decline. The fall of the Ming awaited only the reappearance of Mongol invaders, the incursions of the emerging Manchus, and the growing power of Japan. The first phase was the Japanese invasion of Korea. In 1644, Manchu armies captured the capital, Peking, and made themselves the new masters of China. This Manchu dynasty lasted for almost three hundred years (1644-1911).

For some time after the Manchu triumph, local pockets of anti-Manchu resistance continued to operate largely out of Fukien in South China. A Ming stronghold had been located on Taiwan as late as 1664, ruled by the warlord Koxinga (Cheng Ch'eng-kung), who had established himself by driving out the Dutch East India Company. By 1683, however, this rebellion was quelled by the Manchus. Koxinga died and his descendants were captured. From this time onward all of China came under the rule of the Manchus. This marked the beginning of the second period of barbarian rule over China.

TAIWAN: CULTURAL HISTORY

Unfortunately, until recently, Western historians have given little or no attention to the small island of Taiwan. Its written history merges with myth prior to the thirteenth century A.D. Indeed, there are few clues as to its earlier history. Archeologist Chang Kwang-chih cites some evidence of civilization in Taiwan as early as the Lung-shan or black pottery horizon of neolithic times (1963:87).*

Until recently, little was known of the historical relationships between Taiwan's aborginal cultures and early Chinese civilization on the mainland. The picture has changed somewhat in the light of ethnological and archeological studies which have been done on the Taiwan tribes by Ch'en Chi-lu. In his judgment, their art motifs and carvings have marked similarities with the Shang and earlier civilizations. Concerning their presence on the island, he writes: "It is safe to say that they migrated in waves, beginning a few thousand years before Christ and ending centuries after that" (1968:7). He believes racial and cultural contact between Taiwan and the mainland was rather frequent during the second millenium B.C. The Lung-shan civilization was introduced through a succession of southward ethnic migrations of Chinese during the Hsia, Shang, and Chou eras from about 1500 to 200 B.C. (p. 323). The influence of aboriginal people upon Taiwanese animism from the seventeenth to nineteenth centuries was minimal.

Extensive Chinese colonization of Taiwan began during the reign of Koxinga (1624-1661). He encouraged settlers from various regions of Fukien to homestead on the fertile western plains of Taiwan. This colonization expanded

*J. Campbell, quoting other sources in his work *The Masks of God*, suggests the dates 1900-1523 B.C. for this period (1962:2:377).

rapidly during the eighteenth century, so much so that the whole western plain was included in the Ch'ing administrative system.   Between 1684 and 1875, prefectures had been established at Chu-lo (Chia-yi), Chang-hua, Hsin-chu, and Taipei (Chen 1968:8).

During this period, the aborigines of the plains (the *p'ing-pu*, "plains tribes") retreated to the foothills and the eastern coast. Those who remained were acculturated to the Taiwanese-Chinese. Thus, the ethnic and cultural structure of the plains and foothill areas developed into three strata: the lower level of aborigines, the middle level of mixed race, and the upper level of Chinese or Taiwanese.

In order to appreciate the historical developments in Taiwan from the seventeenth century onward, some knowledge of the earlier period is necessary. When the Ashikaga dynasty was overthrown in Japan (1443), many Japanese were deprived of their property and livelihood by the civil war that followed. Not a few turned to piracy and trading for their livelihood. In their search for a base of operations, they settled on Taiwan. From the port of Keelung in the north of Taiwan they worked the southern coast of China, combining legitimate trade with piracy. They discovered that in southern Taiwan there were Chinese engaged in similar activities. Before long, pirate raids on the China coast had become so numerous that the Chinese government formally broke trade relations with Japan. But the trade and piracy continued. In time, Taiwan became the natural link between these two nations, functioning as a neutral port, open to all countries, where trading was possible without fear of official disturbance.

Meanwhile, three great European powers, Portugal, Spain and Holland, began to extend their colonial holdings into the Orient. In 1557 the Portuguese established a trade center at Macao. The name "Formosa" (Portuguese for "beautiful") is traced back to the late sixteenth century, thus

indicating that the Portuguese seamen were not unaware of
the island's existence.* It is very likely that their trading
activities included Taiwan, though the available data is
inconclusive.

There are four major periods of Taiwanese recorded
history. Rather than focusing only on historical events,
I will also trace the social and religious developments of the
period. The folk religion of the Taiwanese people, while
closely related to that of Fukien on the South China
mainland, has had its own unique development within the
historical framework of the Chinese colonization of Taiwan.
In this context, Ch'iu Ming-chung sees four distinct periods.
They follow below.**

*The Period of Migration and Early Settlement (Early Seven-
teenth Century)*

Significant numbers of Fukienese did not begin to
migrate to Taiwan until during the Dutch occupation (1622-
1664), when laborers were needed to build Dutch fortifi-
cations as well as farmers to cultivate the land. The greatest
influx, however, occurred during the reign of Koxinga, who
captured Taiwan from the Dutch in 1664.

These early Chinese pioneers were careful to bring with
them the ancestor tablets and icons (images) of their chief
divinities in order that the continuity of their traditional
religion might not be broken. The two gods Ma-tsu (媽祖
Goddess of the Southern Sea) and Wang-yeh (王爺 God of
Pestilence) soon became greatly revered because of the
protection which they afforded the pilgrims in crossing the

*The name "Formosa" was the most common name for the
island and used extensively until after 1945, when "Taiwan" became
the common name.
**Ch'iu Ming-chung is author of a doctoral dissertation entitled
"Two Types of Folk Piety: A Comparative Study of Two Folk Religions of Formosa" (1970).

dangerous straits of Taiwan. These two divinities still rank highest in the folk pantheon in Taiwan today.

Other gods also grew in status during this period. As the Chinese faced the task of pioneering in a strange land, they confronted many dangers. Their struggle for survival involved savage tribal headhunters, floods, droughts, and earthquakes. Naturally, they sought the assistance of their gods, especially those who give protection to settlers in frontier lands and help avert national calamities. These gods included Kuan Kung(關公 God of Warriors) and T'u-ti Kung (土地公 God of the Earth) (Ch'iu 1970:153). These gods, whom they felt were responsive to their needs, inevitably gained in popularity and stature.

In addition to seeking the help of these gods, the Taiwanese also relied on the practice of magic to deliver them from the hazards of life. Living conditions of early Taiwan exposed them to recurring plagues and pestilence. Doubtless their lack of a reliable praxis of medicine drove the people to folk religion for magical healing. This provided ample scope for the shaman and the Taoist priest to use their occult arts in expelling demons and healing diseases.

The Taiwanese had to cope with the hostile, dominating presence of the Dutch. Life under those cruel taskmasters was made bitter because of the burden of an excessive taxation. Indeed, together with their interclan feuds, this drove the early Taiwanese to find spiritual refuge in the village folk temple. The temple soon became the symbolic center of all Taiwanese communal resistance to the world outside.

With the coming of Koxinga in 1664, conditions for the peasant improved somewhat. Eventually, however, a new enemy appeared—the Manchu invaders from the mainland. This development necessitated that the Taiwanese maintain a constant state of preparation. Since local officials and other leaders apparently gave little assistance in response to the pleas of the harassed people, they became accustomed to taking their complaints to the temple where Ch'eng-huang and other administrative deities resided, believing that the latter would be more responsive in hearing and answering their pleas.

The above factors served not only to strengthen the existing folk religion of the peasant but to cause it to develop in a dynamic fashion according to the changing needs of the times. Their religion provided, and refined, techniques in "astrology, . . . dream divination, geomancy, witchcraft, palmistry, phrenology, the recalling of the soul, fortune telling and charms" (Ch'iu 1970:155). Each god in the pantheon had its particular function in meeting the needs of the masses.

We might summarize by stating that religion in this early period was primarily a matter of the family and the temple. Each day was begun with the casting of prayer blocks to ascertain whether the day would be free from hostile men and impersonal calamities. Those gods who were responsive and whose directions proved especially efficacious were not long in being promoted to temples of their own. Naturally, they drew a wider group of devotees. Non-productive deities were downgraded. Obviously, there was nothing permanent in a deity's hold on the "mandate of heaven."

The Period of the Early Ch'ing Administration (1682-1820)

The early Ch'ing was a period of internal anarchy and intermittent rebellion. Factors making for such conditions were at least three: tensions between Taiwanese and other Chinese groups, linguistic differences, and incompetent rulers. New settlers were either Hokklos from Fukien or Hakkas from Kwangtung. The differences which existed between these groups, together with frontier conditions of competition and rivalry, were sufficient to create on an average one major uprising every five years and one minor one every three. Before long, the clan and village groups were venturing out to war under the protection of the village god much like the children of Israel marching against the Philistines with the ark of the covenant in their midst (I Sam. 4). Clan warfare thus took on religious overtones. Victory or defeat was a matter of life or death not only for the people but for their deities as well.

Uprisings directed against the corrupt Manchu leadership were supported by temple organizations as well as by other religious societies. Summons for rebellion were clothed with religious sanction, ostensibly by the decrees of the gods. Temples became headquarters for the concentration and distribution of supplies. Morale was often raised by making images of Taiwan's anti-Manchu generals who had died in battle, thus elevating them to the status of gods and installing them in the folk temples. Taiwanese folk religion thereby became identified with the rebel ideology of the restoration of the ancient glory of the Han people. This desire to expel foreign rule became a strong innovating factor in community dynamism, a characteristic that would continue in later periods of Taiwanese history.

Through the vicissitudes of this early period, folk religion with its temples, gods, and experts grew together with the people, often being identified with their deepest feelings of nationalism as well as their religious longings. It became more than just a set of beliefs and religious ritual. Actually, it was part and parcel of their collective cultural and historical experience as a people. To forsake it would have been to cut themselves off from the solidarity of their own historical identity and social coherence. It is significant to note that over half of the present day temples were established during this early part of Taiwanese history (Ch'iu 1970:159).

The Period of the Later Ch'ing Administration (1820-1895)

This period marked the beginning of mutual tolerance and understanding among the clans and ethnic groups, even though a measure of social ferment continued. In 1820 an event occurred on the I-lan plain of northeast Taiwan which contributed much to unifying the people. At that time, three ethnic groups of Taiwanese moved into a mountain area close to the aborigines. These included both the Fukienese and the Hakkas from Kwangtung. After a brief initial period of cooperation against their common enemy, the Hokklos and Hakkas began bitter feuding between themselves. This resulted in thousands of deaths year by year. Eventually, a magistrate named Yao Ying summoned members of all three groups together to participate in a ceremony of reconciliation. Upon an altar he placed the icons of each group together with the tablets of those who had been killed. He then gave a moving speech and knelt before the altar to offer sacrifice to its spirit and the gods, pleading for unity among his people. All in attendance were deeply moved. They henceforth resolved to live in peace (Ch'iu 1970:160).

Evidently from this event onward religious tolerance and unity characterized the Taiwanese and Hakka people. During this period, the Manchu government sponsored many temples and shrines dedicated to eminent scholars, soldiers, and even nature deities. Territorial deities were also established to solidify local groupings of people and make public education possible. Government officials were made responsible for annual festivals of the spring equinox and winter solstice. Although Confucian in appearance, these festivals actually functioned as expressions of folk cults and their rituals.

The vegetarian halls of the Buddhist movement also drew many devotees among the Taiwanese and were likewise incorporated into the folk religion. These halls were built entirely by laymen. This was in contrast with the Buddhist monasteries, which were usually sponsored and controlled by the government. They propagated a form of Buddhism which was eclectic in that it contained Confucian and Taoist elements. Since this type of Buddhism was readily practiced in the home it spread rapidly. By 1895 there were 250 halls in Taiwan (Ch'iu 1970:162).

The Period of Japanese Occupation (1895-1945)

With the ceding of Taiwan to the Japanese in 1895, a new era began. The secret societies and temple organizations which formerly resisted the Manchus were now directed against the Japanese. Before long the Japanese recognized that the continued existence of folk temples was a hindrance to the consolidation of their rule. With an eye towards their eventual total destruction, a census was begun to ascertain their number and location. Concurrently, a program for the Japanization of Taiwan was launched, a program which by 1937 had forced a Shinto shrine into the home of every Taiwanese. That same year marked the beginning of a systematic destruction of temples and confiscation of temple lands. By 1942, 1,140 temples, 33 vegetarian halls, and 1,593 religious societies had been closed. Meanwhile, the Japanese built 179 Shinto shrines all over the island (Ch'iu 1970:164). The result of this anti-folk religion movement was to drive the folk religion more thoroughly into the homes and the secret societies more deeply underground. Feelings of hostility against the Japanese caused the masses increasingly to turn with greater devotion to their own gods. The Japanese had obviously failed. In the light of this intense struggle, it is amazing that Protestant missionaries throughout this long period were so casual in their easy dismissal of folk religion as an obstacle to the Gospel.

The Post-War Period and Current Resurgence (1945-1978)

The post-war years witnessed a marked revival in Taiwan's folk religion. Damaged temples were repaired, icons restored, and many martyrs were deified as heroes and protectors. By 1969, eighty-nine percent of all temples had been restored. Throughout Taiwan it was apparent that ancient art and architecture had been revived with an average annual increase of three to four new temples (Ch'iu 1970-166). This rate of new temple building compares with one per year during the Manchu period. Lest one tend to minimize the importance of this, he needs to be reminded that one new temple dedicated to the God of Pestilence cost an equivalent of over $3 million U.S.

With the increase of urbanization and rapid transportation, pilgrimage and tourism to folk temple sites has become increasingly popular. Such visits combine sight-seeing with merit earning. It was reported that on one occasion in 1966, the famous Matsu shrine in Pei-kang was visited by over 300,000 people (Ch'iu 1970:168).

Religious festivals, formerly proscribed to a large degree by the Japanese, have become increasingly popular. Celebrations relating to one festival alone, the Festival of Hungry Ghosts in the seventh lunar month, occupy the larger part of that month. When the festival is at its height in rural areas, roadsides are lined with people with their sacrificial offerings, thus bearing witness to the serious manner in which the people regard this yearly fete. Despite government pressure to reduce this "consumption" spending, the people seem to be spending more than ever. Since money used on these occasions is considered a meritorious act, the people feel little sense of waste. Hard-headed economists regard this as a subtle way to pour capital into the money market and thereby stimulate the economy. Karl Marx would doubtless agree with them.

Sacred dramas and puppet shows have been transported from local stages traditionally erected in front of temples to the island's major theaters. Many have appeared as television programs. But their religious content and significance continue to be strong.

Religious experts such as the shaman, fortune teller, Taoist priest, and Buddhist monk may be seen plying their arts from the heart of urban Taipei to the isolated fishing village of Kun-shen on the southwest coast. Moreover, the occult techniques of these experts have now been popularized and publicized in book form for public consumption. In a real sense this is nothing new. The Apostle Paul encountered this practice in Ephensus more than nineteen hundred years ago (Acts 19:18, 19).

These few details of the lengthy historical development of the Taiwanese folk religion should be sufficient to indicate the dynamic way in which it has functioned as the integrating factor of peasant life on the island. Since World War II its growth and elaboration have continued unabated.

STRUCTURE OF TAIWANESE FOLK RELIGION

Basic to an understanding of the religion of the Taiwanese peasant is what C. K. Yang calls its "diffused" nature (1967:20-21). By "diffused" he means that the religion of the people with its beliefs and rituals has by and large developed as integral to its composite social structure. There is a sense in which the folk religion pervades every aspect of social life. Beyond the "diffused" religion, however, Yang also finds an institutionalized form of religion which is independent of other social institutions, having its own theology, rituals, organization, and leadership. Ch'iu finds both forms present within Taiwan folk religion and distinguishes them as "natural" and "specifically religious" (1970:178).*

Natural Religious Groups

The family cult serves as the common denominator of the total religious community and stands as a link between its "natural" and "specifically religious" groups. In many respects, the home functions as a small temple and is equipped with the equivalent basic paraphernalia of altar, icons, prayer blocks, and the ancestral tablets.

Besides the usual icons and images in the average home, one may also find the eight trigrams symbolic of the seat of Heaven.** Frequently, they are inscribed on a paper wrapped around the supporting ridge beam of the roof. They frequently encircle the two words *t'ai chi* (太極), pointing to the "supreme ultimate" as the origin of the universe. This is symbolic of the cult of Heaven, centered on T'ien Kung (天公 God of Heaven). He is held in highest honor and presides at the center of Taiwanese family life, thereby making the family not just the basic kinship group but also the fundamental religious entity. It is the medium for man's integration with the cosmos and for the identification with his ancestors.

Within the family cult, the father functions as high priest even though much of the actual ritual is performed by the mother or daughter-in-law. It is his responsibility, however, to insure that belief and practice are preserved and passed on to the next generation. Above the family, the next

*Ch'iu adapts these two terms from Joachim Wach, *Sociology of Religion* (1944:4-5). Ch'iu is the only English source of any note which I have found in this area. While I have followed his material quite closely, I have done so somewhat hesitantly, feeling at times that Ch'iu becomes highly theoretical at points. He fails also to make clear whether the various religious structures which he describes are current or whether they existed only in the past.

**See Figure 3 for a likeness of the eight trigram design.

level of social organization is the immediate kinship group, which finds its unity in the worship of common ancestors at the ancestral shrine. The leader in this ritual is the chief and most respected member of the oldest family in the kin lineage. Worship generally takes place at the spring equinox and other memorial days of the kin group.

Above the immediate kin group is the clan-cult with its clan association. This may include several clans in a given area having the same surname, such as the Lin clans of Taichung. The organization may also extend throughout the whole island. Officials are chosen annually and their chief religious task is to summon the heads of households and clan patriarchs to worship clan ancestors at a central shrine. While the religious relationships of these clan associations are usually loose, they are becoming increasingly important in the political and economic affairs of Taiwanese life. This arises from their deliberate policy of cultivating the official bureaucracy and their collective striving for dominance in some segment of Taiwan's economy.

Above the clan association is an even larger social grouping called the association of the same nativity. These associations function to preserve the separate identity of ethnic groups and make the places of origin on the mainland the focal point of their organizational life.*

Over the years, these associations of the same nativity have maintained organizations in the major cities of Taiwan for the purpose of integrating and assisting newly arrived city-dwellers. They have come to exert a powerful influence on urban and national life, vying with each other to control economic and political power. Cohesion and inner discipline within each group is maintained by means of the corporate

*See Fig. 2 for a description of the manner in which immigrants from particular areas in China tended to settle in distinct districts in Taiwan.

worship of the major deity of their native districts on the
occasion of his birthday (Ch'iu 1970:188).

Another social grouping, quite out of character with the
above, is based upon personal friendships wherein individuals
covenant together to give mutual help and protection in all
times of need. This group is called the fraternity (結拜
chieh-pai).* By taking vows before gods or ancestors, sealed
with the drinking of blood, they create exceedingly deep
bonds of loyalty among themselves. Again, as with other
groupings, this association has religious as well as social
connotations.

The guild association (同業公會 *t'ung-yeh kung-hui*)
is yet another social organization. It cuts across all lines of
kinship and is based entirely upon similarity of occupation.
The objective of the association is to promote the work and
welfare of all members. These guilds have their own cults
and patron deities. During the Japanese occupation of
Taiwan, they numbered at least twenty-one and included
associations of scholars, medical doctors, pharmacists,
farmers, and fishermen. The patron deity of each group was
believed to be the founder and idealized representative of
the skill of each particular guild. Some guild patron deities
have their own temples, but more often include the guild
icon in their family pantheon at home.**

To summarize this section, "natural" religious groups
find their identity in such relationships as kinship, family,
place of clan origin in China, friendship, and occupation.
With the exception of the fraternity cult, membership is
compulsory. Their function is to lend integration and solidarity to all natural social groupings. The cementing factor

*Literally, a "binding together for worship."
**These guilds have had a long history in China. In Taiwan today
they are playing an increasingly important role in political affairs.

in each case is to a large degree the common bond of religious loyalty to and worship of patron gods or common ancestors.

Specifically Religious Groups

Under this heading, Ch'iu includes folk temples, secret societies, vegetarian halls, consciomancy halls, and the society of gods.

The folk temples in Taiwan have developed out of local and family cults. In each area they have tended to grow with the population and have developed functionally according to the changing needs of the people.

Historically, the temple has been the symbolic center of community life and interest, uniting people both in their social and religious activities. The temple functions today as the political and religious core of local autonomy. In urban areas the simple social structure of village folk temples has given way to more pluralistic forms. Town and city temples have been dominated by the larger guild associations and their patron deities. Some have risen to prominence and have exercised a dominant role in bringing together lesser cults of similar nature. The Ma-tsu temple complex in Pei-kang is a good illustration of this coordinating and unifying process.

The society of gods (神明會 *shen-ming hui*) is a group of from fifteen to twenty-five religious societies organized to promote particular cults. The societies often root back in the early experiences of Taiwanese immigrants who claimed supernatural deliverance through the intervention of gods of this pantheon. Cults formed to preserve the memory of these historic occasions have survived down through the years. Each has its own rituals and annual day of festival. In 1917, 5,420 such religious societies were functioning in Taiwan (Ch'iu 1970:194). Despite their decreased numbers today, they continue to play a significant role in Taiwanese folk religion.

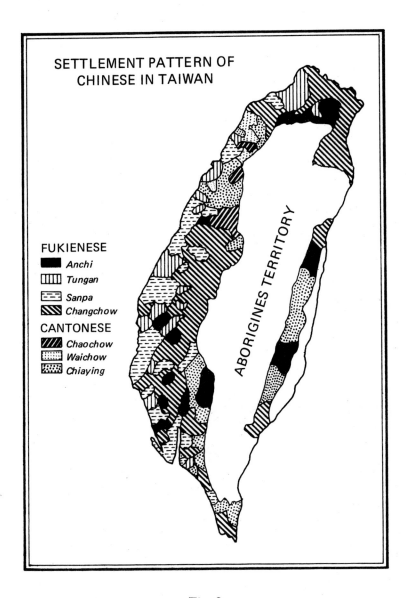

SETTLEMENT PATTERN OF
CHINESE IN TAIWAN

FUKIENESE
Anchi
Tungan
Sanpa
Changchow

CANTONESE
Chaochow
Waichow
Chiaying

ABORIGINES TERRITORY

Fig. 2

As already noted, secret societies have played a vital role in the politico-religious history of Taiwan. Most of them were originally organized to resist the encroachments of foreign rule and to promote autonomy. Their specifically religious activities were often regarded as a means of insuring the cooperation of supernatural powers in their struggle for political objectives. The Boxers of mainland China were a classical example of this kind of politico-religious society.

During the fifty years of Japanese occupation, Taiwanese resistance movements were generally spawned by these secret societies, headquartered in the folk temples. In times of outright rebellion, the folk communities could usually be counted upon to support the cause. My studies could easily lead me to generalize and state that secret societies are not numerous in Taiwan today. Who is qualified to judge the vitality of a secret movement? Suffice it to say, the I-kuan Tao (一貫道 Way of Pervading Unity) is apparently not a somnolent organization. This esoteric cult has secret rites which the initiates alone are permitted to witness. Its major divinity is a shaman god, a sort of patron of patriotism who is powerful in divination, healing, and exorcism. It is indeed significant that the icons of the founders of the five great religions, Confucius, Lao-tzu, Buddha, Mohammed, and Jesus, comprise its pantheon. They are all subordinate to the main deity. Naturally, this society is kept under close scrutiny by the government.

Another particular religious society is known as the consciomancy hall (扶箕廳).* Ch'iu defines this as a "syncretistic folk cult combining the elements of Confucianism, Taoism, and Buddhism together with the spiritmedium planchette" (1970:197). These halls have been organized to make the services of the shaman available to the public. They are not unlike other temples; the deities worshipped are

---

*Also called 鸞堂 or 飛鸞堂. See Hsü Ti-shan (1971).

common to the folk pantheon. The term "consciomancy" refers to the technique used by the presiding shaman of writing words on a sand-covered tabletop while in a state of trance. These words are then interpreted by his assistant, usually in the form of moral exhortations given in reply to the questions of clients. These oracular utterances are often recorded and published in book form. This cult has made a strong impact upon Taiwanese throughout the island.

The vegetarian hall (齋堂 *chai-t'ang*), while Buddhist in origin, combines Buddhist beliefs, Confucian ethics, and Taoist ideas of immortality. Great numbers of common people have adopted this form of Chinese eclecticism as the rule of their religious life. The vegetarian hall movement spread to Taiwan around the middle of the eighteenth century and over the years grew to number around two hundred fifty halls with three distinctive branches. Following the Japanese era, these were united into one association. This religious society is distinguished by the strict observance of vegetarian diet, the chanting of scriptures, and a system of work leading to one's salvation.

In summary we might point out that this survey of the structure of Taiwanese folk religion confirms the thesis that when the peasant is ignored by the elite in institutionalized Buddhism and Confucianism, over a period of time he can be expected to organize religious structures to meet his personal needs. His religious groupings, while based upon the family cults of earlier history, eventually reach beyond family ties and seek to sacralize his larger social relationships. While the masses visit Confucian temples and Buddhist monasteries, their primary commitments are to the local folk cults. Although the peasant is free to choose his cult, he cannot, nor would he wish to, be without one. The person or group unrelated to a folk cult is without identity. Unrelatedness leads to disintegration unless something of comparable nature is put in its place.

FOUR DIMENSIONS
OF TAIWANESE FOLK RELIGION

I will now seek to ascertain the general condition of folk religion in Taiwan today. In particular, my objective is to discover if possible those areas in which it is demonstrating growth, decline, or change.

Manifestations of folk religion are seen most clearly in the ancestor cult, activities of the religious experts, especially these of the shamanic tradition, home and temple worship, and the great festivals of the lunar year.

The Ancestor Cult

As already noted, the ancestor cult in traditional Chinese society has been a central part of the diffused religion of the common people. The importance of the cult derives largely from the way in which the people view the soul, especially with respect to the departed.

Views of the Soul. The Chinese of the ancient world tended to have a dualistic view of the universe. Seeing himself in a sense as part of the cosmic structure, he very possibly saw within his own body the same *yin* and *yang* elements which regulated the universe. Thus he may have conceived of his soul in terms of *yin* and *yang*, that is, *kuei* and *shen*, the essentially heavenly part and the lower or earthy part.

De Groot reminds us that from the earliest written records, the *yin* portion of the soul is denoted by the word *kuei*. This part returns with the corpse to the earth at death. In fact, de Groot sees the *kuei* concept as more primitive than the *shen* and suggests that in it we find the first kernel of Chinese animism, "the seed out of which China's system of ancestor worship, and even its whole religion has grown up" (1892-1910:4:8).

At some point of time, however, the complementary idea of the *shen* or *yang* portion of the soul emerged also.

The *shen* or immaterial soul expresses itself in its activity in the living body, as the *ch'i* (氣 breath). It is also called the *hun* 魂. Separated from the body after death it is called the *ming* (命 refulgent spirit) (p. 5).

The material aspect of the soul derives from the earthy or *yin* substance. In living man it is manifested as *p'o* 魄 and upon death returns to the earth. There it is regarded as *kuei*.

The above were the views of the ancient writers and to a large degree were probably basic to peasant thinking as well. These same concepts of the soul underlie present-day folk religion of the Taiwanese. In a vague way, they also regard the soul at the time of death as dividing into its constituent parts, the *hun* soul returning as *shen* to the other world and the *p'o* soul as *kuei* returning to the *yin* or terrestrial part of the universe. Hence this rather confusing picture of the soul may be summarized by saying that functionally, the Taiwanese have two souls.* One is the superior soul called *hun*. The other is the inferior soul and is called *p'o*. Differences of view begin to emerge when one asks what becomes of the souls at death, at which point the deciding factor becomes the Buddhist or Taoist influences in one's beliefs.

While the Taiwanese believe in the continued existence of the soul after death, there is no coherent body of ideas as to the ultimate fate of the soul. Diamond writes (1966:238):

> Aside from the belief in the existence of trials in Hell, there is considerable confusion as to the fate of the soul and its journey after death.

However, the following views seem to be held by most Taiwanese peasants. First, it is generally believed that for

---

*The question of the number of souls in man is greatly complicated in Taoist teachings. However, this manner of delineating the various parts in a systematic and analytic system is strictly western.

Ancestor tablet of Kuang-hsing Village 廣興鄉. The tablet belongs to the founder of this village in Yün-lin County 雲林縣, central Taiwan. He arrived at the site of Kuang-hsing between 1755 and 1765 and established the village, where his tablet is kept in Chui-yüan Hall *(Photo by Rev. Liao P'i-t'ien 廖毗田.)*

Ancestor tablets in Ch'ung-yüan Hall 崇遠堂 in Erh-lun
Village 二崙鄉 The temple is specifically for the tablets
of the many Liao 廖 clans of central Taiwan. *(Photo by
author.)*

Close-up of an ancestor tablet. *(Photo by author.)*

a period after death one of the souls wanders around aimlessly in the vicinity of its former home and must be fed and offered incense and money to show that the family is in sorrow. The other soul takes up its dwelling in the grave or in the ancestor tablet. Second, it is believed that ten days after death, the wandering soul crosses the bridge into hell, there to face various ordeals finally to be released into heaven or to be sent back to earth again. Third, the people feel a very real obligation to do everything in their power to save the soul which may be in danger of remaining in hell. Fourth, they believe that the soul, after death, may become a *kuei* or evil spirit which can return to inflict trouble upon the living. This will be seen more clearly under the Cult of Bereaved Spirits.

The many questions which occur to the analytical mind of the westerner do not trouble the Taiwanese—for example, the relationship between the *p'o* and the *hun* after death, or how the departed ancestor may change from a good *shen* into a malevolent *kuei* or into a popular god who in turn may be worshipped by many or even become the patron god of a medium. Such matters are seldom questioned.

Nevertheless, many attempts have been made to structuralize Taiwanese beliefs concerning the supernatural. Thelin sees the Taiwanese supernatural world in terms of two broad categories: gods and spirits (the terms I presume denote *shen* and *kuei*). The gods, he says, are essentially good and the spirits evil. Thus a man upon death may become either god or spirit depending upon the kind of life he has lived. He further subdivides spirits into devils and ancestors and observes that ancestors may become either devils or gods (1963:47).

The question yet unanswered is that of the genesis of those spirit beings denominated by a multitude of names like *hsien* 仙, *ling* 靈, and *kuei* which apparently have no human origin. Harvey's comments are worth noting here (1933:55):

The Chinese concept underlying both *kuei* and *shen* is that of the disembodied ghost, built upon the human prototype and traceable to a specific human being who only gradually lost his specific worldly identity.

Harvey evidently traces most, if not all, supernatural beings to human origins. The question needs much more investigation before any firm conclusions may be drawn. Questions of origin, genesis, and classification of supernatural beings are probably largely concerns of the western mind, answers to which the Taiwanese is neither interested in nor able to provide.

Kulp's list of core beliefs central to the ancestral cult concludes this section (1925:206):

(a) The immortality of the departed spirit.

(b) The spirits live on in the other world as they did in this and so need the things for existence there that they used here.

(c) The spirits depend upon living descendants for their necessities.

(d) Spirits can control human affairs according to their pleasure.

(e) If the descendants do not supply the necessities, the spirits become angry and wreak vengeance upon the living by sending misfortune.

(f) The living must carefully perform those rites that provide the spirits with their necessities, then happiness and prosperity may be achieved.

(g) The honor and respect which is accorded the dead persons before their departure must be continued.

(h) It is only a step for the aged members of the familist group from this life to the next. At any moment they may be powerful spirits. Persons must, therefore, be filial toward them in every way.

(i) Worship of the dead involves duties to one's elders who are alive.

(j) The elders enjoy prestige with religious sanction, which gives them favored position and power in the community.

CEREMONY AND PARAPHERNALIA. The ancestor cult is composed of two parts, the mortuary rites performed immediately following death and the sacrificial rites which maintain the long-term relationship between the living and the dead. The reader will find an excellent description of both in Thompson (1969:46-52).

The most important paraphernalia of the cult is the ancestor tablet. Burkhardt gives the following description for the tablet as he observed it in South China. Apparently, the tablet has changed but little in its diffusion to Taiwan (Burkhardt 1958:3:30-31):

> The ancestral tablet is generally a slip of plain wood, rounded at the top, and fixed at the base in an oblong cross socket. The title is written with an ordinary Chinese brush and is headed with the reign in which the subject lived—now the Republic. Then comes the word 'deceased' and the full name of the departed. If husband and wife are commemorated, the names are inscribed in parallel columns. Below them, in a vertical line with the reign are the three characters Chih Shen Wang (之神王) 'their spirit prince'. On the back of the tablet are given ages, date of death, and any honorific posts they may have held.

At an appropriate date following the death of the kinsman, a traditional "dotting ceremony" has been performed to mark the entry of one of the souls into its new place of abode, the ancestor tablet. Burkhardt describes it (1958:3:31):

The officiating priest, with a brush dipped in blood drawn from a cock's comb, adds a scarlet dot to the character 'Wang' (王) converting it into 'Chu' (主) or Lord. It is then placed on a shelf above the family altar, with the other ancestors, and becomes part of the family.

Just how widespread this "dotting ceremony" is in current Taiwanese society, I am not sure.

CURRENT TRENDS. Until recent times, the ancestor cult has continued to be the core of folk religion in Taiwan, an abiding symbol of the filial piety which has been the hallmark of Chinese society. As to the present status of the cult, however, opinions differ. For example, Ch'iu Ming-chung writes, "Ancestor worship is still the most vital factor in Taiwanese folk religion: it continues to hold a position of much consequence in the religious and social life of the people" (1970:226).

This seems to be confirmed by a description of the ancestor cult in the Hsin-hsing village of western-central Taiwan made in 1958. Bernard Gallin noted that "ancestor worship . . . is a form of religious belief to which virtually all Hsin Hsing area villagers adhere" (1966:233). Gallin further pointed out that whereas villagers frequently disagree in their convictions of the effects which the ancestors had on their descendants, there seemed to be a unanimous feeling about the evil results which would surely result if ancestors were neglected.

In contrast, Norma Diamond analyzed the ancestral cult of Kun-shen, a coastal village, around 1960 and reported that "in most households the cult of ancestor worship is not highly elaborated" (1966:114). But did this mean that the cult was entirely without influence? Hardly. She observed that in some households "only the head's parents were remembered" (p.115). This seemed to indicate that the dead did not dominate the living nor serve as models of behavior for the living descendants. And yet her conclusions must all be judged in the light of the fact that in no home in the village of Kun-shen did the people admit that they completely ignored their ancestors.

A more recent observation has been made by Chen Chung-min. After studying the relationships between ancestor worship and clan organization in a west-central village near Chang-hua, he concluded (1967:193):

> Ancestor worship, one of the most important traits of Chinese society is now in the process of declining. And although the clan organization still exists in those rural villages which have dominant surnames, its social functions, such as, serving as an agency for social control, providing psychological security for the individual members, working as a main group for its members' social activities, are almost lost or in the process of dying out.

If it is true that the social structures of clan and family are weakening as Taiwan becomes progressively more industrialized, then it is difficult to avoid the conclusion that the ancestor cult is weakening also. The observation of Radcliffe-Brown supports this conclusion: "The disintegration of the social structure and the decay of the ancestral cult proceed together" (1952:164).

This pattern of decline is observable in other parts of Asia as well.* Describing the cult in Singapore (85% Chinese), Elliott writes: "Ancestor worship has lost most of

---

*An interesting comparison is provided by Roy Shearer, who indicates that ancestor tablets have virtually disappeared from Korean life over the last fifty years (1968:70-71).

its significance as the basis for household or any other religion" (1955:37).

I would conclude, then, that the cult of the ancestor, while still retaining much of its traditional vigor and influence in the more conservative areas of Taiwan, has decidedly entered upon a period of decline. Whether or not the cult will be ultimately eclipsed, however, remains to be seen.

Religious Experts Among the Taiwanese

There is good reason to believe that Taiwanese shamanism before 1895 drew its influence chiefly from Amoy and to a lesser degree from neighboring coastal areas. Indeed, this linkage had been forged from the outset of the immigration of Fukienese to Taiwan during the seventeenth century and continued to the Japanese occupation. Data for this is provided by de Groot, whose researches were done in the Amoy area (1892-1910: 6:1234-94).

There are primarily two classes of religious experts: the *sai-kung* 司公, generally known by the term Taoist priest, and the *tang-ki*, variously termed medium or shaman.* The *sai-kung* class appear to have been the most important representatives of the *wu*-ist priesthood and occupied themselves almost exclusively with "sacrificial work and exorcising magic" (p. 1244). On the other hand, the *tang-ki* functioned more as devil expellers, seers, soothsayers, and diviners.** They operated with the help of spirits whom they allegedly incarnated during periods of trance. Let us examine the *sai-kung.*

De Groot sees in the term *sai-kung* reference to the *wu* of early periods, referred to as *wu-hsi* 巫覡. Evidently, the

---

*The literal meaning of *tang-ki* is "divining youth." The Taiwanese pronunciation of these two names will be used from here on.

**De Groot gives little data on the *tang-ki* of Amoy. However, the work of the *tang-ki* appears in detail in the section under Taiwan.

characters *wu* and *hsi* were abbreviated to *hsi* alone. Subsequently, this was added to *kung*, thus giving the term *sai-kung*.

By T'ang times the functions of the *wu*-ist priesthood had largely been incorporated into popular Taoism. They flourished in and around Amoy, largely under the name *sai-kung*.

The *sai-kung* of Amoy were married men and fathers, wearing no distinctive garb except when officiating. The services of the *sai-kung* were made known through a signboard carrying the notice, "There is a Taoist altar here" (de Groot 1892-1910: 6:1245). The home of the *sai-kung* also served as his workshop where he and his family made the sacrificial items of paper, charms, and other religious paraphernalia for sale to the public. This, however, was usually a part-time job since the *sai-kung* often had some form of secular work which he pursued as well.

Since the office of *sai-kung* was largely hereditary, each priest chose one of his male children to succeed him. In this way the secrets of this mystical knowledge were kept within the family. Moreover, it was widely believed that the magical power necessary for effective use of charms and spells was transmitted from the father to the spirit or soul of his son.

The power wherewith the *sai-kung* commanded spirits and gods by prayer and sacrifice was supplied by his patron god. He has often been described as a magician "obeyed by gods, believed in by men, feared by spectres" (p. 1245). All of this status, however, was premised upon the fact of his priestly power and authority having been known and acknowledged by gods, men, and spectres. Thus it was necessary at the beginning of his career for the *sai-kung* to make a public display of his powers before the visible and invisible world. This was the event of his initiation.

The initiation ritual as observed in Amoy around 1900 included taboo, fasting, purification, isolation, and finally a display of spiritual power through climbing a ladder of swords. The period of taboo and fasting lasted from seven to ten days and was accompanied with frequent ritual cleansings of the body, chanting of invocations, spells, and conjurations. This preparation period served to perfect the "vital spirit and the intellect" so that it might enter into communication with the gods (de Groot 1892-1910: 6:1247).

By climbing the ladder of swords the candidate gave evidence of his superior power over all evil spirits. When he had thereby demonstrated his ability and willingness to enter into the warfare against all demonic powers on behalf of his fellow man, the initiate was pronounced qualified to enter the priestly office of *sai-kung* (p. 1245):

> And the spectral world having thus seen a barefoot man on so dangerous a ladder without incurring even the slightest wound now tacitly confesses itself beaten and thoroughly convinced of his enormous magical competency, will henceforth flee before him with the utmost terror wherever he shows himself.

In Amoy, the *sai-kung* were organized into a *Lao-chün hui*. This society incorporated "Lao" into its name after the patriarch Lao-tzu whom the *sai-kung* worshipped.

The bulk of the *sai-kung's* religious services were taken up with rites of sacrifice and exorcism by magic. Their sacrifices consisted largely in the celebration of "mass-like" ceremonies by which the gods were appeased, their assistance invoked, and hopefully, catastrophes and misfortunes averted.

Exorcising magic on the other hand involved the making and selling of charms and pronouncements of "powerful spells" over the sick. Of all the evil spirits which afflicted the people of Amoy, none drew so much attention as the "spectres of the ground and the womb." These hid in every conceivable corner of the home and assailed babies

and pregnant women. When all household methods of
dealing with these malignant spirits failed, the *sai-kung* was
called in to produce a substitute spirit in the form of a small
puppet. He passed this over different parts of the victim's
body, chanting as he did: "Substitute, be thou in place of the
fore part of the body, that he or she . . . may live to a green
old age, with greater strength than the dragon's" (de Groot
1892-1910: 6:1260).

The relationship between the *sai-kung* and the civil
authorities was, at best, one of tolerance. Because of the
intolerance of the Confucian gentry, the government passed
and enforced strict laws by which the *sai-kung* were registered
and controlled. Each priest was allowed only one pupil,
who also had to be registered. The government thus sought
to keep the number of priests from increasing.

There is no evidence to indicate that the activities
of either the *sai-kung* or the *tang-ki* decreased perceptibly
in Fukien before 1900.

THE *SAI-KUNG* AND *TANG-KI* OF TAIWAN. Among the
great numbers who migrated from Fukien to Taiwan during
and after the seventeenth century, there doubtless were numbers of religious experts, particularly the *sai-kung* and *tang-ki*.
Thompson finds evidence for their presence among Buddhist
and Taoist devotees as early as the reign of Koxinga, 1664-
1668 (1970:4). Early official sources give the impression
that religious experts, whether Taoist priests or exorcists
(called *wu*), were all looked upon as of inferior status. In
Amoy disrespect towards the religious experts was common
among officials. This does not mean, however, that in times
of need these men were not called upon to exorcise, divine,
and heal. Overnight, they could become men of great power
and widespread influence.

There is abundant data to demonstrate that the *sai-
kung* and *tang-ki* exercised a dominant role in animistic
folk religion up through the turn of this century (Mackay

1895:129-30, 312; Moody 1907:104-5). The Japanese apparently drove many of their activities underground, but they certainly failed to stop or greatly diminish the work of the religious experts among the masses.

A growing body of data exists which deals with the person and work of the religious expert among present-day Taiwanese. In working over some of the major sources, however, I have encountered a measure of semantic confusion because of the wide range of terms used to describe the same phenomena. Some writers hesitate to use the term "shaman" at all (Freytag 1969:86ff).* Others use the term but do not agree as to which category of religious experts it refers. For example, while Gallin uses "shaman" to translate the Chinese *t'iao-t'ung* 跳童,** Thelin (1963) uses the same word to translate *fa-shih* 法師. Gallin uses "interpreter" to translate *fa-shih* and Thelin uses "interpreter" to translate *shu-cho t'ou* 豎棹頭. As a general rule, I will follow Gallin's terminology except that I will continue to use the Taiwanese romanization for the Taoist priest and the medium. As for English, the term "medium" is preferred to "shaman" for the *tang-ki*. While it appears that both the medium and the Taoist priest stand directly in the tradition stemming from the *wu* of ancient times, I agree with Eliade that neither *sai-kung* nor *tang-ki* are true shaman types. The *tang-ki*, who in many respects comes nearest to the qualifications of being one who deals in ecstasy, does not control the spirits. Rather he is "possessed" by them (Eliade 1964:450).

Like the above mentioned, most recent studies pertaining to the Taiwanese medium have been done in rural areas reflecting a largely traditional religious setting. The question arises, how does a young man find his way into the role of medium in an urban area like Taipei? The following data

*Freytag used the term "spirit medium."
**This is the Mandarin equivalent of Taiwanese *tang-ki*.

may shed some light upon this question. Those interested
in Christian missions will not fail to notice similarities with
the ways in which young people enter the Christian faith as
well as the Church.

Located in downtown Taipei on a secluded side street
is a tiny folk temple (慈惠堂 Tz'u-hui T'ang). On any
evening after the supper hour, one can see a number of
people in and around the temple precincts. Some will be
simply visiting and sharing neighborhood news while others
are taken up with activities and ritual pertaining to the
temple cult. Among the group of predominantly middle-aged
females, one will observe three or four young men, regular
devotees of this temple. At least two of these have entered
into the life and worship of the temple with a deep sense
of involvement and spiritual participation, perhaps to a
degree not far removed from the temple medium himself.
I discovered one of these young men to be quite friendly and
interested in sharing his religious experience with others.
Following is an account of his spiritual pilgrimage and that
of his friend.

In 1975 Mr. Ch'en attended the Billy Graham meetings
in Taipei largely out of curiosity but interested to learn
something of the techniques of the great evangelist. Subsequently, his interest in religion remained little changed—
curious but largely agnostic. One evening while strolling by
the Tz'u-hui T'ang, he decided to go in and burn incense
just for the fun of it. In the process, he became "possessed,"
he used the term *shen fu shen* 神附身, indicating that one of
the temple deities had come upon him. At this point he
entered into an ecstatic trance-like experience which lasted
for several minutes before he returned to his normal state.
This experience dispelled all unbelief in the existence of spirit
beings, especially the deities of that temple, of which there
are upwards of fifteen. It also left him with a feeling of
having bridged over into the world of gods. In short, religion

for him had taken on a dimension of reality. As a result of this "conversion" experience, he is now a fairly regular devotee of this temple.

A classmate of Mr. Ch'en's moved into the area and began working in a refrigerator repair shop. It was not long before Ch'en had shared his experience with his friend, Mr. Chang, who also was "converted" and now comes often in the evening to the temple. According to the reports of these young men, they experience possession by specific gods of the temple pantheon. Sometimes more than one god will come upon them, but only one at a time.

Observing Mr. Chang in possession one evening, I was struck with the likeness of his movements, facial expressions, and sounds to those of a monkey. Suddenly, he changed movements and sounds to something else. In talking with him afterwards, I learned that he was first possessed by the spirit of the monkey god Sun Wu-k'ung 孫悟空.* He was then taken by a wolf god whose image was to be found beneath the god shelf.**

Both Ch'en and Chang assured me that they were not seeking the role of the medium, though they acknowledged that they were open to being chosen. The experience of possession had a number of values as they saw it. While possessed, one may sometimes "see" the deity in some extrasensory way. One's body is refreshed and invigorated by the strenuous movements of jumping, rolling, and crouching, and one experiences a certain communion with the deity and in some sense gains merit toward one's own salvation as well as opening possibilities of helping others. Finally, one has the feeling of belonging to a group of mutually concerned persons.

*Sun Wu-k'ung figures prominently in the famous Chinese epic, Hsi-yu chi (西遊記, The Westward Journey).

**Chang claims to have been fully aware of my presence and my taking pictures of him while he was possessed.

Two views of a neophyte concentrating his spiritual force.

Possession by the Monkey God in Taipei's Tz'u-hui Hall 慈惠堂
(*Photos by author.*)

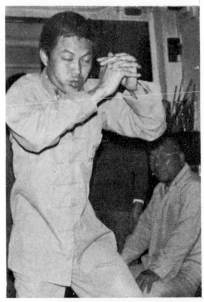

Two views of the neophyte possessed by the Monkey God's spirit.

However, the point of interest here is the pattern by which young men may become involved in a folk temple via a kind of "conversion" experience involving a form of possession which in turn prepares them for a possible further call to the role of medium.

Folk religion is adapting itself increasingly to the individualism of urban areas. An individual may become a medium with no prior contact with the neighborhood, the temple, or other religious experts. The pattern of calling differs considerably from that often described in rural areas, which typically involved experiences of sickness and healing.

When we investigate the call and training of the *sai-kung* in rural Taiwan, we discover that except for local variations in detail, the pattern of Amoy around 1900 still holds. Candidates for the Taoist priesthood in the Lu-kang area of western-central Taiwan receive their training from older members of the priesthood, under whom they serve as novices. According to Gallin, the medium is chosen by the god, who decides to use him as a means for communicating with human beings (1966:244). Writing from a fishing village on the west coast, Diamond notes that the calling of a young man to serve as a medium often involves his being cured from a sickness. He is then chosen by his future patron god. The *tang-ki* in K'un Shen received no formal training but was taken to the house where the god was kept and remained there for a month, receiving instruction from the god (Diamond 1966:125). In the Lu-kang area, training for the medium is received from a master *fa-shih* and lasts for seven days during which the novice *tang-ki* learns the language of his patron god (Gallin 1966:244). Jordan also indicates that the initiation of the *tang-ki* varies from place to place (1972:72).

The *fa-shih* serves as interpreter to the medium. He is trained by the elders in his art. He learns magic rituals and the use of potent charms and instruments of coercion for exorcising demons. Quite often he possesses a modicum of knowledge and tends to be politically oriented in his associations in the village (Freytag 1969:51).

The role and status of these religious experts varies. Most of them only serve part time in their religious calling and engage in secular work on the side. I would differ with Nida and Smalley and challenge the view that these men belong to the "lunatic fringe" of Chinese society (1959:58). Actually, they appear as fairly normal individuals, though possibly they are more aggressive than the average (Gallin 1966:243).

Freytag found the status of the priest and medium lower than that of the laymen since the former was always invited at the laymen's initiative. While the Taoist priest may be given more respect in the community, the power and influence of the medium-interpreter team should not be underrated.

The work of the *tang-ki* includes divination, exorcism, and magical diagnosis (Freytag 1969:87). The Taoist priest may preside over funerals if he belongs to the "black-headed" group. If he is a member of the "red-headed" group, his work will involve less religious but more magical ritual (Thelin 1963:52). Writer Kuo Ho-lieh reflects a decided disrespect for the Taoist priesthood of Taiwan. He describes them as generally unlearned and unworthy of being religious leaders of the people (1970a:247-48).

As to whether these men are declining or increasing in Taiwan today, I have not found data that would indicate one way or the other. Suffice it to say, one may encounter these practitioners all the way from the large cities like Taichung to isolated fishing villages such as K'un Shen.

THE GEOMANCER OF TAIWAN. Before leaving the religious experts, one word should be said about a very important figure. The geomancer and his work complements that
of the *sai-kung* and *tang-ki* and falls under the general term of
feng-shui 風水 (geomancy). Thelin describes his work as "a
form of divination, . . . a pre-scientific way to meet some of
the problems of daily life" (1963:52).* He identifies three
schools of geomancy found in central Taiwan: *jih-chia* 日家,
the school for selecting lucky dates and hours; *hsing-chia*
形家, a school with specializes in topographic studies identi-
fying land forms with certain animals (hence good and bad
luck); and *fa-chia* 法家, a school expert in determining propitious sites for graves (Thelin 1963:53). The geomancer
relates to the problem of animism in a negative yet interesting way, since he recognizes that his skill is limited to the
natural forces of nature as they bear upon the life of the
family. Although he admits that his skill is of no value in
counteracting bad influences resulting from evil spirits or
immoral behavior, he brings a scientific dimension to the folk
religion with his knowledge of the heavenly bodies, his
almanac, and his compass. "In an age of science, this side of
folk religion receives much attention by the people" (Freytag
1969:90).

Taiwanese Folk Temples and Folk Deities

The most visible and audible aspects of Taiwanese
animism are to be found in the folk temples. These are the
temples which house the popular icons of the masses in
contrast to the temples which are purely Buddhist or
Confucian. Since the folk temple is the focal point of the
peasant's religious activity, it provides a good index whereby

---

*The use of "pre-scientific" implies evolutionary assumptions
which to date are lacking validation. To us of the West, "unscientific"
might be a better term.

one may measure the trends of growth or decline of religious life among the masses. I shall attempt to interpret some of the available data on temples and gods with a view to drawing some tentative conclusions as to present trends.*

DESCRIPTION OF FOLK TEMPLES. Even the most casual observer is impressed with the great numbers of folk temples which are to be found in Taiwan's remote villages and lofty mountain valleys. Thompson's excellent description catches something of the color and shape of these remarkable structures (1970:322-23):

> There is general similarity to their appearance, despite a thousand variations. The larger ones adopt the customary courtyard plan; their gatehouses and main buildings are designed in a triple arrangement of central hall flanked by subsidiary halls which are somewhat lower and smaller; they utilize the traditional Chinese construction features of raised platforms, prominent pillars, swinging gates. Above all it is the roofs which give the outward aspect a striking picturesqueness. These roofs overhang the walls in the usual Chinese style, while their eaves soar boldly upward in the southern manner, quite unlike the restrained curves of the eaves one recalls from Peking palaces. Eaves and ridges are profusely decorated with animal and human figures from the rich store of myth and legend, while entire roof—and for that matter practically all of the temple save for floors and outer walls—is luxuriantly alive with color: gold, red, green, blue, black, and white. There are gleaming sweeps of colored tiles, great dragons curling about the

---

*I am indebted to L. Thompson's article, "Notes on Religious Trends on Taiwan," for much of the data on Taiwan temples and gods. However, he does not make a distinction between folk and other temples, a fact which lessens the value of his data for the purposes of this study.

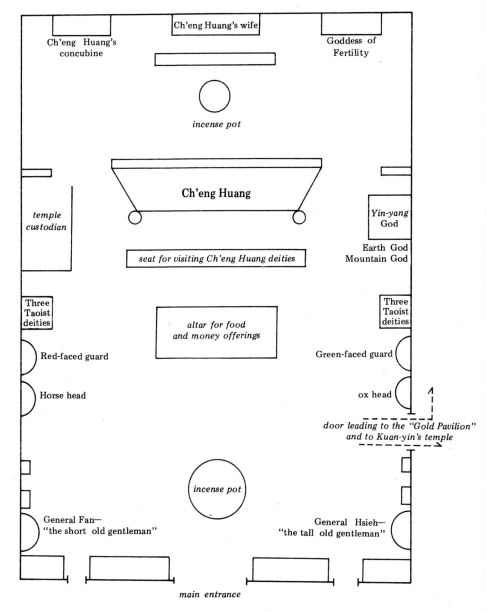

Fig. 3

pillars at the front, truly incredible intricacies of wood carving everywhere, especially under the roofs and adorning the shrines within the sanctuary.

As to the arrangement of icons, the chief deity is usually placed in the center on the throne, flanked by two or more attendants. Thus, Ma-tsu, Goddess of the Southern Sea, may be flanked by her two attendants Ch'ien-li Yen (千里眼 God of All Seeing), and Shun-feng Erh, (順風耳 God of All Hearing).

Paraphernalia for the average temple include such items as the altar table, candles, ornate holders, vases of flowers, a brazier for incense sticks, small wine cups, vessels for sacrificial food, prayer blocks, and wooden slips in a bamboo vase.

MAJOR AND MINOR DEITIES. One convenient way of handling the folk deities is to classify them as major and minor according to the number of counties or municipalities in which they are worshipped. Accordingly, we find from a 1960 survey that there were 4,041 temples whose chief deities were worshipped in one or more counties. Secondary deities, that is, those worshipped only in a single county, numbered only 179 out of a total of 4,220 temples (Thompson 1970:324).

The term "chief deity" is used in three ways: it may refer to an individual god, it may include a group of gods worshipped under one title, or it may be a multiple deity in which several gods of different surnames share the same title.

While there are upwards of three hundred deities in the folk pantheon, the number of gods who reign in the temples is very small. If major deities be reckoned as those for whom over 100 temples have been established, we find only nine. These nine account for 2,756 of the 4,220 temples in 1960. Secondary deities, for whom there is a minimum of 20 temples, number only nineteen and account for 863 temples. While they make up only a fraction of the folk pantheon, these twenty-eight major and secondary deities are found in nine-tenths of the temples.

The important thing for us to measure, however, is the relative increase or decrease in popularity of these gods. By comparing surveys from 1941 and 1960, we learn of those gods which declined and others which have increased. In our handling of Thompson's data, however, one important factor needs to be kept in mind. The 1941 temple survey, as Ch'iu reminds us, was done by the Japanese with the express purpose of eclipsing the politically resistant folk religion and placing in its stead Japanese State Shintoism. To this end, they succeeded in closing 1,140 temples, 33 vegetarian halls, and 1,593 religious societies between 1937 and 1942 (Ch'iu 1970:164). It would seem, then, that by the time of the survey in 1941 many of the temples actually listed were already shut down, if not confiscated or destroyed. And certainly by 1945 other temples had been destroyed by bombers. If these observations are correct, then the figures for 1960 actually represent even greater growth than appears on the surface.

While data from the 1960 survey is incomplete, indications are that Fu-teh Cheng-shen 福德正神 shrines have dropped in popularity possibly as much as 50 per cent. Shrines to Yu-ying Kung (有應公 Gods of the Evil Spirits) have decreased by a ratio of 1:2/3. The Ch'ing-shui Tsu-shih (清水祖師, a group of water deities) and Ta-chung Yeh (大眾爺 General of Evil Spirits) have both declined by a ratio of 1:4/5. Several other gods could be included in the category showing a loss of popularity.

On the other hand, some deities have gained immensely in popularity. Reckoned against a population gain from 1941 to 1960 of four million for a ratio of 3:5, the Buddhist Shih-chia Fo 釋迦佛 temples increased 3:11 2/5; San-pao Fo 三寶佛 temples increased 3:8 1/4; Fu-yu Ti-chun 孚佑帝

君 temples increased 3:7 1/2; and A-mi-t'o Fo 阿彌陀佛 temples increased 3:12 2/5 (Thompson 1964:325-26).*

We should point out that nearly all the above increases are Buddhist deities. Thompson suggests that this is the result of two million Buddhist-oriented mainlanders who flooded into Taiwan between 1948-1949 along with the official backing of the Chinese Buddhist Association of Taiwan. It would be interesting to know what percentage of the Taiwanese peasantry has been drawn into the Buddhist form of religion in recent years. The answer might possibly indicate a current instability of Taiwanese affiliation with the folk religion.

One conspicuous gain is recorded by a folk deity which usually goes under the group name of Wen-shen (瘟神 Gods of Pestilence).** This cult registered an increase from 458 temples in 1918 to about 800 temples in 1967 (Hsü 1968: 219). This is an interesting example of a deity which has managed to survive through change of function. Originally, the Wen-shen protected only against pestilence. Now they have come to function as protectors against all forms of disease.

The geographic spread of the various deities suggests in some cases a definite correlation between environmental problems and human needs on one hand, and the nature and function of the deity on the other. Thus, in the wind-swept fishing villages of the Peng-hu Islands, the most common deities are those of the Gods of Pestilence and the Goddess of the Sea, both chosen obviously for the help they give to fishermen facing danger and disease.

---

*Most of these are Buddhist deities and are popular among the masses.

**This deity is referred to on page 99 as Wang-yeh.

One final word on the number of folk temples in
Taiwan today. Admittedly, it is very difficult to make any
comprehensive statements. Kuo Ho-lieh deals with this
problem in his recent work on Taiwanese folk religion. He
feels that the only accurate survey ever done on the temples
of Taiwan was the Japanese survey of 1919 which recorded
a total of 11,271 temples. The Japanese survey of 1936,
listing a total of only 3,700, was not accurate since it excluded all temples not registered with the government (Kuo
1970:261-62). The 1941 census was inaccurate for reasons
previously noted; it recorded a total of 3,815. The 1960
survey is admittedly incomplete: "The figures for many
temples in the rural areas are not half of their actual amounts"
(Thompson 1964:321).

Kuo concludes with the judgment that by 1970 folk
temples greatly increased over the 1919 figure of 11,271.
He bases this statement on the following (1970:262-63):

1. An estimate by Lin Heng-tao who says the number of
   temples has doubled since 1949.
2. A statement by the editorial department of the
   Taiwanese Presbyterian Church to the effect that the
   "mushrooming of temples in Taiwan since the Restoration (1949) is a very natural phenomenon."
3. A statement by a government official recommending
   the proscription of secret altars being set up for the
   use of shamanistic methods of healing the sick
   (1968).
4. The statement of a city official to the effect that
   he had observed an increasing number of Buddhist
   halls, and ancestral halls in which were found very
   strange icons, used for deceiving the people of the
   city. He also urged that the police take action
   against them.*

*Author's translation.

CONCLUSION. Depending on which data one uses, different pictures emerge of the condition of temple worship in Taiwan. While there is evidence of decline among certain deities, others most certainly are holding their own, if not increasing. Despite an evident resurgence of Buddhist-type deities and temples, the weight of evidence seems to indicate an overall growth of folk temples. The new million dollar Wang-yeh temple complex in Tainan is a good example. The increase, however, will likely affect those areas where the deities concerned are already popular, although some are already universally worshipped throughout the island.

Since the temple is a focal point of identity for folk society, this current resurgence may in large part be related to nationalism. It may also be fed indirectly by the government through its current emphasis upon cultural revival. However, should all the statistics prove false and we discover that folk temples are actually decreasing, we would still be faced with another important factor, folk worship in the home. Almost every home occupied by Taiwan's lower classes contains within it the basic paraphernalia of the folk temple. "Thus in actuality every home is a temple" (Thompson 1964:331). In order to prove decisively that the folk religion of Taiwan is dying out, one would have to prove that such was also the case in the home as well as the temple.

The Festival in Taiwan

Another important part of animistic folk religion is the festival. This refers to the principal feast days of the lunar calendar when large numbers of Taiwanese participate in social and religious activities popularly described as *pai-pai* 拜拜. Saso defines *pai-pai* (n.d.:iv):

> The whole set of rituals and prayers offered for the spirits and ancestors. . . includes the offering of a banquet-sacrifice, the burning of incense and paper

money, the casting of the moon-shaped wooden blocks, and the prayers offered by the participants.

The term *pai-pai* may be used to refer to the simple offering of prayer before a shrine, but its chief use is to identify festival celebrations.*

While the lunar year includes a number of feast days, I have chosen only one as representative. This festival falls on the fifteenth day of the seventh month. It is known by such names as the Feast of Hungry Spirits and the Hungry Ghost Festival. It is one of the chief expressions of the Cult of Bereaved Spirits, the activities of which occupy the entire seventh month and include other forms of temple worship throughout the year.

I have chosen this particular festival for several reasons: first, because it demonstrates an aspect of ancestor worship not often recognized by many writers; second, because this festival ranks next in popularity to New Year's among the Taiwanese; third, because it demonstrates their effort to cope with the problem of the broken relationship between the living and the dead which has arisen through abnormal deaths or failure of descendants to care for the spirits of their dead; fourth, because the analysis of this festival will afford us considerable insight into the communal aspect of folk religion; and fifth, because this festival has gone through considerable change in form in recent years although in function it has remained constant.

DESCRIPTION. The Taiwanese call the day on which the Hungry Ghost Festival is held K'ai kuei-men (開鬼門 opening the ghost gate) (Saso n.d.:66). According to their belief, this is the day when the souls of those suffering in the Buddhist or Taoist purgatory are released from their prison

---

*The Chinese character *pai* 拜 is made up of the two hands together, suggestive of the way the hands are held during worship.

to roam freely upon earth. A banquet must be prepared for them to alleviate their sufferings and also to effect for some an early release from their purgatorial punishment.

The giving of the banquet sacrifice with prayers and incense is called *p'u-tu* 普渡 and marks the release of the souls from suffering. The gates of hell which have been opened on this day are supposed to remain open until the thirtieth day of the seventh month. This is the birthday of Ti-tsang Wang 地藏王, the god who presides over purgatory and exercises a positive role by seeking to release suffering souls from torment.

Besides the feast, there are also many processions in which Ch'eng-huang, the chief administrative god of the city, together with his official court are carried about the city. This allows Ch'eng-huang and his helpers to oversee the hungry ghosts and to insure their good behavior at a time when they are potentially malevolent.

The actual offering of sacrifice takes place in front of each home and is celebrated by the burning of incense and paper money. Particular sacrifices are given to the souls of those who have been drowned in the vicinity and who are believed to be particularly present. Lanterns are floated on rivers and carried in processions along river banks. The object is to conduct these souls to their final resting place. There, ceremonies are held not only on this day in the year of drowning but also once every three, ten, or twenty years thereafter.

ORIGIN OF THE CULT OF BEREAVED SPIRITS. The origin of this cult and its relationship to Buddhism is a interesting question. One name used to designate the festival not mentioned above is Yü-lan-p'en hui 盂蘭盆會. Some trace this to the Sanskrit word *ullambhana*, referring to the journey of Ti-tsang Wang down to Hades to save his mother.* He

*Ti-tsang is usually found on a side altar in Buddhist temples in gold robes and a crown with a jewel in one hand and a staff in the

is supposed to have been one of the disciples of Buddha who renounced nirvana to help suffering souls out of hell. Actually, Ti-tsang Wang is the name given posthumously by the Jade Emperor to a very famous Korean hermit named Mu-lien who lived in China during the reign of Emperor Su-tsung (756-763; Saso n.d.: 68). According to the Taiwanese version of the story, Mu-lien begged Buddha to be allowed to rescue his mother from purgatory, whereupon Buddha commanded him to "cook some fragrant meat" together with five kinds of fruit. These were then offered to the starving ghost of his mother with the result that her soul was released from torment. It seems then that an Indian figure has been completely taken over by Mu-lien.

Other writers find the origins of the cult much earlier than the time of Mu-lien. Eberhard suggests that it may have originated in some locale as a harvest festival, or that in another area it may have been a repetition of the Lantern Festival of the fifteenth day of the first month celebrated exactly half a year earlier. At any event, he contends that, like the Spring Festival, the Festival of Hungry Souls has come to be devoted not to the living but to the dead (Eberhard 1952:129).

Thompson finds the basic idea underlying the cult in a passage of the *Tso-chuan* (*ca.* 500 B.C.). Here the opinion is expressed that "when a ghost has a place to go (*kuei* 歸), it does not become an evil spirit" (Thompson 1970:2). This principle was subsequently elaborated by high authorities. One of these was the Hung-wu Emperor of Ming, who in 1370 gave instructions for the building of an altar to bereaved spirits with the stipulation that sacrifices should be offered on it three times a year, "at Ch'ing-ming, on the 15th of the 7th month, and on the 1st of the 10th month" (Thompson 1970:2).

---

other.   He is not to be confused with Yen-lo Wang (閻羅王 King of Hell), who exercises the negative role of overseeing all punishment.

It is of interest to include at this point a specimen of
the prayers offered to the bereaved spirits in Ming and Ch'ing
times (Thompson 1970:3-4):

And now we bear in mind the bereaved souls who dwell
in the midst of darkness. Formerly they were living
persons; we know not how they died. Some among
them were wounded by weapons of war; some died
from water, fire, or at the hands of bandits. . . .

Their names have been blotted out of a sudden; the
sacrificial rites to which they are entitled are unknown
and unrecorded. These lonely souls [ching-shen] have
not dispersed [to heaven], but remain attached to
their yin souls [yin-ling], and so they live in plants
or trees. . . .*

[His majesty] pities their loneliness and has therefore
decreed that officials throughout the world shall at the
appropriate times offer sacrifices.

The bereaved spirits are then invited to partake of the
sacrificial foods and wine. They are further implored to act
as the moral arbiters in matters pertaining to social justice,
such as severe punishment of those who violated the five
relationships (that is, between ruler and subject, father and
mother, parent and child, elder and younger brother, and
friend and friend) and protection and material blessings for
those citizens who "obey parents, . . . stand in awe of magistrates, respect the li and the law" (p. 5).

---

*It is interesting to note how the ancients looked upon the
"bereaved soul," that is, in terms of the higher yang soul's failure
to be separated from the lower yin soul.

Several items of importance emerge from the above. First, the status of the spirits may be determined by the manner in which they died, particularly if it was some form of abnormal death. Second, they become hostile if they are thereby deprived of the sacrificial rites to which they are entitled. Third, bereaved spirits can only be delivered from their state of torment through the correct performance of sacrifice and ceremony by officialdom. Fourth, significance must be seen in the "clear intent to use the awe of the bereaved spirits as an instrument for governmental control of both people and officials" (Thompson 1970:5).

From all accounts, it would appear that this cult had weakened or disappeared from officialdom before the nineteenth century on mainland China. On the peasant level, however, this was not the case. Obviously, they would feel a measure of indifference to any cult restricted to officialdom. As Thompson notes, however, the necessity of appeasing the vengeful natures of bereaved spirits was a "self-evident proposition." Hence, even the humblest peasant was concerned to maintain the ceremony.

There is evidence of this cult dating back to the early Ch'ing. During that time, the cult still functioned at the official level. It was the duty of officials to create public cemeteries and store coffins awaiting shipment back to the mainland. But these services were insufficient. Pioneer conditions inevitably resulted in the death of multitudes of people due to epidemics, local feuds, and attacks by aborigines. Moreover, wood for coffins was not always available. The resulting sight of corpses and skeletons not properly buried and without continuing sacrifice aroused the people. Compelled by feelings of pity and fear, they began to provide for the adequate burial of their dead and build shrines at which the bereaved spirits could receive their rightful sacrifices from the local people.

The Cult of Bereaved Spirits grew and gained in popularity among the Taiwanese people. Today it is represented by several thousand temples to be found everywhere throughout the island and continues to sink its roots ever deeper into Taiwanese culture.

The temples referred to here are often nothing more than tiny shrines, usually lacking either spirit tablet or image. They usually contain a "golden peck measure" which is a large earthenware jar for the bones. Over the shrine is draped a red cloth on which are written the words, *yu ch'iu pi ying* (有求必應 "Ask and ye shall receive"). The group name given to the main god of these hungry spirits, Yu-ying Kung 有應公, is taken from this motto. Other deities of the bereaved spirits include Ta-chung Yeh (大衆爺 Lord of the Multitudes) and Wan-shan Kung (萬善公 Lord of the Myriad Virtues). Besides these there are numerous other gods and cult objects.

Various writers have pointed out that the help given by these hungry spirits in return for sacrifices is unlike that given by the *shen* because it is not restricted by moral qualifications. One need not ask for that which is morally right. Neither must the devotee be one of upright character or good intention. For this reason, Yu-ying Kung temples are frequently patronized by gamblers and disreputable characters.

The high point of the bereaved spirit cult is the great feast and the performance of the *p'u-tu* cermony mentioned earlier. This is usually celebrated on the fifteenth day of the seventh month. Today's version of this feast day is a far cry from what missionary George Mackay witnessed around 1880 (Mackay 1895:130-31):

The custom prevailed in all the cities and towns in North Formosa of erecting, in an open space of several acres, great cone-like structures of bamboo poles, from five to ten feet in diameter at the base, and sometimes fifty or sixty feet high. Around these cones, from bottom to top, immense quantities of food, offered to the spirits, were tied in rows. There were ducks and smaller fowl, dead and alive, pork, fish, cakes, fruits, bananas, pineapples, and all manner of delicacies in season; and fastened everywhere in the mass were hundreds of huge firecrackers. On one occasion I saw fifty such cones at a feast at Bang-kah. It was a gruesome sight. When night came on the time for summoning the spirits approached, the cones were illuminated by dozens of lighted candles. Then the priests took up their position on a raised platform, and by clapping their hands and sounding a large brass gong, they called the spirits of all the departed to come and feast on the food provided. 'Out of the night and the other world' the dead were given time to come and gorge themselves on the 'spiritual' part of the feast, the essence, that was suited to their ethereal requirements. Meanwhile a very unspiritual mob—thousands and thousands of hungry beggars, tramps, blacklegs, desperadoes of all sorts, from the country towns, the city slums, or venturing under cover of the night from their hiding-places among the hills—surged and swelled in every part of the open space, impatiently waiting their turn at the feast. When the spirits had consumed the 'spiritual' part, the 'carnal' was the property of the mob, and the mob quite approved of this division. . . . At length the spirits were satisfied, and the gong was sounded once more. That was the signal for the mob; and scarcely had the first stroke fallen when that whole scene was one mass of arms and legs and tongues. Screaming, cursing, howling, like demons of the pit, they all joined in the onset. A rush was made for the cones, and those nearest seized the supports and pulled now this way, now that. The huge, heavily laden structures began to sway from side to side until with a crash one after another fell into the crowd, crushing their way to the ground. Then it was every man for himself. In one wild scramble, groaning and yelling all the while, trampling on those who had lost their footing or were smothered by the falling cones, fighting and tearing one another like mad dogs, they all made for the coveted food. It was a very bedlam, and the wildness of the scene was enhanced by the irregular explosion of the fire-crackers and the death-groan of some one worsted in the fray.

In its old and barbarous form, this feast was outlawed by Governor Liu Ming-ch'uan sometime before 1900 (p. 131), but this does not mean that the feast disappeared. Indeed, one may visit the huge and ornate temple of Yi-min Yeh in Hsin-chu County and there witness three days of religious ceremony and feasting attended by thirty thousand people annually (Thompson 1970:8). While the cruel and dangerous aspects of the feast have disappeared, the same atmosphere of excitement and religious fervor prevail as before.*

Returning to earlier observations of Buddhist influence upon the Cult of Bereaved Spirits, it should be noted that this influence now dominates. In Eberhard's opinion, the early Chinese did not believe that the soul of man possessed eternal life. Rather, they believed it declined from a period of powerful life and influence immediately after death until with the death of the last person who had known the deceased, the soul in a sense died a second time (Eberhard 1952:130). With the coming of Buddhism to China, however, souls no longer died but lived on in purgatory until reincarnation took place. But this accentuated the problem

---

*This demonstrates change in form but not in function.

of those dying abnormal deaths and those with no living descendants to provide filial care. In response, the pattern developed of inviting a Buddhist priest to read a kind of "mass" for all the dead, but especially those forgotten by the living. This situation prevails in Taiwan today.

From time to time the authorities have attempted to persuade the Taiwanese against the excessive consumption spending involved in these festivals. Reports from early Ch'ing officials indicate similar efforts. When Gallin described the Festival of Hungry Souls in Hsin Hsing village of west-central Taiwan in 1958, he felt that it had decreased in size and expenditure. He reckoned this to be the result of government restrictions which forced all the villages of the area to hold the feast simultaneously on the same day. This made it impossible for any one village to invite outsiders.

Today, thirteen years later, it is questionable whether this festival and indeed the whole Cult of Bereaved Spirits is declining at all. Personal observations indicate quite the contrary. It seems that various factors contribute to this: Taiwan's growing affluence, the persistence of the Buddhist stress on gaining merit, and the opportunity the festival affords to express a distinctly Taiwanese identity.

Ch'iu not only confirms the growing popularity of this dimension of the folk religion, but also lists the following reasons (1970:260):

> The rapid increase in the number of festivals and pilgrimages after World War II leads me to think that these ceremonial festivals are still major occasions by which Taiwanese folk retain their fellowship and preserve their identity. Since there is no other occasion for Taiwanese people to meet together freely, . . . these festivals have become the sole occasion for their fellowship, and the temples have become the symbolic centers for their corporate identity.

FUNCTION OF ANIMISTIC FOLK RELIGION IN
TAIWAN TODAY

From the above description of animistic folk religion, I believe we may safely conclude that, even today, the religion of the masses is still the integrating factor of their corporate life, especially in rural areas. While the ancestor cult shows definite signs of weakening in certain aspects, it continues to provide the family with socially and religiously acceptable means of integrating life during the shattering experience of death. This is especially true of the burial ceremonies performed by the Taoist priest.

The temple with its pantheon of deities and religious rituals is still the focal point of individual and communal religious life. The religious function of the temple is well expressed by Elliott: "Propitiation of the *shen* in conjunction with recourse to divination is the accepted means of resolving problems and overcoming hardships which do not appear to have an immediately practical solution" (1955:40).

Apart from the religious function, the folk temples of Taiwan serve as centers for social and political activities. The temple is the hub of economic, political, social, and religious relationships. Indeed, the temple tends to be symbolic of the Taiwanese sense of historic ethnic identity and serves as a potential rallying point for nationalistic feelings.

In many respects, the festival complements the function of the temple. It is uniquely during the great festival occasions of the lunar year that the Taiwanese find opportunity for reaffirmation of their ethnic and religious identity. What lends cohesive quality to the Taiwanese as a people is the deep religious feelings which are visualized and experienced in the ceremony surrounding each *pai-pai*.

Taiwan's religious experts continue to function as the mediators between society and the spiritual powers that surround the lives of the people. As such, they are indispensable, particularly to the peasants. The Taoist priest comes into his own when there is a death. At this time of crisis, he provides the bereaved with a sense of having met all filial obligations as well as having restored harmony through correct and adequate provision for the departed.

The medium and his interpreter assist those who seek knowledge of those things which are beyond the human ken. Discovering the causes of illness, giving medical prescription, communicating with the gods above or the departed below, or speaking some moral maxim—these are his stock in trade.

The function of the geomancer in society is unique. He alone possesses the means of handling the natural forces of the earthly and heavenly spheres which allegedly bear so heavily upon man's fate. While the others provide answers concerning life, health, fertility, and the future, the geomancer provides important answers concerning propitious days and hours for important events and suitable sites for building and burial.

The priest, the medium, and the geomancer all serve the whole community. They deal with forces outside of the layman's control. Each has his own rather well-defined areas in which he is expected to operate. They are, in short, the physicians of Taiwanese society, experts in all matters pertaining to both body and soul. Together they aim to "control nature, make people sick or well, organize human behavior, save souls and revitalize society" (Wallace 1966: 167).

WORLD VIEW OF THE TAIWANESE

There are several factors which tend to complicate one's efforts to delineate what might be called a world view of the Taiwanese today. First, one must distinguish between that part of society which functions as the bearer and preserver of the folk beliefs and the elite who tend to scorn folk religion and feel themselves superior to it. I suspect that Ch'iu is not far off when he reckons the elite as constituting approximately 15 percent of the population. This leaves 85 percent who are still "faithful adherents of the folk religion" (Ch'iu 1970:3).

Second, one must not overlook the face of social change. The Taiwanese, especially the 85 per cent mentioned above, are living in a state of growing tension between the old and the new. In many homes television is commanding large blocks of time and attention from the people. The world as conceived in animistic thought is being continually bombarded with scientific data and ideas, many of which are potentially destructive of current religious beliefs.

Finally, one must not think that the average Taiwanese has conceptualized his world view into a neat system which he can verbalize to others. I once sent out a class of students, mostly Taiwanese, to collect data from the surrounding area to determine current Taiwanese views relating to the soul and the future life. Failing to obtain any kind of meaningful data, I erroneously assumed that this part of the world view was non-existent, or that it was not an issue of importance to the Taiwanese peasant. Subsequent research has changed my conviction. The inability or, in some cases, the unwillingness of the Taiwanese to verbalize his world view does not prove that he does not have one. Every people, whether consciously or unconsciously, has a world view. The problem is how to discover and draw out its constituent parts. I have chosen three separate sources from which to elicit the necessary data for reconstructing a Taiwanese world view: the symbolism which surrounds the Taiwanese use of the trigram, Taiwanese mythology, and the ritual which is performed at the time of funerals and great festivals.

According to Ch'iu, the world view of the Taiwanese is reflected in their use of the *t'ai-chi* 太極 (Grand Ultimate) diagram incorporating the eight trigrams (*pa-kua* 八卦)

(Fig. 3). The whole diagram is made up of two components: the two Chinese characters for *t'ai chi* in the center and the trigrams, which surround the center and represent the *yang* and *yin* elements of the universe by permuting broken and unbroken lines in sets of three. The trigrams first appeared in the *Book of Changes* (*I Ching*) and were subsequently taken over and adapted by the folk religion. This symbolism is found in many Taiwanese homes inscribed on the highest beam of the house. It is also used as a seal of security in the amulet, an emblem of divinity in iconography, a tool for divination, and a seal on the coffin to signify the finality of man (Ch'iu 1970:206).

The two words *t'ai-chi* convey the idea of primeval origin or the ultimate reality of all things. The *t'ai-chi* is at the center of the universe and harmonizes all things in itself. The concept of the *t'ai-chi* is dynamic. From it all things have come into being in an orderly manner. The Taiwanese, says Ch'iu, identify this idea of the ultimate reality with T'ien Kung, the high god of the Taiwanese pantheon. Below T'ien Kung, in order of descending rank, is the entire hierarchy of folk deities organized into a system remarkably parallel with the officialdom of the ancient Chinese monarchy. These gods are responsible for directing the affairs of heaven and earth.

Further dimensions of the Taiwanese world view may be discerned in the rituals of the funeral and the festival. These rituals are the most important of all Taiwanese religious activities. Ch'iu sees them as the "means by which man can transcend his profane world and have rapport with the sacred" (1970:321). By these activities, he says, man's individual and social life is, in some sense, reintegrated in harmony with the ultimate reality or with T'ien Kung.

This preoccupation with the restoration of harmony is a prominent aspect of the funeral ceremony. Elaborate rituals are performed to assist the departed soul to its destined

CHART OF THE GRAND ULIMATE

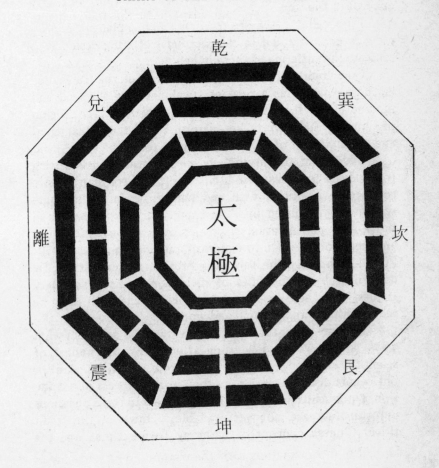

Fig. 4

place, lest the soul should become malevolent and disrupt the harmony of the living. This suggests the dualism which runs throughout the Chinese world view. Man as a microcosm includes within himself elements of the *yang* and the *yin*, an idea which, as we have seen, appears most clearly in their concept of the soul.

Firm belief in the life to come and in a place of punishment is demonstrated in the sacrificial offering designed to mitigate the suffering of those in hell.

One could further illustrate by way of the Taiwanese language which has a copious vocabulary for the soul and kindred ideas. It seems that animism, which was the religion of China at the dawn of her history, is still the fundamental and principle part of Taiwanese religion today.

Finally, in the mythology we discover models setting forth ideals for Taiwanese life. One finds here man's desire to become identified with and participate in the ultimate reality as symbolized by T'ien Kung. Ch'iu explains this in terms of euhemerization, a process by which mythical gods are metamorphosed into historical authentic persons (1970: 204). In this way, the Taiwanese provides for himself specific and concrete personalities of divine origin and exemplary virtues. On these he may model his life and with these he may identify through ritual and worship.

In conclusion, the question may well be asked: in what ways is this world view being affected by the impact of scientific knowledge and ideologies from the West? Are the old beliefs disappearing or are they in the process of adaptation if not reintrenchment? Clear answers to these questions unfortunately are not yet available. However, the traditional Chinese concept of harmony between man and the universe has very likely been altered in recent times. It is inconceivable that the impact of the West has not in some way affected the Chinese and Taiwanese world view of life even among the masses. Hodous, writing in 1936, observed (1936:340):

> The impact of the West upon the East has disturbed the mental and spiritual equilibrium; men are confused and distressed. For ages the Chinese lived in a homogeneous culture which they regarded as being in harmony with the fundamentals of the universe. This culture is now being destroyed under their eyes.

This, of course, is more true of the mainland than it is of Taiwan, where traditional culture has been largely preserved.

R. P. Kramers, writing in 1961, locates the possible breakdown in the Chinese concept of harmony with a particular time and event in history: "The break with the harmonious total world picture of the past began with the proclamation of the Chinese Republic" (1961:38). While this was primarily a mainland political event, it nevertheless represented to all Chinese peoples a break with the traditional realm of the monarchy and the concept of unity under the Son of Heaven. Is it not likely then that the Chinese and Taiwanese religious concept of the universe, patterned as it was after the monarchy of China, also suffered some disrupting influences? Indeed, this process in Taiwan may have been accelerated by the period of colonial rule under the Japanese (1895-1945).

As for the other aspects of the world view, I find no evidence that would point to significant change. A provocative word from Schoeps (1968:197):

> Beneath all the Buddhist overlays and the abstractions of the great philosophical systems, these elements of the folk religion have proved to be the really permanent

constituents of the religious life of China. They are part of the innermost nature of the Chinese peoples and it is difficult to imagine that they will ever be displaced.

And a more recent observation from Jordan: "Taiwan folk belief is fluid and adaptable, capable of providing explanation for and means of dealing with a wide range of human problems in conditions of changing values and practices" (1972:xviii).

5

Animism and Christian Missions in Taiwan 1865-1978

INTRODUCTION

THE HISTORY OF Protestant missions in Taiwan is a story of struggle. After one hundred years of concerted effort by both Protestant and Roman Catholic missionaries, the Christian community does not exceed five percent of the population. Meanwhile, indigenous forms of folk religion continue to flourish. While the Church has been planted, Christianity is still an alien presence, a stranger in the land.

In this chapter I am assuming that the animistic folk religion of Taiwan has yet to be effectively encountered by the Gospel. And let me remind the reader that I am speaking of the peasant Taiwanese of Chinese extraction, not the hill tribes who have turned to Christ in great numbers. This absence of encounter seems self-evident from the present size of the Church as well as the recent burgeoning of temple construction, religious life, and festival activities, and the absence of any popular movements away from traditional religion. The question I wish to ask is, why has the mission-

153

ary enterprise experienced only limited success in penetrating the religious life of the Taiwanese? Granted the existence of animistic powers antagonistic to the Gospel, why has the power of the Gospel not yet been demonstrated as sufficient to the disarming of these "principalities and powers" (Col. 2:15)? The question is all the more valid when we recall the great number who have turned to Buddhist or Neo-Buddhist options in preference to Christianity as I have shown in the last chapter. This turning shows they have not been resistant to religious change.

Answers to this riddle could be pursued in many directions. Some would look for lack of dedication and spiritual power on the part of the missionaries. Others might point to inadequate missionary strategy. Lack of sufficient personnel would suggest another cause, while others might point to insufficient funds to sustain vigorous evangelistic outreach. Obviously a wide range of possible factors has contributed to the limited growth of the churches. Nor would I presume to have final answers to this problem. Nevertheless, there is one area which invites our attention. In our description of the Taiwanese folk religion, we found religion to be the integrating factor for the life of eighty-five percent of the people. I suggest that a major reason for the slow growth of the churches has been the failure of missionaries to recognize this all-important fact. Nor have missionaries appreciated the fact that the displacement of the religious integrator of life necessitates that adequate functional substitutes be made to meet the needs of Taiwanese at least as thoroughly and effectively as did their ethnic religion. Coupled with this has been their tendency to discount, overlook, even reject as unreal the animistic nature of Taiwanese religion. The net result has been a continuing absence both of power encounter and effective displacement of animistic folk beliefs and practices.

THE FUNCTION OF
ANIMISM UNRECOGNIZED, 1865-1900

In fairness to the men of God who initially brought the Protestant faith to Taiwan (to the south in 1865 and to the north in 1872), we must recognize the fact that during their lifetime the concept of animism and its function in society were not widely known. Actually, the idea of animism was first developed by Sir Edward B. Tylor in his epochmaking book, *Primitive Culture* (1873). However, the form in which he developed his unilinear evolutionism lent itself readily to existing ideas of western superiority. If those missionaries had heard of Tylor's work, the probability is that they would have rejected it for these reasons. We should not judge them for failing to have an adequate concept of animism.* How they actually regarded the religion of the Taiwanese, however, is another matter. It is in this area of their attitudes that we must make our evaluations.

In order to appreciate missionary attitudes, a word must be said about the western world which produced these men. England in the latter half of the nineteenth century was in her ascendancy as a world power. Canada was only a fledgling nation, but due in part to her proximity to the United States shared in the mainstream of western culture. To these lands had come new streams of religious vitality. England and Scotland, swept a century before by the Evangelical Awakening under the Wesleys, were soon to experience new life again through the Moody revivals. Eastern Canada had felt the impact of men like William Burns whose missionary preaching had awakened many Presbyterians to a new sense of responsibility for the unevangelized world (Band 1948:1:90).

---

*This would have been true of the whole "culture concept" which was then only beginning to develop in the minds of historians and anthropologists.

Western society in the 1860s was already marked by strong individualism, a product in large measure of the pioneer conditions in which many were still living, especially in Canada. Varg writes: "The individual was more or less a self-contained entity loosely tied to his family, medieval manor, urban community or nation state" (1958:16).

Missionary candidates came largely from middle-class society and brought with them a particular set of ideals. They unconsciously assumed the superiority of western culture and technocracy. Thus, Christian dogma was interwoven with the ideals and patterns common to western civilization. Hackett sums up the general attitude of western peoples: "The advanced, superior peoples of the West looked upon themselves as saviors of the heathen, and motives of political domination, economic exploitation and religious conversion became so confused that we are still having a try to divorce them" (1969:64-65).

The dichotomy between science and religion was another characteristic of those days. The missionary helped to export it overseas. For instance, when the missionary doctor healed the sick he was oblivious to his invasion of the domain of the shaman. What he did had religious significance, though he too often didn't know it.*

Evangelical doctrine of the nineteenth century centered around the bankruptcy of the human heart, the judgment of God on all sinners, and the grace of God unto salvation offered in Jesus Christ. With this went the concept of "instantaneous conversion," by which one was changed in a moment. This change, it was confidently affirmed, would be marked by a complete rejection of all past beliefs. The corollary to this was that many well-intentioned missionaries condemned all that was strange and unfamiliar to them, usually without much investigation.

*See Horner, *Protestant Cross Currents in Mission* (1968:212ff).

In the West, knowledge of the Orient was fragmentary. The picture painted by those returning from China was usually one of poverty, suffering, and spiritual darkness. It is little wonder that the missionary of 1865 went out with not only a sense of Christian "oughtness" but also a sense of cultural superiority. He saw himself responsible to bring the Gospel and also ideas and methods which would improve the lot of Chinese life in general.

But prior to 1900, what was the typical missionary's attitude towards the religion of the Taiwanese as he encountered it in their villages? George L. Mackay's reactions are representative. In short, he regarded it largely in negative terms (1895:125-26):*

> The heathenism of Formosa is of the same kind and quality as the heathenism of China. It is the same poisonous mixture, the same dark, damning nightmare. The original element was Confucianism—a system of morality, with its worship of heaven, its deification of ancestors, and its ethical maxims. Centuries after, Taoism was added—a system of demonolatry, with its spirit-superstition and wretched incantations. Then from India Buddhism was brought—a system of idolatry, with its shrines and smoking incense. These three systems existed side by side until the dividing-walls began to crumble; and now the three are run together, a commingling of conflicting creeds, degrading the intellect, defiling life, and destroying all religious sentiment.

When writing to a western audience, Mackay could be scathing in his criticism of the grosser aspects of the folk

*Mackay pioneered the work of the Canadian Presbyterian Missionary Society in northern Taiwan in 1872.

religion. However, when in Taiwan preaching the Gospel, he did not make the mistake of deriding the people's faith as so much superstition. In fact, he sought points of value he might possess for the Gospel and built his preaching on points of contact he discovered in it: "It has been my custom never to denounce or revile what so sacredly is cherished, but rather to recognize whatever of truth or beauty there is in it and to utilize it as an 'open sesame' " (Mackay 1895: 133).

Whether or not Mackay was fully aware of the centrality of folk religion and its integrating function in the life of the people is still another question. Indeed, as a child of his day, unaware of the science of religion, it may be that he did not think Taiwanese religion worthy of careful analysis as to its essence and function.

As one examines the writings of the Taiwan missionaries prior to 1900, several impressions emerge. There is a consensus that the Gospel has power to emancipate men from degrading superstitions. There is a general recognition of some kind of powers which seemed to bind men in their religious beliefs. In fact, many were so impressed with the powers of evil that they expected "only an occasional faithful convert" (Varg 1958:16). And yet these powers, so vaguely recognized and poorly understood, were rarely made the subject of careful research or given serious consideration in evangelistic strategy.

Hoping to find evidence of how missionaries felt about the folk religion, I read through a set of mission minutes covering a period of some thirty years. Apart from a reference to idolatrous practices witnessed in a Christian funeral and other similar incidents, I found nothing. It appeared that missionary committees were too busy with organizational, administrative, and other matters. The matter of residual animistic practices among Christians was handled with a brief note encouraging missionaries to "exhort the brethren against heathenish observances."

Actually, it is difficult to find any missionary of either English or Canadian Presbyterian missions, apart from a few like Mackay, William Campbell, and Campbell Moody, who made any serious attempts to investigate the religion of the Taiwanese. None apparently ever raised the question as to how one should go about presenting the Christian faith in such a way as to challenge through encounter the animistic powers that controlled the people. Nor did the missionaries grapple seriously with the cultural and spiritual void which must be filled should any considerable segment of the population turn to Christ.*

I conclude that the function of Taiwanese folk religion remained largely unrecognized by these pioneers.** Failing to see how animistic beliefs and practices were the peasants' only means of access to divine counsel and intervention in problems of poverty, disease, and death, they presented the Gospel in the only way they knew. A few were reached and the Church was planted, but the multitudes remained largely untouched.

THE FUNCTION OF ANIMISM NEGLECTED, 1900-1940

According to Varg, the purpose of mission among mainline denominations changed after 1900. Before 1900

---

*This had been a pressing issue with early group movements among the Pepohoans of Taiwan. There, effective encounter occurred and thousands turned to Christ, only to find themselves culturally and spiritually adrift through being inadequately incorporated into the new faith and the new way of life.

**In fairness it must be said that some Protestant missionaries on mainland China had done serious research on the ancestor cult but, except for a few like W.A.P. Martin, most could see the problem of the ancestor cult only in negative terms.

major stress was laid upon the doctrine of eternal punishment of the unconverted. Much was made of the fear of perishing as a motivation to conversion. Varg quotes J. Hudson Taylor, founder of the China Inland Mission, 1865, to illustrate this viewpoint: "The Gospel must be preached to these people in a very short time for they are passing away. . . . There is a great Niagara of souls passing into the dark in China. . . A million a month in China are dying without God" (Varg 1958:68).

After 1900, however, missionary preaching began to reflect the changing theological and social moods of the West in which the spiritual and physical benefits of the Gospel were coming into increasing prominence. In 1879 Dennis's three-volume work, *Christian Missions and Social Progress*, appeared and exerted great influence upon missionary thinking. The purpose of missions, according to Dennis, was to elevate human society, modify traditional evils and introduce reformatory ideas (Varg 1958:72). This was the beginning of a social view of missions which eventually stressed the humanitarian aspects of the Gospel to the almost total eclipse of the evangelistic mandate.

Behind the changing views on mission goals lay a shifting theology. By 1917 a humanistic form of higher criticism was being taught in the colleges and seminaries of the Presbyterian Church of Canada. This brought controversy between "fundamentalists" and "modernists" and drastically influenced both home church and foreign missions (Goforth 1937:232-33). The new anti-supernaturalistic approaches to the Scriptures began to influence some to look upon belief in the spirit world as a thing of the past. One reads of inquiries arising in the West in which belief in Satan and spirit beings is denigrated (Lin 1911:145). How much this new emphasis influenced missionaries in Taiwan is difficult to ascertain. It seems probable that they, like their co-laborers on mainland China, were all affected to some degree.

Presbyterianism in England and Scotland was not spared the eroding influences which had undermined evangelical theology in Canada. Even Scotland, which had provided the early missionaries both to China and Taiwan via the English Presbyterian Mission, was beginning to experience decline after 1914.

It was during this period following 1900 that some European theologians began a concerted attack upon the supernatural elements in the New Testament, especially the doctrine of demonology in Jesus and Paul. Among the early writers, Renan, Dibelius, and Harnack stand out. While the liberalism represented by these men was largely rejected following World War II, many of the same ideas on demonology have been reproduced in recent years by Rudolf Bultmann.

Strange as it may seem, some of the prominent conservative theologians of the period were reluctant to give serious attention to the subject of demonology. James Denney is a case in point. Perhaps in this he reflected the optimism and compartmentalized thinking of his age. His monumental work, *The Death of Christ*, contains frequent illustrations of this.

For instance, Denney was a firm believer in what he called "the physical theory of evolution," although he sought to check any theological deductions from it. He resisted those who argued that because they had been physically evolved they were therefore free to "discredit the conception of moral responsibility for sin embodied in the story of the Fall" (1902:277). When the first edition of this book came out in 1902, he was chided by a friend for its serious omission, "the want of any reference to the death of Christ as a victory over Satan" (p. 203). In reply, he added a paragraph to a subsequent edition of his exposition of the death of Christ in the Johannine writings and stated that a person with his mind set "does not naturally personalize the principle

of evil—turning the principle into a prince." He also confessed
that he had experienced "embarrassment" in dealing with the
subject (p. 203), although he was willing to affirm that "Jesus
demonstrated by his death that the Prince of this world
has no rights at all" (p. 204). When discussing Paul's references to the powers, Denney concedes that they must have
had "some sort of reality for him" although he assigns this
to Paul's "background of Jewish unbelief" (p. 142). When
he raised the question as to Paul's actual convictions, Denney
concluded (p. 142):

> If Paul had definitely held such a view as has just been
> expounded, the probabilities are that it would have
> told more decidedly on his thinking, and found less
> ambiguous expression in his writings. He could not,
> for example, have given that complete account of his
> Gospel without so much as alluding to these vaguely
> conceived beings. At best they could belong only to
> the quasi-poetical representation of his faith.

Obviously, Denney did not really have any place in his
thinking for the realities of the spirit world. The men he
trained for missionary service most likely reflected his
agnosticism on this subject. How could it have been otherwise? Naturally, therefore, they were ill-prepared to cope
with the animism they found when they got there.

However, this neglect of animism can also be traced to
a new preoccupation that quite absorbed the hearts and
minds of the missionaries. During this period, both in
northern and southern Taiwan, missionaries were profoundly
influenced by institutionalism. Hospitals, schools, and
other mission-related works were being multiplied. They
effectively absorbed the majority of mission personnel.
In 1907, Campbell Moody wrote (p. 249-50):

The Christians of Europe are little aware of how much the missionaries are drawn off from that which is supposed to be their peculiar business, the work of preaching the Gospel to the heathen, . . . and sometimes almost the only man who carries on except at odd times, any sort of work among heathen, is the missionary doctor in the hospital.

Writing at a later period, Edward Band voiced the same concern: "The prospects of aggressive evangelism are bleak indeed. Our missionaries are all occupied inevitably it seems in institutional work. Even those who came out definitely to do evangelistic work have been swallowed up by the 'lean kine' of institutionalism" (1926:249).

The picture of church growth (1900-1935) reflected the above problem. Communicant members for both Canadian and English Presbyterian Churches grew only from about 5,000 to 13,000 over this thirty-five-year period (Gates 1966:74).

It appears, then, that very few missionaries found themselves often engaged in direct evangelistic work and confrontation with the folk religion. Most of the work of evangelism and church planting had been relegated to the national pastors, who themselves were fully occupied with the pastoring of their young congregations. Few, it seems, were concerned to inquire into the function of Taiwanese animism. Indeed, it may have appeared to many, and at that time justly so, that the oppressive measures by the Japanese during this period to stamp out folk religion at the temple and home level were sufficient, together with the influence of Christianity, to turn the Taiwanese populace away from their ancient ways. Moody's account of temple worship in one area seems to confirm this: "Japanese rule and Christian preaching have already reduced the temple pilgrims to a third of their former numbers" (1907:116).

Apparently, missionary methods continued to emphasize individual conversion despite what Varg observes as a "shift of emphasis from the individual to society" (Varg 1958:73). There is little evidence that they saw much vital relation between social structures and religion. Neither was there an awareness that it would be impossible to effect social change without grappling seriously with the integrating factor of Taiwan's culture—its religion.

Again, I should not stand in judgment upon missionaries for failing to be aware of anthropological insights which the professional anthropologist did not begin to formulate before 1937.* I do, however, observe the possibility that lacking such insight into the integrative role of religion and being confined largely to institutional-type labors, and with a vocal minority continuing to stress individual conversion, little substantial encounter with the animist religion took place. This absence of encounter is best demonstrated by the absence of any people movements to Christ during this period. Except for the occasional winning of whole families, there is little significant evidence of any Taiwanese group movements.**

THE FUNCTION OF
ANIMISM OVERLOOKED 1940-1976

The picture of missions in Taiwan following 1940 is complicated by World War II. Immediately following the war, there was a rapid influx of new mission societies, some fifty or more by 1964. However, the largest church con-

---

*Radin introduces the idea of religion as the "integrating factor" (1937:15).

**It is possible that minor group movements may have followed the Sung meetings in 1936, a period when communicant membership rose sharpy. The term "people movement" or "group movement" is used here in the sense of a multi-individual turning to Christ of small or large groups of people.

tinues to be Presbyterian. In 1964 it accounted for over sixty percent of the total Protestant Christian community (Hwang 1968:15).

The Presbyterian church on the plains grew from a membership of 56,591 in 1954 to 100,547 in 1964 (Hwang 1968:15). Other Protestants increased from about 20,000 to 106,970 in the same period.* Remarkable as these statistics are, the fact remains that most churches have ceased to grow significantly since 1960. Moreover, the total Protestant community in 1964 did not exceed two per cent of the total Taiwanese population (Hwang 1968:15). Thus, while the Presbyterian Christian community on the plains doubled (1954-1964), I find little evidence that would point to a people movement, nor is there any indication that folk religion during the same period received any significant setback. On the contrary, it appeared increasingly alive and growing. Witness the increase in temple building as well as public participation in festivals and pilgrimages.

What then have been the prevailing attitudes of missionaries and national church leaders toward animism during this post-war period? What is the attitude of Taiwanese Christians?

Taiwanese theologian Song Choan-seng, writing on Protestantism in Asia in 1970, appears at first to appreciate the centrality of folk religion within his culture. He quotes Tillich: "Religion is the content of culture and culture is the form of religion" (1970:73). However, he sees a dialectical relationship between culture and religion, a "tension" which "must not be disrupted." If it is, the argument goes, religion may become "culturalized" or the culture "indiscriminately identified with religion" (p. 73). I find Song difficult to

---

*This figure includes mainland Christians as well as Taiwanese.

follow at this point. Can religion legitimately be seen as an entity in dialectical tension with culture and distinct from culture? Surely, religion in any land must appear within the garb of that culture. The above quote from Tillich seems to bear this out. Song further complicates the picture by inferring that what the Taiwanese really need is not a religion but "Christianity without religion" (1970:74). Is this an unwarranted transplant from Bonhoeffer's "religionless Christianity" into a culture without Germany's long and formal Protestant tradition? Song does not, in my judgment, have a clear grasp of the function of religion among his own people.

It is interesting to contrast Song's views with those of Thornberry, a Methodist missionary writing two years earlier on the subject of religious encounter. He also uses Tillich as his authority: "Study of this indirect cultural encounter may seem awkward for the Western Christian who tries to maintain a division or tension between culture and Christianity. However, it is quite natural for the contemporary Confucianist who sees religion as the core or driving force in culture" (Thornberry 1968:47). Thornberry appreciates the force of the Confucianist who says, "The basic force of cultural life is religion" and demonstrates the fact that Chinese non-Christian writers are not unaware of the importance of religion in society.

Similar sensitivity to the integrating role of religion is not often found among evangelicals. Among most conservative theological journals which might conceivably contain articles on the role of Taiwanese religion in society, one looks in vain for insights suggesting its crucial role in the life of the people. By and large, these lessons are still coming to us from the anthropologists and sociologists.

Finally, we must inquire concerning the attitude of believers within the churches. Freytag's study on churches in rural Taiwan is helpful here. In the course of his research, he discovered a remarkable silence on the part of Taiwanese Christians concerning the folk religion which surrounds them on every side: "The limited attention which folk religion receives from the church stands in sharp contrast to its strong influence in village life (Freytag 1969:74).

. Freytag found popular religion to be closely related to the political power and social prestige of village life. In his judgment, "folk religion unites the community" (p. 74). Strange that Taiwanese believers have chosen to adopt an attitude of passive disregard for the old religion. Freytag suggests several reasons. The churches are pressed to distinguish themselves from the religious practice of their social surroundings, both in belief and worship.* In addition, society affirms that the Christians are regarded as no longer part of that community which derives its coherence from the folk religion.

Modern education has also taught Christians to regard the old ways as inferior and superstitious. Hence, they are embarrassed over their former religion. They are reluctant to discuss it.

The strongest negative influence, however, seems to come from the Taiwanese pastors. By and large, these men have assumed strongly critical attitudes toward folk religion. A sample of such attitudes may be found in *A Guidebook for Christians on Taiwanese Customs and Superstitions* (Albrecht 1965). This is a translation of a romanized book written by Taiwanese pastors for the purpose of instructing Taiwanese believers in correct attitudes towards folk religion. After describing each festival and religious practice, the writer concludes with such remarks as the following: "There is no point for discussion. We Christians must not believe

---

*Then, too, they are reluctant to talk of the old life from which they have been delivered.

this kind of superstition. Not only that, but we should destroy it. . . .The popular traditions mentioned above belong to the realm of fairy tales. We Christians must not believe and follow such customs" (Albrecht 1965:33,44).

It becomes clear from the above that attitudes have been cultivated among Taiwanese Christians which tend to close their minds to any careful evaluation of their non-Christian practices. Doubtless, these attitudes were introduced first by missionaries but later reproduced and continued by national pastors and other church leaders.

CONCLUSION

From the above data, I conclude that even in recent years few have grasped the significance of the integrative function of folk religion. Second, there has been little recognition of the effects of culture change upon religious belief and practice. Third, neither missionaries nor church leaders have developed a theology of power with which to appreciate and handle the spiritual dynamism represented by the many animistic elements in the folk religion. Therefore, little effort has been made to structure the Christian message in such a way as to bring about genuine power encounter. As a power block resisting the Gospel, animism has remained unbreached and unchallenged up to the present.

6

Animism and the Powers: A Theological Approach

INTRODUCTION

IN CHAPTERS 1 THROUGH 4 the animistic dimensions of Chinese-Taiwanese folk religion have been examined. We encountered its massive, ubiquitous, and powerful presence. In Chapter 5, I explored missionary attitudes towards animism in Taiwan from 1865 to the present. I concluded that certain deficiences have existed in missionary understanding both of the nature and function of animism in the popular religion of the Taiwanese.

In this chapter I will describe briefly four approaches which some theologians and missionaries alike have adopted toward non-Christian religions. Following an evaluation of their positions, I will then set forth an alternate approach growing largely out of the theology of Paul. As Addison has pointed out, a missionary's approach to other religions will be determined by his understanding of their nature and origin: "Who is responsible for the beliefs and practices of

169

these alien peoples—God or Satan? How you will act when confronted with them will naturally depend on what answer you give" (1938:110).

The first view, which prevailed until the middle of the nineteenth century among orthodox missions, ascribed non-Christian religions largely to Satan. Addison traces this viewpoint largely to the writings of Calvin, who while conceding a certain knowledge of the true God among all peoples, nevertheless saw the non-Christian religions as having passed through a long process of decay and corruption under Satan's direct influence. This understanding of non-Christian religions, as we have seen in the last chapter, tends to create obstacles to an open-minded approach, theological or otherwise: "Convinced that heathenism was substantially Satanic, missionaries found no motive to view it sympathetically or to search for its redeeming features" (Addison 1938:111).

When missionary and theologian alike possess such negative views and feelings, they see little use in working out any concrete theological approach to the powers present within animism. These are dismissed as satanic, and the case is closed. One wonders if this viewpoint is a subtle form of satanic deception designed to cloud minds and create fog lest a sounder approach to animism be developed that conceivably might result in the growth of the Church around the world.

A second and more balanced view which emerged in the early twentieth century saw a measure of value in all religions. Addison quotes from a sermon delivered by Bishop Wescott at a missionary conference of the Anglican Communion, 1894 (1938:117):

Each people has its own peculiar gift which will, we believe, be brought in due time to Christ through the Church. There are great nations—China and India—

inheritors of ancient and fruitful civilizations endowed
with intellectual and moral powers widely different
from our own, which have some characteristic offering
to render for the fuller interpretation of the faith.*

Another earnest Christian missionary, Monier-Williams,
expressed his views at the same conference: "Beware of
speaking evil of whatever is good and true in Hinduism. . . .
No missionary . . . ought to make the mistake of despising his
adversary. He ought rather to set himself to penetrate the
inner meaning of the system which he is sent to controvert"
(Addison 1938: 117).

Records from the Edinburgh Conference of 1910
strongly reflect the view that one should recognize in all
religions a modicum of truth since God has nowhere left
Himself without a witness. Encouragement was given missionaries to study the national religions with sympathy.
Edinburgh marked the beginnings of movement towards
some form of rapprochement between Christianity and the
non-Christian religions. This second view was more whole-
some and positive in its regard for animistic peoples and,
doubtless, took seriously the demonic powers encountered
by missionaries.

A third view was debated at the International
Missionary Council Jerusalem Conference of 1928, largely by
men from orthodox Continental Lutheranism and the
Reformed Faith. This was partly a reaction to liberalism in
Great Britain and America and was most fully articulated by
Barth. The Barthian position, firmly based upon theological

*Our reference to Wescott in no way implies that he was deficient
in his views on demonology.

concepts, denied *in toto* the idea of any revelation of God within the non-Christian religions (Addison 1938:120).:

> 'Heathenism' is the great attempt of man to get united again with God by his own effort.... 'Heathenism' is a form of 'religiousness' but it proceeds from man.... The message of Christ, therefore, spells sentence and judgment on all 'religions' first and last. ... It is therefore of not much use to speak of 'elements of truth' in other religions.

The above view of the uniqueness of the Christian revelation as a concept for missions was well developed in Kraemer's *The Christian Message in a Non-Christian World*. However, Kraemer did little towards developing a theological treatment of animism per se. In fact, his entire book—a monument of missionary insight and wisdom—is singularly lacking in serious discussion of the theological significance of spirit powers operating within animistic religions.

The fourth view was developed in the early thirties by left-wing liberals of Britain and America. Their approach to the non-Christian religions is well articulated in the Laymen's Commission Report, *Rethinking Missions*. Addison quotes the author Professor W. Ernest Hocking of Harvard University: "The missionary will look forward not to the destruction of these religions but to their continued co-existence with Christianity, each stimulating the other in growth toward the ultimate goal—unity in the completest religious truth" (1938:120). Hocking did not see any need for dealing with animism as a missionary problem. This would not be necessary with religious coexistence.

In retrospect, I find little help in the first, third, and fourth views above. I may certainly emulate the attitude of openness and biblical integrity of the second view. Beyond that, however, I must move into relatively new territory as I

attempt to develop a theological approach which will deal
intelligently with the phenomenon of animism and the
problem of "the powers."

A THEOLOGY OF "THE POWERS"

I shall now explore the biblical concept of power and
"the powers" in hope of finding a theological framework and
conceptual basis from which to approach more intelligently
the power-reality which is animism.* It is my conviction that
the powers encountered and described by both Jesus and
Paul in the first century are essentially the same as the
animistic powers active within Taiwanese folk religion today.

After reading current theological works on the powers,
I am impressed that many theologians have largely failed to
give any place in Pauline theology to a study of the powers.
John H. Yoder, writing the introduction to Berkhof's *Christ
and the Powers*, observed this hiatus (1962:3):

> Few realms of biblical thought have until very recent
> years been so resolutely ignored by the main streams of
> Protestant theology as that which provides the theme of
> this booklet. For an age which no longer believed in
> spooks or Santa Claus, there was something embar-
> rassing about the way in which the Bible—and especially
> the Apostle Paul—spoke of the 'powers', that is of some
> sort of undefinable superterrestrial beings, not only as
> if they existed, but in fact as if they mattered and were
> somehow involved in the work of Christ.

*I am indebted to my professor, Dr. Arthur Glasser, for the idea
of developing a missionary theology of "the powers" as well as many
helpful suggestions along the way. The term is taken from Ephesians
6:12.

It appears that most theologians, not knowing what to do with the problem, especially in an age of scientific advancement, merely set it aside as being out of date. This being the case, as Berkhof observes, they were then free to develop their own philosophy of history, culture, the state, and even theology itself, unhampered by what in their sophistication were outdated superstitions or remnants of "rabbinic metaphysics or apocalyptic angelology" (Berkhof 1953:3).

True, a number of works were hastily written in the years following Hitler's rise to power. These were largely by German theologians and reflected their reactions to the demonic powers of the state which Nazi Germany unleashed upon the world. However, as Berkhof notes, too much of this was written under the "impress of post-war attitudes and too little disciplined by exegesis of lasting importance" (p. 59).

It is my observation that many of these men, including Berkhof himself, have been influenced overmuch by a sociological interpretation of the powers. Berkhof seems to agree that Satan "rules the course of this world" and does so with and through "the powers" (Berkhof 1953:24). However, the primary dimensions of Pauline demonology are almost entirely lost sight of. Bultmann's demythologizing school has also made its negative contribution through its exclusion of Satan and demonology from its theologizing. Kallas, in his work, *The Satanward View* (1966), regards the current rejection of demonology as one of the tragedies of contemporary theology.

"Power"—Its Background and Biblical Meaning

The apostle Paul's use of several Greek terms, commonly referred to in English as "the powers," must be understood against the larger concept of power, both in the Old and New Testaments. Moreover, since my purpose is to develop a theological approach to the animism of an oriental people, it will be instructive to look also at the concepts of power in the Great and Hellenistic .world where oriental influences were not wanting.

First consider the several Greek words from which the concept of power has arisen. Grundmann defines them as follows (1964:284):*

1. *Dunamai* a) "to be able," "to be capable of," sometimes indicating the "concept of might or power" or "a specific form of power"; b) "to be able," with reference to the "subjective spiritual or moral attitude which either makes able or not," in this sense it may even mean "will"; c) when used of things it has the sense of "to be equal to," "to count as," "to signify."

2. *Dunatos*—"one who has an ability, a capacity of power"—"one who is powerful." This is a verbal adjective of *dunamoi*.

3. *Dunateō* is a verb derived from *dunatos* and means "to have great ability."

4. *Dunamis* is by far the most important word in the group. Here the original idea of "ability" or "capacity" is fully developed. The word may also mean "possibility" or "capacity." With its implications of "power" the term can be applied to the whole range of human experience, including the "powers of hearing and seeing" and to "spiritual and intellectual powers." In this sense, "all moral and intellectual life may be traced back to the *dunameis* of man." This is only part of the powers of the cosmos, for animals and plants also have their *dunameis* as do the underlying forces

*My primary source for data in this section is Kittel's *Theological Dictionary of the New Testament*. In particular, I am indebted to Grundmann for his many insights into the concept of "power."

of the cosmos itself. *Dunamis* may also have the meaning of "power," "competence," "host," or "power of a host."

5. *Dunastēs* refers to "the one who can do something," "ruler," "might," "dominion," "the one who is powerfull, . . . who exercises authority and rule." It is used of both human rulers and of God.

6. *Dunamoō* and *endunamoō*—both simple and compound terms mean "to endue with power," "to make strong," "to strengthen".*

It should be noted that the above terms all are derived from the root *duna* and share in the basic meaning of "being able" or "capacity."

THE CONCEPT OF POWER IN THE GREEK AND HELLENISTIC WORLD. The various uses of *dunamis* in Greek and Hellenistic writings reveal a tendency to make *dunamis* an absolute cosmic principle. This was a natural expression of their world view. As they conceived the various aspects of life in terms of *dunamis*, the inevitable result was to regard *dunamis* as a cosmic principle. On one occasion, Plato declared *dunamis* to be "the absolute mark of all being (Grundmann 1964:286). The Stoics conceived of it as "the invisible force which is self-originating and self-moving" (p. 287). In the writings of Aristotle and the Stoics the idea of *nous* remains behind the idea of *dunamis*, but in Poseidonius the process is complete and *dunamis* becomes an absolute cosmic principle, an entity in and of itself, dependent upon nothing. Here we find a whole system of powers which both create the world and operate in it. Its base is the *dunamis zōtikē*, the "original power of all being," which inwardly holds the world together

*The above Greek terms are found both in biblical as well as profane literature.

(p. 287). This is similar in part to the Chinese concepts of *t'ai-chi* and *tao* 道.

The development of the Greek concept of god resulted from the merging of the cosmic principle *dunamis* with the idea of deity. The resulting deity is entirely neutral, devoid of any personal element. Since cosmic material is fashioned by cosmic force or deity and equated with it, the result is an universal pantheistic force. This at least was how the Stoics viewed deity, differently to be sure from the transcendent being of Platonic and Aristotelian philosophy.

The neutral concept of God held by the Stoics proved a fertile ground for interaction with pagan belief in gods. Thus individual gods became *dunameis* of the universal force and were conceived of as "personifications of the capacities of a neutral deity" (p. 288). This process of identification between principle and divine power became complete in the philosophy of Poseidonius where the original life-giving power, the *zōtikē dunamis* is the deity. Thus, the forces which in earlier thinking were but part of the cosmic system now became its master, and the mystery of the cosmos was dissolved in them. The forces then became "spirits, energies, chains, sources, original forms and emanations of the inexpressible, of the original mystery of existence" (Grundmann 1964:288). Here is to be seen some of the oriental influence which was active in changing Greek thought in the direction of later forms of Hellenistic Gnosticism and animism.

This influence of oriental religion needs to be underscored. To the Hellenist the universe itself was a manifestation of the forces working in and by and on it. He saw the world as forming a great nexus of power, "a single supreme power of which the different demonic powers were emanations" (p. 289). He saw all occurrence as comprised in these forces. Hence, to accomplish anything one had to participate in the powers and control them. This required special knowledge of the powers and led very naturally to the use of magic. Man believed himself to be nearer to the demonic and cosmic forces than to the deity under which they operated. Hence his preoccupation with them obscured to him the higher but more removed deity.* Within this activity, the magician or shaman came to play an important role. These religious experts, knowing the cosmic, divine, and demonic forces and their interconnections, stood as mediators between man and the powers which influenced the world for good or for ill.

The presence of the religious expert did not hinder the gods or demons from intervening directly in the affairs of man. Witness the healing activities of the god Aesculapius, widely acclaimed in the Greek Hellenistic world of Paul's time. These acts were called *dunameis*, acts of power. Similar acts of punishment are given the same name. In this kind of a universe, man found himself increasingly at the mercy of the powers. His struggle to identify with the powers and to obtain the help which he believed they could bring gave rise to the question of salvation. What would lift him above mortality or, as the Hellenists saw it, what would redeem him from the bondage of matter? A solution was found in the "ten saving forces" related to the astral bodies. By means of secret rites of initiation these forces or *dunameis* entered into man, giving him immortality and deification.

I see behind the whole Greek conception of power the idea of a force which controls, moves, and determines the cosmos as well as the life of man within it. The origins of these views of power appear to be oriental but were fully indigenized within Hellenistic thinking.

---

*This is a common characteristic of most polytheistic religions even today. Note Chinese concern for the more immediate ancestor and patron gods as against his little occupation with Tien Kung, the high god.

THE IDEA OF POWER IN THE OLD TESTAMENT. Turning from the Greek and Hellenistic world to that of the Old Testament, one finds oneself in a different atmosphere. No neutral god is here. Rather, we meet a people who have been overtaken by a personal God who has disclosed Himself to them. Power and might have been created by the will of Yahweh and take the place of natural forces operating according to immanent law. In short, the world of the Old Testament has in a sense been demythologized. The forces of nature have returned to their proper places as servants to the Creator and are no longer gods. The Old Testament is unique in that it portrays God as completely independent of His creation, although His presiding providence fills all its dimensions. This radically new concept of God is vividly expressed in terms of His relationship to history and in the subjection of all power to His will (Grundmann 1964:291):

> In contrast to the surrounding deities which are essentially nature gods, the God of the Old Testament is the God of history. The result is that the personalistic character of the idea of God is decisive and that it absorbs the underlying naturalistic elements. This gives us the further result that the important and predominant feature is not force or power but the will which this power must execute.

God's power among His people Israel is linked from the very beginning with His mighty acts: their deliverance from Egypt and subsequent crossing of the Red Sea on foot (Dt. 3:24). According to His own will and purpose, His power works to shape and fashion their history. And He creates in their hearts confidence in the future deployment of His power on their behalf in times of need.

This view of God as related to a lineal concept of time, and the utilizing of His power to further His purpose also determines His relation to nature and nature's forces. How important this is can best be appreciated when contrasted with the conceptions of the Canaanite when he encountered the powers of nature. G. E. Wright's description is excellent (1950:17):

> The polytheist saw the problem of his life over against the powers of nature which he could not control but on which he was utterly dependent. The awesome power of a great thunderstorm, the majestic expanse and depth of the heavens, the mysterious brilliance of the moon and stars, the wonderful blessing of the sun's warmth, the miraculous fecundity of the earth, the terrible reality of death, all these awakened in him many feelings of awe and wonder. He did not distinguish between reality and the force in or behind it. In the storm he meets the God Storm. Nature is alive and its powers are distinguished as personal. . . . They are known to him because he has experienced them not as objects but as personalities so much greater in power than his own that of necessity he worships them.

In the Old Testament revelation, all astral bodies are demythologized, dethroned, and returned to their rightful places as servants of the High God. Whereas the sun, moon, and stars were gods to the Mesopotamians and the Egyptians, to the Hebrews they were revealed as the handiwork of God manifesting His greatness and glory—His servants, totally subject to the will of the Creator. Indeed, all nature and the universe at large is subject to the transcendent God and sustained by His word. The prophet Isaiah writes: "Lift up your eyes on high and behold who hath created these things, that bringeth out their host by number: He calleth them all by names by the greatness of His might, for that He is strong in power; not one faileth" (40:26).

As the power of Yahweh initiates and guides the course of history and as His word upholds the material universe, so He also controls the life and destiny of man. Man's religious quest now comes to focus upon this personal God whose right hand is powerful to save (Isa. 59:1) and in whose power there is holiness and righteousness, judgment, and grace. In this connection, Walter Freytag succinctly observes (1957:42, 43):

> Man lives in his religion because he knows that he depends on God. It is because God does not let him go that he cannot manage without Him. His religion rests upon the fact that God has not left him.... But (in his long history) he forms notions, and he makes his own gods. He exchanges God for his own gods. This always takes the form of his not being prepared to face fully the questions inherent in his own existence.... According to the testimony of the Bible there is thus no religious awareness without God, neither is there any religious attitude which is not, in face of the Christian message, unmasked as self-assertion.

The Old Testament view of the concept of sanctified power is in sharpest contrast with both oriental and Hellenic ideas. God is never equated with impersonal power. Notions of magic and pagan cultic ritual have no place in the personal relationship of the Jewish people with Yahweh, which is expressed through holy faith, obedience, prayer, and sacrifice: "Only on a personal view of God is the frontier maintained between God and man, Creator and creature. Prayer and sacrifice are aware of this frontier; magic and deification remove it" (Grundmann 1964:294).

This view of power no longer creates fear except for the rebel. Rather, it evokes doxologies of praise to the one whose power has brought salvation and purpose to an elect people within an otherwise fearful and apparently chaotic world. "One generation shall laud thy works to another, and shall declare thy mighty acts" (Ps. 145:4).

CONCEPTS OF POWER IN RABBINIC AND HELLENISTIC JUDAISM. Much of the Old Testament view of power carries over into the period of Rabbinic and Hellenistic Judaism. The mighty acts of Yahweh which marked God's self-disclosure to Israel and their exodus from Egypt are seen as manifestations of His power. The word of God remains the instrument by which God creates, sustains, and otherwise manifests this power. However, during this period new strands of thought and significant departures from the Old Testament revelation appeared which warrant our critical attention.

The first strand which later came to play an important part in the New Testament is that of the "eschatological deployment of power" (Grundmann 1964:295).* This is based on God's deliverances of Israel from hostile powers during the Old Testament period. They are now seen as his intimations that He will at some future date demonstrate His power in one final apocalyptic conflict in which all hostile powers are overthrown.

Another line of thought arose out of the Hellenistic Greek world, although it is likewise rooted in the Old Testament—belief in the power of demons (represented in Judaism by Satan) and in the ministry of angels. These powers have a dual role: standing between God and man, the angels work for God whereas the demons work against Him. These powers bear different names: *arkai, kyriotētes, ekklektoi, exousia, thronio,* and *dunameis* (Grundmann 1964:295).

The use of *dunameis* for these powers is of uncertain origin. It first appeared in Jewish writings in order to designate the angels. In its broader context, however, the term

---

*There are intimations of this in the Old Testament, in Isa. 2:19 and 40:10, for instance.

is used both for angels and demons, and largely focuses
on the single aspect of power possessed by these spirit beings
In the apocryphal literature, angels are sometimes regarded
as personified natural forces.

The angelic powers belong to God and constitute His
host. They share in His worship and service and rule over the
realm between heaven and earth. The demonic powers
belong to Beliar or Satan, and by means of them he rules
over men. "Human existence is the battlefield between
angels and demons, between God and Satan" (p. 296).
Although the oriental influence is somewhat evident here,
we must underscore a distinction from the Hellenistic view
with its neutral concept of God. In contrast, Judaism
fiercely held to a personal God and saw Him as the Creator
of the demonic powers. Judaism in general regarded the
heathen nations as worshipping these intermediate creatures
along with astral bodies instead of the living God (Dt. 4:19).

Although Judaism uniformly maintained the supremacy
of God as Creator and Lord, the introduction of angelic and
demonic conceptions led to a neglect of Him. His person
tended to fade into the background, especially since the Jews
were reticent to use God's name. In its place they substi-
tuted the term "power." However, there was no hypostatization of the concept of power in Rabbinic Judaism.*

The question of "saving power" in Judaism draws our
attention to the Torah, since it was given this designation:
"The Torah is power because it is the cosmic order with
which God creates and sustains the world . . . because He
gives to those who do it sanctification and power. . . . The
Torah becomes saving power as the revelation of the will of
God" (Grundmann 1964:297).

---

*The term "hypostatization" indicates the attributing of personal
existence to something impersonal, in this case, power.

The hypostatization which Rabbinic Judaism avoided is found in Philo. The growing tendency to shun God's name and the increasing emphasis upon God's transcendence made "power" into an independent hypostasis. Philo's god, while still personal, became pure being. He saw the powers both in unity with God (Jewish) and independent of Him (Hellenistic). Philo also severed the Old Testament concept of power from history. He conceived of the world as a "great nexus of divine powers which create and sustain life and being" (p. 299). Behind this teaching we detect the philosophy of Poseidonius, which at this point serves as a bridge between Greek philosophy and the Jewish view of God.

We will better understand the influences from the Hellenistic world upon Judaism if we review briefly the state of Hellenistic religion around 300 B.C. During this period, popular religion was moving in the direction of astralism. Gilbert Murray calls this the "failure of nerve" which followed the collapse of the anthropomorphic religion of the masses (MacGregor 1955:20). Having lost confidence in the deities which they had regarded as responsible for the ordering of life's affairs, the people were shut up to ideas of chance or fate. This proved a very fertile ground for astrology, "the scientific theology of waning heathenism" (p. 20). The old gods which had lost their appeal reappeared as deities and planets now enthroned as arbiters of human fate. Finding themselves trapped in the "prison house of the stars," men increasingly turned to systems of magic. Thus, during the intertestamental period, this pseudoscience increasingly dominated the minds of men prior to the coming of Christ.

THE CONCEPT OF POWER IN THE NEW TESTAMENT. Power in the New Testament takes on decisive meaning in the Christ event. Various aspects of this power in Christ are delineated in the synoptics and by John. First, however, I should trace the continuity of the power concept from the Old Testament idea of Messiah to the New Testament.

Power and might in the Old Testament are frequently ascribed to Messiah. This power is given to Messiah by Yahweh for purposes of battle and the deliverance of His people (Ps. 18:32, 39). Messiah is thus pictured as a mighty king (Ps. 2). A prophetic power is also given to Messiah by which He is enabled to give testimony to the Lord (Mic. 3:8; Lk. 24:19). In Christ, however, more is seen than a mere prophet endowed with power. His very existence was determined by the power of God. In the virgin birth, we see, according to Luke, a miracle of the power of God. In the incarnation, the *dunamis* of God took on the character of substance; God was revealed in the flesh as Jesus Christ, the Son of God (Jn. 1:14).

As the Son of God, Jesus became, through His miraculous birth, the "Bearer of Power" (Grundmann 1964:310). The source of His power was the Holy Spirit. He imparts to the Son not only power but authority, *exousia*, a "definite personal authority which He had in substantial terms the *dunamis* to exercise" (p. 301). The healing of the woman suffering with the flow of blood demonstrated such power (Mt. 8:46). In this miracle, we see the saving power of God which overcomes the demonic power in sickness.

The miracles of Jusus are often referred to as *dunameis* and *dunamis* (Mt. 11:20ff), as were the pseudo-miracles of others of His day. Important differences, however, distinguish the miracles of Jesus from the works of others during this period. Jesus' miracles have no connection with magic. They are evoked by the word of His power. He spoke with power and overcame the power of magic as well as the demonic powers ruling in sin, sickness, and death. The power unleashed in the miracles of Jesus was nothing less than the kingdom of God invading the kingdom of Satan.

We must also observe, moreover, the personal element of faith present in the exercising of Jesus' miracles. There is evidence to show that faith of some sort is a requirement for the performance of magic. Indeed, the shaman must somehow believe in the workability of the rituals which he uses. However, the dimension of holy, sanctified faith, trust, and obedience is entirely foreign to magic as a system.

The Johannine concept of power dovetails with the synoptics and enlarges certain aspects. The emphasis shifts from the term *dunamis* to *exousia* and *sēmeion*. John calls attention more to the subjective capacity of Jesus' power than to His objective acts (Jn. 3:2).

The power of God in the Son is nowhere demonstrated more fully than in His resurrection. The power of death is unable to hold Christ in the grave. As the Father empowered Him in life, so He is given power for new life. The Apostle Paul regards Him as "designated Son of God in power according to the Spirit of holiness by his resurrection from the dead" (Rom. 1:4): "In His power which overcomes all the might of darkness and death, He is the power of God. As such He is the theme and content of the Christian *kerygma*" (Grundmann 1964:304).

As a New Testament concept, power is developed in the full light of the Old Testament. The power of God working in history and for the consummation of history bridges into the New Testament as the kingly and prophetic powers of Messiah. As Messiah, Christ regards His power as derived from God. It is in fellowship with God through dependence on His power that Christ fashioned redemptive history and showed Himself champion over the powers, both in His life and by His death.

Paul's Concept of "the Powers"

In Paul's writings, I find the positive concept of power unfolded yet more in consonance with the testimony of the Old Testament and the Gospels. As for its negative aspects,

Paul's treatment is in many respects more developed than any
of the earlier biblical writings. Paul took the reality of power
with life and death seriousness. He relied wholly upon the
power of the Spirit in his preaching (1 Cor. 2:4). He reckoned the message of the cross as the power of God for man's
salvation. But he also recognized the powers of evil arrayed
against him in his efforts to bring the Gospel to Jew and
Gentile. Like Jesus, Paul encountered Satan and knew the
measure of his strength. By Christ, he overcame. When he
refers to Satan, he uses significant terms such as "the prince
of the power of the air" (Eph. 2:2) and "the god of this
world" (2 Cor. 4:4). Often in the same context in which he
refers to Satan, Paul also speaks of angels (*angeloi* Col. 2:18),
"principalities and powers" (*arkai* and *exousia* Eph. 6:12),
"powers and dominions" (*dunameis, kuriotētes* Rom. 8:38;
Col. 1:16) and "thrones" (*thronoi* Col. 1:16). Two other
terms of significance are the "world rulers of darkness"
kosmokratoras tou skotous Eph. 6:12) and the *stoicheia*
(Gal. 4:3, 9; Col. 2:8, 20). Others could be included, but the
above are the most important terms for our study.

Our understanding of Paul's use of the above terms will
be facilitated if we look first at his ideas of the cosmos and
second at the prevailing beliefs of those to whom he writes.
MacGregor suggests the following Pauline uses of *kosmos*
(MacGregor 1955:17-18):

a. The whole of the created universe (Rom. 7:20);
b. The stage upon which human life is played (1 Cor.
5:10); c. The epitome of earthly interests which con-
sume the affections of man (1 Cor. 7:32-33); d. The
description of mankind in bondage to earthly claims and
interests, the sphere of anti-godly powers, the "rulers of
this age" (1 Cor. 2:6, 8), and the "god of this age" (2
Cor. 4:4).

The prevailing religion of Paul's day was largely characterized by forms of astral worship. References to worship of heavenly bodies, even within Israel, are found in Acts 7: 42-43. When we read Paul's reference to the powers, we must keep in mind these astral beliefs and the Chaldean astrological lore which were so widespread in the first century. The idea of "cosmic salvation" was common knowledge to many. The idea of solidarity between man and the physical universe was taken for granted. Man saw himself as a microcosm of the macrocosm or, in Poseidonion language, "the world is a great man and man a little world" (MacGregor 1955:25). Between the two were mysterious relationships which so controlled man's destiny that he believed his fate was fixed as firmly as the orbits of the stars. Thus he felt himself trapped by malign influences of the astral powers. Never did a people long more deeply for a Savior who would deliver them from the demonic *kosmokratoros* and the dualistic dilemma of life.

How then does Paul look upon "the powers"? How much of the earthly demonology of the Gospels does he retain? To what degree have his "powers" become cosmic beings whose activities include the very government of human life? Are we to see these powers in some Pauline contexts as referring to the sociologic powers of state, tradition, public opinion, law, and secularism, as well as supernatural intelligences? Are they to be seen as instruments by which the "prince of this world" rules the course of human life?

This brings me to the most crucial question of all: do we find in Paul's thought dependable theological concepts and categories with which to approach the powers resident within the various levels of Taiwanese animism?* Should we find an

*I use the term "the powers" from here on as a convenient term broad enough to include all aspects of "power," especially in the negative sense.

acceptable theology of "the powers," is there adequate
provision made for overcoming their influence so that men
may be taken captive by Jesus Christ? This question, I
believe, lies at the heart of the missionary mandate for Taiwan.

I am not suggesting that one may find absolute parallels
between all forms of Taiwanese animism on the one hand and
those encountered by Paul on the other. At the same time,
I am convinced that the sum total of the powers as found in
Pauline theology is broad enough to encompass every
conceivable form of power to be found in the folk religion of
Taiwan, be it demonic or otherwise. I would like to look at
the powers under two headings: "the primary powers" and
"the secondary powers." These will designate the same
powers but will distinguish the way in which they operate,
on the one hand directly and the other indirectly.*

THE PRIMARY POWERS. Two terms of importance in
this section are *daimōn* and *daimonion*. The use of *daimōn* in
the Greek and Hellenistic periods was shot through with
animistic ideas of popular belief. It was used for major and
minor deities, often for protective deities. Once these
popular ideas were brought into philosophy, the abstract
forces of the *kosmos* were seen as personal, intermediary
beings: *daimones*. These demonic beings were then set over
against the heroes—*hēroes*—the messengers from the gods. In
time, the demons became closely related to animistic forms
of religion and magic and were associated with misfortune.
They were the rulers of life and destiny, and were essentially
evil. They operated in the heavenly regions close to the
earth.

Frequently, the demons were considered to be the
spirits of the departed, especially of those whose death was
violent. Most forms of evil, especially illness, were attributed
to the demons. Magic was the only method of control of the

*An alternate appellation of these two expressions of the powers
might be "the powers: direct" and "and powers: indirect."

demon powers. (One cannot miss the similarities here to Chinese folk religion and the concern over "bereaved spirits," "hungry ghosts," etc.)

The whole sphere of demonology appears only on the margin of the Old Testament. While the existence of such beings was not denied, God's people were forbidden to have dealings with them through magic or divination. In the Old Testament the term "angels" was used to describe those beings who functioned as God's messengers, somewhat parallel to the *hēroēs* of the Greeks. The lesser demons *daimonion* (Septuagint) came to be regarded as the evil spirits of popular belief, the gods of the heathen.

The New Testament unfolds further this Old Testament revelation of demonology. It contains no reference to the spirits of the dead other than that they sleep until the resurrection (1 Thess. 4:16). The *daimōn* as an intermediary between God and man is dropped, and a distinction between angels and demons is formulated. The possibility of human communication with demons is recognized (1 Cor. 10:20), but the primary emphasis in the synoptics is with demon possession. All demons are subject to Satan and Satan's power is restrained by God.

The New Testament sees two kingdoms: one of Satan and one of God (Col. 1:13). It is against this world view that we must consider Paul's experience and writings in the area of demonology. Paul was acquainted with the existence of Satan and the nature of his activities. Doubtless, he saw Satan very much as did Jesus—as the champion and leader of all demonic beings. Paul's encounter with the slave girl in Philippi provides a case study similar in many respects to spirit possession in Taiwanese shamanism. Consider Bruce's description of the slave girl (1954:332):

She is described by Luke as a 'pythoness,' i.e. as a person inspired by Apollo, the god particularly asso-

ciated with the giving of oracles, who was worshipped
as the 'Pythian' god at the oracular shrine of Delphi
(otherwise called Pytho) in central Greece. Her invol-
untary utterances were regarded as the voice of the god,
and she was thus much in demand by people who
wished to have their fortunes told.

The above description conforms well with the oriental
pattern of female shamanism, even the detail of the group of
parasites who associate with the unfortunate person, hopeful
of easy income. However, I would substitute the phrase
"possessed by Apollo" as possibly more accurate. She was
the medium into whom and through whom the "Python
spirit" spoke when occasion warranted.

In this encounter, Paul exorcised the "Python spirit"
from the slave girl. The idea of spirit exorcism is common to
the Taiwanese peasant. However, one does not usually think
in terms of exorcising the patron spirit from the shaman.
Ordinarily, the medium or the Taoist priest, as we have seen
in an earlier chapter, is himself the expert exorcist. The spirit
which possesses him leaves voluntarily after each performance, in contrast with classic demon possession. A remarkable example of spirit exorcism by a Taoist priest is carefully
documented in Thompson's *Chinese Religion: An Introduction* (1969:30-32), but this is somewhat aside from our
subject. I mention the matter of exorcism here only to point
out that exorcism is a familiar concept to the Taiwanese,
and can be utilized in any way necessary in our witness to
the Lordship of Christ over all demons.

One other reference to demons is important. In 1
Corinthians 10:21 Paul relates idols and demons by teaching
that sacrificial offerings made to idols are made "to demons
and not to God." He is speaking here about the ordinance
of holy communion. The argument is that if one would
participate at the Lord's table, he cannot offer sacrifices to

idols. Sacrifice means communion and determines the
Communion (*koinōnia*) to which one belongs.* Communion
with demons through sacrifice to idols precludes the possibility of communion with Christ at His table. However,
the truth of the idol-demon relationship goes beyond this
context. It seems to me that it should be applied to non-
Christian religions in general. In short, we are not to exclude
the possibility that associated with the Taiwanese pantheon
of idols is the reality of extensive demonic activity.

I find the problem of ancestor worship less clear-cut.
Serious theological difficulties arise when one concedes the
possibility that communion with the living spirit of the
departed is possible (Eccl. 9:4-10). Conversely, it is difficult to conceive of the ancestor cult as having survived these
thousands of years if it did not involve the reality of some
form of spirit communion between the living and what was
regarded as the spirits of the dead. The account of Saul and
the witch of Endor (1 Sam. 28:8-19) provides a possible clue,
though one is reluctant to be dogmatic.

On the surface, it would seem that Saul truly conversed
with the spirit of Samuel. But one hastens to point out two
things: first, the possibility of a counterfeit. Saul did not see
Samuel. The woman saw someone but called him a "god"
(28:13). Was this really Samuel? Second, this was not a
form of ancestor worship. There was no kinship relation
between Saul and Samuel, nor was Saul's purpose in coming
that of worship. This is a poor model upon which to establish
the possibility of actual communion with the spirit of one's
ancestor.

Although this incident has little similarity to ancestor
worship as such, it does present a form of behavior which
is frequently associated with ancestor worship in Taiwan,
and often termed necromancy. This involves a calling upon

*See Tippett's *Verdict Theology* (1969:27-28)

the dead for information relating to an unsolved problem. The reply received usually relates the problem to the neglect of the ancestor by the living descendants.

The appearance of Elijah and Moses on the Mount of Transfiguration is related to the power of God and offers even less evidence to substantiate real communion between living and dead kin. I find the following quotation by Beyerhaus rather compelling (Beyerhaus 1966:145):

> It is the unanimous consensus of Rabbinism, the New Testament and the Church Fathers that the spiritual forces behind mediumistic and occult phenomena are not the souls of the departed but the power of the fallen angels or demons who are masters of disguise.

I conclude then that in Taiwan today it is very possible that wherever the ancestor cult still includes forms of worship, prayer, and sacrifice, some form of spirit contact takes place. I would agree with Beyerhaus that the spirits involved are other than those of the departed.

Turning to those terms more peculiarly associated with Paul's concept of the powers, we find four which are often grouped together: *exousia, arkai, dunameis,* and *kuriotētes.* The first two are not found in Hellenism or pagan Gnosticism but occur in Jewish apocalyptic writings where they are used to designate ranks of angels in the seventh heaven (Kittel 1964:2:571). These powers are often distinguished from the demonic. The former find their place in the heavenly regions, while the demons operate in the earthly sphere.

The New Testament usage of the above terms, including *thronoi,* reflects the Jewish background. *Exousiai* and *arkai* are cosmic powers usually separate from the *daimones* whose region does not extend beyond the *aēr.* Several aspects of these suprahuman intelligences may be defined:

a. They are part of the creation which is created *en Christō* and *eis Christon* (Col. 1:15f).

b. As part of the created world they share in its fallen-ness, and function in part to seduce, enslave, and keep men from the love of God (Rom. 8:38,39).

c. In some contexts, these powers are demonic in function, being closely allied to Satan in his opposition to God's purpose (Eph. 6:11-12).

d. In other contexts, they are seen as needful of reconciliation (Col. 1:16, 20), and as destined to have their negative power annulled (1 Cor. 15:24).

e. Some powers are seen as beyond reproach (1 Tim. 5:21).*

Schoonhoven conceives the powers as falling roughly into three categories: (1) essentially good angels who pose no threat to man; (2) imperfect beings who nevertheless stand on the side of God; or (3) definitely demonic intelligences who belong with Satan (1966:57). The fact that Paul can use the same terms for demonic powers as for good angels is because the former are in fact "fallen angels, once loyal but now among the demonic host" (p. 60).

The remaining two terms, *kosmokratoras* and *stoicheia*, point to the cosmic, if not solely astral, dimension of the powers. MacGregor sets forth considerable evidence to indicate a first century Hellenistic source for both terms. The first word, which may be rendered "world potentates," is found in Hellenistic mystical writings and represents the "seven supreme astral deities." The *stoicheia* is used

---

*This assumes the inclusion of angels among the powers.

in Orphic hymns of "elemental deities or demons." The two
terms come together in the Hellenistic Jewish writings, the
Testament of Solomon. Here certain spirits come to Solomon and confess that they are "some of the thirty-three
stoicheia of the *kosmokratoras tou skotous*, . . . and our
stars are in heaven, . . . and we are invoked as goddesses"
(MacGregor 1955:22). Considering the religious background
of Paul's converts, it seems likely that his use of *stoicheia*
may in some cases be understood as referring to cosmic
spirit intelligences.

We must now inquire how Paul regards these powers and
how we should look at them, especially within the context of
animism. One thing is clear: he admits their existence but
denies their divinity. Moreover, he brings clearly into focus
the New Testament distinction of tension with the powers
working both with and against God. Although part of God's
creation, they have to a large degree lost their original function of serving both God and man. They are active in and
among men as demonic forces, opposing both man and God,
seeking to destroy and to undo all that is of God. In their
cosmic dimensions, they seduce man with false systems of
religions. Posing as deities, they direct worship toward the
heavenly bodies. Failing this, they lead men into magic and
sorcery, in short, into anything and everything that might
divert man's attention away from his Creator to that which
He has created (Rom. 1:20f).

We have in this aspect of the more cosmic type of
powers ample scope for including the remaining aspects of
animism within the Taiwanese religion. Certainly, those
common Chinese deities of the sun (T'ai-yang-hsing Chün
太陽星君), moon (T'ai-yin Niang-niang 太陰娘娘), and stars
(Hsüan-t'ien Shang-ti 玄天上帝) worshipped within Taiwanese folk religion fit this category well.

More important perhaps than all of the astral deities is
the dualistic concept of the *yin* and the *yang* with its many

manifestations. Here indeed is one of the most powerful elements in Chinese religious thinking, a concept which has been deified in the sense that all created beings are allegedly the issue of the interaction of these two forces. This has become a natural vehicle for possession by the powers. From our study of Chinese religion, we have already noted the influence of the *yin-yang* idea upon Taiwanese thinking. Throughout Chinese history this concept has served to replace the idea of God as Creator in Chinese religion. It has directed the thinking of millions away from the Creator and focused it on an impersonal, dualistic, philosophic concept.*

I conclude, then, that there is within Paul's teaching of the supernatural adequate scope for all the levels and aspects of the powers we have found functioning in Taiwanese animism.

THE SECONDARY POWERS. In the last section we saw that the spirit powers, whether demonic or angelic, could have direct access to men, especially within the non-Christian religious context. It seems that we should posit the possibility that this direct access is not the sole way of approach. After all, Satan is a master of disguise and deceit (2 Cor. 11:14). As such, he is not to be expected to reveal himself in any manner which would make him vulnerable to counterattack. The same would be true of all spirit intelligences serving under his leadership. Should they not be expected to prefer operating indirectly within existing human structures in their ceaseless activity of diverting men from God? This activity I have called the "secondary powers."

*It is interesting to read Geusen's prediction concerning the possible continuity of the oriental concept of *yin* and *yang* as against that of *kuei* and *shen*: "Though the old *kuei* and *shen* might disappear in the near future, the basic Chinese dualistic philosophy is undoubtedly going to endure and reappear in other popular superstitious forms and religious or pseudo-religious expressions" (1969:246).

But what are these structures by which the powers operate? They would be the institutions of man, including all socio-religious, economic, or political structures which he has constructed for the purposes of ordering his life on earth. Jacques Ellul's book, *The Meaning of the City*, develops the thesis that man in his fall and flight from God has built the city as the sign and symbol of his ethical and spiritual failure. The city with its manifold structures not only reflects man's fallenness but becomes vulnerable to possession by the powers. "All the cities man constructed are marked with the same stamp—power" (Ellul 1970:13). This power is not of flesh and blood but "a spiritual power which is the essential characteristic of the city" (p. 15). In his work entitled *Violence*, Ellul is more specific in affirming that the powers invade man-made institutions (1969:163-64):

> For the powers are incarnated in very concrete forms and their power is expressed in institutions or organizations. . . .The *exousia* of the State is incarnated in a government in the police force, the army.

Ellul's usage of the term "power(s)" tends to be symbolic, leaving little room for the demonic. And yet, while his hermeneutic is inadequate, he does make the point that man since the fall has created an amazing number of structures. These would include social customs, kinship patterns, civil laws, the state with its coercive institutions, and economic grids, among many others.

Ironically, all of these structures are basically good. Some, like family and marriage, are even stamped with the imprimatur of God. Others have arisen for pragmatic reasons. But all fill important and powerful roles in the ongoing life of man. Unlike the powers, these structures and institutions are neither intelligences nor do they possess any inherent power of their own. Although originally designed to serve man, they have become increasingly open to the control of the powers. As man himself may be possessed by demonic beings, so his institutions are equally vulnerable. A vivid illustration of demonic possession of a man-made institution in Paul's day would be the state: "To the Jewish, as to the early Christian outlook, the totalitarian State is precisely the classic form of the Devil's manifestation on earth" (Cullmann 1955:74).

Recent German history witnessed the unleashing of demonic powers through Hitler's Nazi state machine. Indeed, this experience drove German theologians to rediscover "the powers" in Pauline theology, the most neglected part of Protestant thought for over one hundred years!

But what about other aspects of life, even in Paul's day? On occasion, Paul had to warn his Galatian converts against the danger of falling back under the Jewish Law (Gal. 4:8-11) and the Colossians against old traditions and customs (Col. 2:20), for it was crystal-clear to him that these were ready-made instruments for the *stoicheia* powers, waiting to enslave the unwary pilgrim who might look back to such laws and traditions for assistance in his salvation.

We are on safe ground when we affirm that any man-made structure provides potential access for the dominance of the powers over the lives of men. This would be doubly true of non-Christian peoples. One thinks of Chinese institutions—the family, clan, ancestor cult, custom, and tradition. The social, economic, and religious bonds which knit the Taiwanese culture together can be very strong. And yet, not too strong to prevent their penetration by the powers. Kept in their proper place, these structures serve the Taiwanese by giving unity, direction, and content to life. But due to the activity of the enemy they have gotten out of hand. They have become like gods, securely enthroned to the point where individuals come under a bondage comparable to that of the

Jews under the law or of today's westerners caught up in the pursuit of mammon or pleasure. Once a man subjects himself in this way to his own institutions, his life comes under the dominance of the powers. In turn, the measure of his subjection marks the measure of his alienation from God in Christ as well as the unpredictable and self-destructive aspects of his own behavior. We are thus brought back to Paul's words in 1 Corinthians 6:8 and their reminder that long ago civil authorities in Jerusalem were taken captive by the demonic. Under this controlling presence, the state structure impelled them to crucify the Lord of glory. Nevertheless, there has to be a state and its system and officials. Paul says Christians should pray for them. The fact that they need to be upheld in prayer shows not that they are bad, but that they are vulnerable to the demonic.

One other aspect of importance should be mentioned before I conclude this section. Is there a sense in which the forces at work for cultural change in Taiwan can also be included within this framework? I have in mind here the impact of secularism upon Taiwanese religion. As we have seen in Chapter 4, the secularizing forces of industry and scientific knowledge are working against the popular religion in certain areas, such as the ancestor cult. The integrative function of religion in life is thus being eroded. I would suggest the possibility that secularism, insofar as it functions in the process of turning lives from God, may also become a vehicle for possession by the powers.

I close with a brief consideration of the biblical solution to the powers encountered in Taiwanese animism. We have already observed several basic truths about them. First, they were created in Christ, through Him and for Him (Col 1:16f). Second, they have shared in the fall with all of creation as implied in Romans 8:20-22. Instead of remaining God's servants they have arrogated to themselves the role of gods

(Gal. 4:8). Third, they, in the mid-point of history, were active in the crucifixion of "the Lord of glory" (1 Cor. 2:8).

Three essential truths remain. First, the good news that in the death and resurrection of Christ the powers were overthrown. The key passage is Colossians 1:15: "He disarmed the principalities and powers and made a public example of them triumphing over them in him." The Greek word for "disarmed" is *apekdusamenos*, a term over which commentators have long debated. Lightfoot favors "having stripped off from himself," which agrees with the Revised Version's "put off from himself." Powell sees the object of this "stripping off" as His body (1963:168). MacGregor writes (1955:23):

> Now that part of man through which the evil powers can lay hold of man and enslave him is his 'flesh.' Therefore, Christ had taken upon Himself the physical condition of man, . . . 'flesh' in which the principalities and powers could find lodgment. In the act of dying He divested Himself of that flesh and with it 'stripped off the principalities and powers' thus breaking their dominion, and carrying with Himself in His victory all those who through faith had come to be 'in Him' and thus shared His experiences.

However one translates this difficult verb, the central meaning is clear: Christ conquered the powers! As predicted, Satan has fallen "like lightning from heaven" (Lk. 10:18). Other writers like Cullman and Morrison view the conquered powers as still alive though bound as to a rope. While they may still exercise a measure of power over men, they are not free to enslave the believer. The powers appear as both good and bad. Good in that they have been subjected to Christ, but bad because of their desire to be freed and to return to their former fallen independence.

The second truth grows out of the first. At the present time, Christians must actively oppose the powers (Eph. 6: 12ff). While the powers have been conquered in Christ, this age is nonetheless characterized by spiritual tension between them and His followers. God's people live between the times; they are "caught up in a tension between the kingdom of God and a sinful world, between the age to come and the present evil age" (Ladd 1964:334).

The third truth is that before the end, the powers will encounter final defeat and nullification at the hand of Christ in His *parousia* (1 Cor. 15:24ff).

We see the powers subjected, *hypotassō*, but not yet destroyed, *katargeō*. "The rulers of this world (1 Cor. 2:6ff) are not yet destroyed, though their power to destroy has been taken from them in Christ" (Powell 1963: 169). In one sense, they are even now being put out of action, *katargoumenoi* (1 Cor. 2:6). Christ has entered the "strong man's" house, bound him, cast him out, and spoiled his goods. He now sits at the right hand of God. All authority and power is now under His sovereignty (Heb. 12:2; 1 Cor. 15:27). Moreover, His power and authority have been pledged to all those who go forth in His name (Mt. 28:18, 20). Indeed, they bear His promise with them that they shall see even greater works than His (Jn. 14:12). Not more people fed miraculously or more dead raised after longer periods in their graves, but more individuals delivered from the kingdom of darkness and incorporated into the kingdom of God.

CONCLUSION

I have endeavored to work out an intelligent approach to animism, one which has been both true to the data of Scripture and applicable to the beliefs and practices of the animist.

The concept of power as it unfolds in both Old and New Testaments offers an excellent means of approach. People trapped by the powers of a hostile universe seek for some form of superior power for deliverance. The Bible points us to the power of God in Christ as sufficient for such deliverance.

In Paul's teaching on the powers, we find concepts readily understood by animistic peoples, especially as they are illustrated from the actual events of power encounter in the lives of Paul and Jesus.

Finally, the great event which demonstrates once and for all the victory of God's power over Satan's power is demonstrated in the resurrection.

As Christ disarmed the principalities and powers, unmasked them, and forced them to participate in his victory procession, so Christians are called today to go forth in His name and power and do likewise, wherever these powers still hold men under their dominion (2 Cor. 2:14-17).

All this brings one final question: Having formulated a biblical theology of the powers and having underscored the reality of Christ's past and ultimate victory over them by His cross and *parousia*, how does the missionary bring this message of redemption and release to Taiwanese animists? Can the powers of their animism be encountered with the *kerygma* of Christ in such a way that many Taiwanese will be released from their grasp and brought into the light and power of Christ's kingdom? It is this question which I shall attempt to answer in Chapter 7.

7

Animism Encountered

INTRODUCTION

THE PURPOSE OF this chapter is the formulation of a biblical *kerygma*, grounded in the atonement of Christ, which may be used to encounter Taiwanese animists in the arena of their religious convictions and commitment. This kerygmatic approach will be deliberately formulated with a view to confronting and challenging the world view of the Taiwanese. It will be elenctic in that its ultimate objective will be to bring Taiwanese to conviction of sin, repentance toward God, and faith in Jesus Christ.

Definitions

I use the terms *kerygma* and elenctic here as they are found in missiology of the reformed tradition and as popularized by Johannes H. Bavnick in his text, *An Introduction to the Science of Missions*. The kerygmatic approach is basically one of preaching Jesus Christ. This leads to encounter within the context of *agapé* love, Christ Himself being the one who encounters the receptor. This was Paul's evangelistic approach: "We preach not ourselves, but Christ Jesus the Lord" (2 Cor. 4:5).

Bavnick defines "elenctics" as "the science which is concerned with the conviction of sin" (1964:222). The word elenctics comes from the Greek verb *elenchein* meaning "to rebuke" (Rev. 3:19) and also "to convict" (1 Tim. 5:20), but implies and includes the call to repentance (Jn. 16:8). Bavnick understands encounter as that which occurs when advocate and receptor permit the light of God to guide and illumine their lives: "In such moments all consciousness of class and rank, of race and color, disappear, and only two people remain standing together before God (1964:128).

Alan R. Tippett develops encounter in terms of power: "Man is the victim. He is bound. He is under an enslaving authority, trapped and imprisoned. The situation is such that it is quite beyond human power for man to save himself or escape. In this desparate plight a Savior from outside must be introduced into the situation or man will perish" (1969: 89).

In this context of encounter, Christ and Satan meet and those who have been enslaved by Satan and the powers are delivered. Encounter conceived of in this way is meaningful against the context of an animistic people who are familiar with the idea of good and evil powers in mutual conflict and the overcoming of a lesser power by a greater power.

Indigenous Factors

In order to be relevant, our kerygmatic approach must take into account several factors from the indigenous situation. There must be an awareness of man's basic nature as created in God's image although alienated from Him. Man is a spiritual being. He must be seen as the Bible declares him to be, a sinner, a rebel, an exile, a person displaced from his proper relationship to his Creator and oppressed by the powers. But man is also a social being. He is a bearer of culture. He lives within a web of social relationships, central to which is his religion. Life for modern man, especially in Taiwan, is dynamic and changing. Secularism has invaded his religion and challenged his world view. He is caught between the ancestor and the computer. This secular challenge of his old values and views has brought anxiety and insecurity. And yet his primary orientation remains animistic. His patterns of life continue to rest unconsciously upon the silent though pervasive authority of mythology.

A Distinction: People vs. System

The effectiveness of any approach to a non-Christian religion is conditioned by the attitude of the advocate. A useful distinction is found in Paul's experience on Mars' Hill. As Paul beheld the city full of idols, Luke states that his spirit "was provoked within him" (Acts 17:16). The Greek word rendered provoked is *parōxunetō*, a strong word connoting feelings of extreme pain or agitation. One is reminded of the reaction of our Lord in the presence of death and its ravages in the home of his beloved friend Lazarus. John writes "he was deeply moved in spirit and troubled" (11:33). Again the terms *enebrimēsato* and *etaraxen* are strong ones. They signify an "indignation of Jesus . . . directed against the power of death and against Satan the invisible enemy who wields this terrible weapon against men" (Godet 1893:184).

When face to face with systems of non-Christian religion or the powers which bring men to death, Paul and Jesus both evinced deep antipathy and agitation. This is in sharp contrast to their treatment of people. Paul looked upon the Athenian religious system as under the powers and unredeemable. Towards the people he felt differently. They shared in the image of the God who "gives to all men life and breath" (Acts 17:25). No matter how deeply fallen into sin and despair, they were still within the circle of God's providential concern. More, He has not "left himself without a witness" (Acts 14:17) and desires that men should "feel after him and find him" (Acts 17:27). Jesus' treatment of sinners was the same. All were regarded as salvable. Nowhere in the Gospels does He despair of any. As His creatures, all have the potential of calling upon God in faith.

This distinction seems valid. All religions and social systems are defiled because they are of human creation and are penetrated by the powers. This is equally true with respect to the social structures and the animistic religion of Taiwan. Of course, the social system in itself is not totally bad. There is a sense in which it is redeemable—it can be improved. The Taiwanese are the object of God's common grace. He utilizes much in their social system to stabilize family, community, and national life. But their animistic religion as a system is another matter. God wills to save the Taiwanese from all the harmful influences of their religion and bring them into His kingdom.

With this distinction in mind—people vs. religious system—we are prepared to tackle the world view, bringing to it the *kerygma* of the risen Christ.

World View: Target for Encounter

The three major elements of the Taiwanese world view which we described in chapter four may be subsumed under three categories: God (spirit world)—Universe (material world)—Man (human world). Our task is to formulate our *kerygma* in the light of each. The importance of what we are about to do must not be missed. The reader will remember our earlier definition of world view: the concept which a people have of the supernatural, of the nature of society and of man, and the way in which these concepts form a system that gives meaning to life and behavior (see page 9). One's world view determines one's norms for life and belief. Therefore, to effect significant changes at the deeper levels of belief and behavior, a radically new world view must displace the old; that is, a view which holds firmly at its center a biblical understanding of the God and Father of our Lord Jesus Christ. As we approach the task of formulating a *kerygma*, we must ask one final question: what have the Taiwanese done with God? In a sense, we are asking what have the powers, working through the animistic system, done with God? These questions require a brief examination of the deity which heads the Chinese-Taiwanese pantheon.

The Taiwanese High God

Geusens in his work, *God the Father Loves Us*, traces the concept of the high god in Chinese-Taiwanese history. He concludes that the high god of today's Taiwanese folk religion resembles the high god of the Shang dynasty. He has four basic functions (1969:40-41):

a. He is the supreme weather god, controlling rain, wind, drought and floods.

b. He is protector of the city and its ruler and is invoked to bring down blessing on its citizens, victory in its wars and calamity on its enemies.

c. He is giver of abundant harvests.

d. He is giver of boy babies.

The last function is peculiar to the Taiwanese high god. The first three are the same as those of the high god of Shang period.

The question arises why the high god of the Taiwanese is unlike the high god of the Chou dynasty, the latter being also the rewarder of virtue and punisher of evil. Geusens suggests that the difference arises from Taiwan's isolation from the mainland and the circumstances under which its pioneers lived. He reasons as follows: The early settlers of Taiwan were fishers and farmers. As such, they were consciously dependent upon the natural elements which they believed to be controlled by sun, moon, and stars. Their natural concern was to control nature and their religion developed in this direction.

Being cut off from the mainland, they were not taken up with obedience and service to the emperor, however divine he might be. Nor did they continue to worship the high god of the Confucian state religion, whose god was the remunerator of virtue and the punisher of evil, essentially the same as the high god of the Chou period. Hence the Taiwanese increasingly "fell back upon pre-state religion, animistic views and practices. It is these which largely survive today in Taiwanese ... religion" (Geusens 1969:44).

Geusens' argument makes good sense, but does not adequately reflect the fact that the state concept of Heaven as publicly promulgated during certain periods was that of a depersonalized deity. What remained, however, was the abiding concept of Heaven and the idea of virtue rewarded and vice punished.

At first glance, there appears to be some resemblance between the Taiwanese high god and Yahweh of the Old Testament. Early missionaries were aware of this similarity. Geusens claims, however, that none of the pioneer missionaries ever completely identified him with Yahweh. Geusens, quoting Saso, writes: "He is more like Zeus than Yahweh. He separates chaos, but he does not create. He is distant from man and the lesser friendly spirits and the ancestors come in between him and mankind. He is not a father but a kind of heavenly ruler" (1969:46). The above portrait of the Taiwanese high god emphasizes the idea of power and justice but lacks the concepts of Creator, Father, and Redeemer.

This is not to say that T'ien Kung has no place in Taiwanese life. His symbol,* the *t'ai-chi* diagram, is found in most homes and his image adorns many temples. The cult of T'ien Kung is part of the folk religion. However, activities relating to him are largely restricted to one ceremony on the ninth day of the first lunar month of each year. He is *deus absconditus*, far removed from the people. Only in times of natural calamity or national crisis is he called upon to help. There is little evidence of loving worship offered in his name. He is reverenced and perhaps feared, but not loved.**

Tendencies to Dismiss God

What then have the Taiwanese done with God? Several tendencies are discernable. First, God tends to be more or less absorbed into the cosmos. That is, He is merged into and identified with cosmic principles—the *tao*, *t'ai-chi*, or the dualistic *yin-yang* concept. In function, God is the dualistic all-pervasive power which manifests itself through lesser deities. This means that the cosmos itself is deified and God "sinks away behind the smog of human effort and fancy." God is dethroned and dissolved in the cosmos and is removed from the moral sphere of man's existence. His very name loses its significance. It no longer instills hope, inspires godly fear, or provides the dynamism for evoking a people's love and worship. Bavnick calls this the "cosmic-centric" world view (1964:255).

A second tendency is also found among the Taiwanese—their propensity to hypostatize the moral order of Confucius and the other sages. This means that numerous commands and prohibitions take on a quasi-deification. God is buried

*According to Ch'iu (1970).
**Folktales exist both among Taiwanese and tribal peoples describing how the once near and personal "heaven" was offended and left to dwell far away, remote from man (Wu 1969:372).

beneath the pile or at best left as a non-functioning appendage, excluded from the moral order. He is obliged to stand outside, looking in. Morality is largely seen as a horizontal relationship, in which sin and guilt are defined and resolved within the framework of social relationships. Vague ideas of Heaven's retribution may lurk deep in the hearts of men, but the resulting sense of sin and guilt rarely lifts the devotee above this practice of divination or propitiation of protector deities.

The third tendency is "the inclination to conceive of God as an ocean out of which all existing beings arise as little waves or ripples, and into which they sink again" (Bavnick 1964:266). Religious Taoism is the chief source of this pantheistic idea. Behind all of being is the eternal *tao* out of which have come the *yin* and *yang* elements. Man contains within himself elements of both the *yin* and *yang*; hence, in a sense he participates in deity. This produces a form of mysticism which robs true religion of its vital force. All is turned inward. The duality of God and man dissolves into a duality within man himself. The essential thus becomes the earthy sensory life; in short, man himself. The transcendent God is made to disappear into the "solitary abyss of the primeval one" (p. 270).

When God is removed from life in this way, people learn to live without Him. They become insensitive to inner longings for fellowship with Him. Who can get excited over interaction with the "god stuff" of which he himself exists? This has been observed among the Taiwanese. Moody described a Taiwanese village (*ca.* 1921) and referred to the villagers as "happy without God": "Why should the heathen desire the blessing of forgiveness? He does not adore or dread, much less commune, with any supreme spirit" (Moody 1921:373).

In view of the three tendencies detailed above, what formulation of the biblical *kerygma* will be most effective in

restoring God to His rightful place in this people's world
view? Let me begin with the Old Testament record.

THE OLD TESTAMENT *KERYGMA*

According to Nida's analysis of culture and communication, we are on good ground when we begin with the concept of God in the Old Testament. In his work, *Message and
Mission*, he talks about various societies and their orienta-
tions toward life. One of these he calls "tradition oriented,"
a society which is characterized by the outlook, "We have
always done it this way" (Nida 1960:124). This is the
outlook of large segments of Taiwanese today, especially in
rural and semi-rural areas. Urbanization has not yet begun to
erase the tradition-centered outlook of the majority. Nida
further points out that with the traditionalist, "one usually
communicates more relevantly by beginning with God, then
the world and finally man" (p. 128).

The traditionalists, says Nida, are interested in such
questions as: What is God like? What has He done? Where
does He live? How can one know Him? Taking a cue from
these questions, I shall explore the revelation of God in the
Old Testament, keeping in mind Taiwanese concepts of the
high god previously discussed. At this point my natural
inclination is to draw up a long list of God's attributes as
found in the Old Testament, especially those which are
lacking in the Taiwanese high god concept. This would lead
to a kind of "comparative religion" approach. We do well to
heed Wright's counsel at this point: "The study of comparative religion can do nothing more than point out the dis-
tinctiveness, and perhaps the superiority of the Biblical God;
it cannot lead us into the presence of this God, nor can it
bring us to worship Him, or acknowledge Him as our God"
(Wright 1950:42).

Something more dynamic than this is needed. Another temptation would be to yield to the westerner's bent for analysis and put God, the universe, and man into separate compartments. But the animist does not think in these terms. Neither does the Old Testament give this analytical view of life. I have chosen rather to give a composite picture, using Israel as a model and making applications to the Taiwanese wherever possible.* God will be our focus at most points, but man and the created universe will find their places as well.

I feel justified in this approach since the Old Testament in large part is the record of a people called by God from an animistic-polytheistic background and led by Him into a monotheistic world view and faith. Important insights for Taiwanese animists will appear, I believe, when asked the basic question; how did Israel become the people of God? What were the factors which placed Yahweh in the center of their world view, and brought Him to the center of their affections? No natural explanation can account for Israel's faith. It was a miracle of God's grace. And nothing short of the same miracle of His grace will be needed to bring the Taiwanese to confess this God as their Lord.

The picture which Wright paints of pagan religion as it existed in Palestine around the third millenium B.C. reflects the basic elements of Taiwanese religion today—all except its animism, which he erroneously suggests would have been outgrown by that time. Cosmic gods, protector deities, complementary powers paired male and female, precisely as the *yin* and *yang*, are all present in great profusion. Around these gods had grown a mythology to which the polytheist ascribed authoritative truth. By means of the yearly re-enactment of their myths, man identified himself with the

---

*I am indebted to G. E. Wright's *The Old Testament Against Its Environment* for many ideas in this section.

gods, who in turn maintained the rhythmic cycles of nature
so basic to life. In this way, he secured the integration of his
social existence with the activities of nature, an act very
much akin to what Granet describes in ancient China.

God

The initial disclosure of Yahweh to Israel—as earlier
to Abraham—came in the form of a divine call, a call which
brought Abraham out of Ur and Israel out of Egypt (Gen.
12:1-3; Ex. 20: 1,2). Yahweh thus showed Himself as the
God who acts in history, entering into the affairs of men
to work liberation and redemption, delivering them from the
world, the flesh, and the devil that they might serve Him.

This truth is of great importance to the Taiwanese, for
in one stroke it removes God from the remoteness and
anonymity of cosmic absorption and the primeval sea.
Although transcendent, He is suddenly revealed as immanent,
near to the life and sufferings of humanity. While the
Taiwanese cannot look back to Yahweh's mighty deliverance
in their own history, nevertheless their forefathers did
experience a great exodus from the mainland in the context
of famine, pestilence, and slavery. The preservation of thousands as they crossed the stormy Taiwan Straits in flimsy
craft can only be ascribed to the gracious protection of a
concerned God. Though they knew it not, in this experience
they encountered the mighty power of Yahweh. It is tragic,
though understandable, that in their gratitude for supernatural help and ignorance of Him, they gave thanks and
made vows to an alleged "protector" deity, Ma-tsu, the
Goddess of the Sea. This points up the task. As Israel
learned to see God's gracious providence in Yahweh's
deliverances from Egypt, the Red Sea, and the wilderness,
so we must encourage the Taiwanese to see in their own
history evidence of God's power, protection, and provision. If
this analogy appears unwarranted, I can only point to Amos

9:7. In his prophesying, God made similar analogies: " 'Are you not like the Ethiopians to me, O people of Israel?' says the Lord. 'Did not I bring up Israel from the land of Egypt, and the Philistines from Caphtor and the Syrians from Kir?' "

Once Israel had settled in the land and become adjusted to an agricultural way of life, she soon learned that Yahweh was the One who gave fertility to the soil and blessed her with abundant harvests. From Him came the fruit of the breast and the womb (Dt. 31:13). And yet He was no mere deity of fertility but the mighty God who provided for His people. Pursuing my analogy further, there is no more fertile island in all of Southeast Asia than Taiwan. The rich soil of southern Taiwan bears three crops a year. Nor are the people ungrateful.* Their thanksgiving, however, is offered more to T'u-ti Kung, God of the Earth, than to the true and living God. Israel's example should be of great significance and usefulness in directing the thanksgiving of the Taiwanese to the true source. In this way, the animist is enabled to see God as Lord of nature as well as history. He transcends both, for He is God of heaven and God of earth (Gen. 24:3).**

With this new concept of God, the Taiwanese will begin to see his existence as it truly is, not as an integration with the forces of nature and harmony with the cosmos, but rather as a relationship to the God who calls him to repentance and faith.

The revelation of Yahweh to Israel was such as to preclude the tendency to develop any dualism in nature conceptualized in the symbols of male and female. Yet, such a

---

*A common proverb in Taiwan goes, "When you drink water, think of the source" (yin-shui ssu-yüan).

**One could also point out the plight of Israel when seduced by the fertility cult of Canaan with its many Baal gods, which made necessary the subsequent power encounter between the prophet Elijah and the priests of Baal.

dualism developed early in the history of China, as discussed in Chapter 1. But now Yahweh challenges this *yin-yang* concept. The duality of sexes is found in the created world, but not in the Godhead. "Biblical Hebrew," says Wright, "has no word for goddess" (1950:23).

The holy nature of Yahweh is clearly seen in the Sinaitic prohibition against the making of images of Him. He was neither to be seen nor touched by human hands. By this law the Israelites were reminded that Yahweh is a Spirit; in contrast, the high god of Taiwan, T'ien Kung, has been conceptualized in an image readily visible in many temples.

Yahweh's place among the gods of the Old Testament is instructive to the animist in his polytheistic world. One finds the names of many gods in the Old Testament record. But these gods are all described as images and idols rather than supernatural beings having an existence of their own. True, on occasion Yahweh is pictured as seated at a heavenly assize together with the gods of the nations (cf. Ps. 82:1). However, these other gods are seen as having failed in their assigned task of caring for the welfare of the nations (82:2). They are sentenced to death (82:7). Moreover, the numbers of the council receive no worship. Yahweh is exalted above all (82:8). His jealousy permits worship of no other god. In the light of His glory and power, all gods fade into insignificance; indeed, they may be regarded as "no gods." They are without power, impotent to help or save, unworthy of man's worship and service. This one God above all others is exclusive in His claim to power and authority. He is the one to whom all the gods must submit. This concept would not be beyond the animist's grasp.

The Taiwanese need to see the implications of such passages as Deuteronomy 32. The worship of other gods means weakness, trouble, and defeat. Yahweh alone is powerful to deliver and lead a people in triumph over all powers.

But the worship of Yahweh is not without its price. He demands that His people sever themselves from all that had earlier tied them in any religious way to nature. The animist lives in a world where all his religious efforts have been directed towards achieving order, harmony, and integration— man, the microcosm, struggling to get in tune with the universe, the macrocosm. His was a world in which nature, human society, and the gods were one in their interpenetration. But the transfer of allegiance to Yahweh terminates all this. His worshippers know that the judgment of God rests upon the social order in its fallenness, upon creation in its travail, and upon the Satanic host that resists His will. Within the tension between God and a sinful world, man must live and, above all, seek to obey the will of God as well as look to Him for solutions to the ills of life.

I mentioned earlier the tendency to bury God beneath Confucian moral and social teaching. In contrast, the Old Testament makes clear that Yahweh alone is the law giver and moral arbiter of mankind. In fact, it traces the beginning of Israel's life as a nation to the Sinaitic covenant, when a redeemed people freely accepted Yahweh as Lord and Savior and promised to obey His law. From this time onward, social order was grounded neither in nature nor the gods of nature, but in the moral law of a Redeemer. Moreover, it was the first law code in human history in which God identified Himself as primarily concerned with protecting the rights of the common man—the poor, the weak, and the defenseless. Yahweh's law was a protest against all social injustice. It was a terror to the oppressor and to those whose life style reached for luxurious self-indulgence. God is concerned that men be rightly related to Him and to one another. His law pointed to a pattern of life based on righteousness, justice, and mercy. Through its sacrificial system it provided grace and forgiveness for the penitent individual and encouraged those things that would further community harmony.

God as lawgiver is at best a vague concept to the
Taiwanese.   In their proverbs there are references to the
"ordinances of Heaven," the "will of Heaven and the law
of Heaven" (Plopper 1969:59f).   I have found no clear
Taiwanese concept that the God who fills all with His
numinous presence is also the God who is the moral governor
of all mankind.

The Taiwanese are also strongly tradition-oriented.
The idea of looking back to the authority of the sages for
light on today's decisions is a common one. The Mosaic
law would seem to be most important as a means, when used
in the light of Israel's experience, for pointing man's attention away from man and to God for the ultimate authority
on life's deeper issues.

The Universe

The tendency to submerge the high god into the "abyss
of the primeval one" has already received its antidote in the
concepts of Yahweh developed thus far. He is now seen as
the "God who is there."   But more, He is Creator of the
heavens and the earth (Gen. 1:1).   Early philosophical
explanations for the creation given by the philosophers of
China have never satisfied the searching peasant mind. For
this reason there emerged out of religious Taoism the
mythical figure of P'an-ku 盤古. Legend has it that he is the
one who divided chaos into the heavens and the earth
(Plopper 1969:20). The animist needs to see the true God as
Creator of the world in which he lives, yet transcendent
above it: nature as His servant (Ps. 90), the earth as the stage
upon which He does His mighty acts. But He is distinct from
that which He has made and is not to be confused with it.
The prophet speaks to this point: "Have you not known?
Have you not heard? The Lord is the everlasting God, the
Creator of the ends of the earth" (Isa. 40:28).

Man

Long before Israel appeared in history, the early documents of Genesis had a clear formulation of man's sinful nature. He is pictured as a fallen creature, living in a continual state of rebellion against and flight from the living God (Gen. 1, 2). Subsequent revelation tells us that man left to his own resources has no righteousness before Yahweh (Isa. 64:6). The result of his sin is a separation from his Creator, a dilemma which only He Himself can solve.

This view of man conflicts in part with Taiwanese thinking. Confucian views of man's essentially good nature still prevail, even among the masses. However, a growing awareness of the holiness of God will go far towards arousing in the animist a true sense of sin and guilt.

The Taiwanese folk view of man as the microcosm striving for harmony in a world of hostile powers is similar to that of the pagan in the ancient world of the Old Testament. Both hold the social order to be tied up with the activities of the various ruling deities, with man vitally concerned to discover the divine will. The animist held this preoccupation in common even with the Israelites of old, but with one great difference—in his animistic polytheism he possessed a method, a technique for influencing both gods and nature. In Taiwan, this same bent has led to extensive use of magic and divination and the employment of the religious expert. Believing sickness to be caused by demons, the Taiwanese has at his disposal a multitude of animistic and magical cures, most of which involve the manipulation of one power against another. The powers of charms, incantations, and potions are naturally measured by the efficacy of the god or goddess whose help was sought in bringing about the desired cure. The Old Testament unambiguously levels its indictment against this traffic. Prohibitions against magic are explicit, as are also the judgments which Yahweh warns will fall upon those who knowingly disobey His will: "If a person turns to mediums and wizards, playing the harlot after them, I will set my face against that person and will cut him off from among his people" (Lev. 20:6).

That the power and knowledge of Yahweh could be secured through any man-made technique, whether of spiritualism, necromancy, astrology, or divination, was a concept utterly incompatible with His nature as revealed to man. He will make known His will where, when, and how He chooses. Indeed, all who profess to have special knowledge of that will, apart from His self-disclosure, are false prophets and deceivers of the people. No lesson could be more crucial for the eighty-five percent of the Taiwanese population who currently have regular recourse to occult forms of divination. Actually, the Old Testament record of Israel's experiences of blessing and judgment under Yahweh provide the Taiwanese with the only viable option to their present practice.

The reality of demonic powers and the animist's obsession with controlling them through ritual methods is too real and existential to him to be handled by mere prohibitions. He must be given some demonstration of power encounter in which the evil spirit powers are defeated in his very presence. Only this would be meaningful to him, for it alone fits his formula of overcoming power with greater with greater power. The account of Elijah and his power encounter with the priests of Baal is a vivid illustration of this. In that dramatic event, Yahweh showed Himself as the mighty God, powerful enough to defeat all powers of evil. He is the God who alone "answers by fire" (1 Kings 18:24).

I have previously noted that festival and pilgrimage play a major part in molding Taiwanese religious views. From earliest times, the festival has functioned to reaffirm man's place in the cosmos. By reenactment of the mythical victories of gods over demons in the past, man seek to place himself on the side of the gods to insure the repetition of a fruitful, prosperous outcome to the current agricultural year. The festival was and is the focal point of meeting between divine and human world, wherein the divine powers are called upon to act on behalf of society. Obviously more is needed than a fruitful harvest. The people need health, fecundity, tranquility at home, and peace with their neighbors.

In contrast, whereas the Israelites had their annual cycle of festivals, the religious focus was different. Yahweh was always central. That which occasioned the festivals of Israel was often some event in history in which Yahweh had acted on their behalf. Their festivals celebrated their deliverance from Egypt and His provision during times of pilgrimage when they lived in "a howling wilderness." The festival was a time of thanksgiving, joy, and worship, and focused the minds of all participants upon the will and acts of God. When I contrast this with the animist pattern, the differences are striking: historical commemorations of God's grace on one hand; the preservation of harmony in the social and natural worlds on the other.

In the Taiwanese view of man-in-the-cosmos, sacrifice plays a supportive role. Unlike the Israelite, however, the act of sacrifice is not accompanied with anything approximating the same sense of sin and guilt. When the Taiwanese experience a sense of shame due to failure in moral and social obligations with others of society, or come under the pressure of some personal problem or family need, or respond to the compunctions of tradition—these situations usually constitute the motivation to offer sacrifice.

To the Taiwanese sacrifice and banqueting are closely related. Not that these are not connected in Israelite worship. God's people were to be happy in their worship. In fact, they had a whole system of thank offerings. On the other hand, on the Day of Atonement, there was to be solemn contrition and fasting (Lev. 23:26f). Central to the

Old Testament view of worship and sacrifice is its emphasis on the holiness of God and the sinful nature of man. When the Israelite broke His law or breached His covenant, his sin required the shedding of the blood sacrifice, but even more, the offering to God of a broken and contrite heart with confession of sin (Ps. 51:17). The Scriptures are eloquent on this subject: "If I were hungry I would not tell you, for the world and all that is in it is mine. Do I eat the flesh of bulls or drink the blood of goats? Offer to God a sacrifice of thanksgiving; . . . call upon me in the day of trouble; I will deliver you, and you shall glorify me" (Ps. 50:12-15; see also Isa. 57:15; 66:2).

Finally, I must speak briefly to the problem of idolatry in which all of these concepts come to focus. The prophet Isaiah describes in dramatic form the burdensome dimensions of idolatry which he saw in his day: "They lift it upon their shoulders, they carry it, they set it in its place, and it stands there, it cannot move from its place. If one cries to it, it does not answer or save him from his trouble" (Isa. 46:7). In sharpest contrast, the worship of Yahweh was largely joyous and was rewarded with God's tender love and care, which was promised throughout life: "Even to your old age I am He and to grey hairs I will carry you" (Isa. 46:4).

While the Old Testament says little about ancestor worship, there is no doubt that Israel struggled with temptation in this area. In Deuteronomy 26:14, the tithe-giver makes this statement: "I have not eaten of the tithe while I was mourning . . . or offered any of it to the dead." It is clear here that the tithe, sacred to the Lord, was not to be connected with the worship of the dead. Nor were the dead to be worshipped at all.

Having surveyed the main dimensions of God, the universe, and man in the Old Testament, we are amazed at the composite picture which emerges. Albrecht sums up in one magnificent paragraph, as quoted by Wright, most of the data (Wright 1950:29):

The belief in the existence of only one God, who is the Creator of the world and the giver of all life; the belief that God is holy and just, without sexuality or mythology; the belief that God is invisible to man except under special conditions and that no graphic nor plastic representation of Him is permissible; the belief that God is not restricted to any part of His creation, but is equally at home in heaven, in the desert, or in Palestine; the belief that God is so far superior to all created beings, whether heavenly bodies, angelic messengers, demons, or false gods, that He remains absolutely unique; the belief that God has chosen Israel by formal compact to be His favored people, guided exclusively by laws imposed by Him.

In conclusion, I find in Yahweh's dealing with Israel a model for the Taiwanese people, currently locked in their animistic-polytheistic world. Were they to turn to Him, they would find under His relentless tutelage that nature and the universe are no longer possessed of fearful spirits but instead are subject to their Creator. Nature would become the stage and scene of His redemptive acts. Finally, they would see themselves as sinful creatures, yet loved by a redeeming God. And into their lives would be written large and clear the spiritual nature of the worship which they owe Him. They would also come to understand that, in His eternal purpose, the worship of all deities, whether idol or ancestor spirit, must come to an end. Every device or practice of man which might conceivably come between Yahweh and His people falls under the divine judgment. Thus, man is called to cast his total lot upon God.

The Old Testament message to the animist is clear. The wrath of God is revealed as against all spirit worship, idolatry, and shamanism. The animist should forsake all to follow Yahweh. God alone must be his refuge and fortress. He will deliver; He will save (Ps. 91).

And yet, one must not fail to see that the Old Testament gives no clear formulation as to how Yahweh would provide eternal salvation for His people. It confronts us with a certain incompleteness. The animist might even feel he has the right to ask: Where is this God today? How can I know Him?

One is thus driven to the New Testament with its record of the incarnation and the atonement for the completion of our *kerygma*.

THE NEW TESTAMENT *KERYGMA*

Our search for a *kerygma* within the Old Testament has been most rewarding. We have found there a world which is familiar to the animist. More than this, we have uncovered models of Yahweh's activity which can be applied to all the great issues of life in his world. We have measured the relevance of the warnings of the prophets by whom God clearly demonstrated the folly of animistic practice and the wisdom of forsaking all to follow in His ways. Pressing on into the world of the New Testament, we discover two other things of great importance: first, the Palestinian world was still essentially animist-polytheistic in its religious orientation, and, second, the unanswered questions we have brought from the Old Testament find their solutions in Christ, His atonement, and His victory over the powers.

God Brought Near

In the incarnation, Yahweh "puts on a human face" and brings God near to man. Nothing can be of greater significance to the animist and the idolater than the fact of

Immanuel, "God with us." *Deus absconditus* has become *deus praesens.*

The idea of a virgin birth is not completely foreign to the Chinese, as we saw earlier in the story of Chiang Yüan (above, page 50). However, their virgin birth stories are never related to the idea of the High God of heaven coming down to live as Man among men. This dimension of Jesus' birth, anchored as it is to time and place in history, is of great importance to the animist, for it fuses together the miraculous and the moral. God in Christ is not only the Miracle Worker and Loving Redeemer, He is also the Moral Arbiter. He comes proclaiming all men as responsible agents, morally accountable to God. He presses the animist to associate God's power with God's judgment and to forsake the sinfulness of seeking to manipulate God's power.

The animist is further made aware of his sin touching Jesus Christ for the whole human race is responsible for His death. When he learns that the very minimal oriental courtesy of receiving a guest into one's home was denied Jesus, he senses the shame of it all. That social discourtesy is followed by crucifixion! And all this took place in the Asian world! The animist's sense of community may even intensify his awareness of personal and social guilt.

Another profound truth confronts the Taiwanese animist when he ponders John 1:1. Every Chinese would agree that "in the beginning was the *tao*." Moreover, he might remember the words of Confucius who said, "*Chao wen tao, hsi ssu k'e yi*" 朝聞道夕死可矣, which loosely translated means, "If in the morning I might perceive the *tao*, death in the evening would be acceptable." But when he discovers in verse fourteen that the *tao* has taken upon itself the form of man and lived as a servant among men (Mk. 10:45), this indeed is a new and notable thing!

Jesus becomes increasingly more real to the animist as he beholds Him in the Gospels, living, teaching, preaching,

and healing. But he will be particularly impressed when he
finds that Jesus is the one who masters all demon powers
and restores possessed men to complete freedom and sound-
ness of mind and spirit.

The animist will also see that Jesus was one whose
religious beliefs permeated every facet of his life. Here is the
true "princely man" of whom the sages spoke, but who previously had not existed on the earth. To the Taiwanese
whose religious ethos is found as much in everyday life as in
his acts of ritual, this will be most meaningful. There is no
compartmentalizing of the sacred and the secular in the life
of Jesus. The will of His Father touched every part of His
life. Only one problem will remain. Where is this God-Man
now? Has God come near only to withdraw again to his
"deep Heaven?" We will deal with this question later.

The Powers Objectified

In the Old Testament, we find a few references to Satan
and the powers but they are tantalizingly brief and incomplete. Not so in the New Testament. Satan, demons, angels,
and other spirit beings are clearly revealed. This is an interesting fact: in the New Testament one finds not only fuller
revelation of God in Christ, but also a more concrete unveiling
of Satan and the powers. Narrative accounts of demonic
activity are varied. Jesus encounters two demon-possessed
men in a graveyard (Mt. 8); the disciples struggle unsuc-
cessfully to deliver a demon-tormented boy (Mt. 17); the sons
of Sceva are overcome by demonic powers (Acts 19); and the
apostle Paul exorcises the python spirit from the Philippian
slave girl (Acts 16).

One also finds in the epistles considerable teaching
devoted to this subject. So real were the powers to Paul that
he wrote about them to the infant churches in Ephesus,
Rome, Galatia, Corinth, Thessalonica, Colossae, and Philippi.
Evidently, Paul felt the importance of stressing in his teaching

of his converts clear concepts of Satan and the powers. We do well to learn from Paul. His theology cannot be understood if one refuses to accept his emphasis on the demonic.

When working among animistic peoples, little is gained by denying the existence of the powers. One must give the same scope to the powers in our preaching as he did. The biblical perspective makes clear the origin of the powers (Col. 1:16) and their basic antagonism towards men and especially toward those who have believed in Christ (Eph. 6:12; Mt. 8:28). This emphasis evokes a deeply felt response among Taiwanese people. One need only observe the time and effort they give to that religious ritual which seeks to control the spirit powers to realize how profound is their fear of the demonic and how great is their expressed need for a sense of security and protection from these powers. The animist cannot but welcome the possibility that there is someone who is greater than all malevolent spirits. He stands in awe before the Christ who expelled demons from the possessed and rebuked Satan to his face. It is this which brings us to the heart of our *kerygma*!

The Powers Conquered

We derive many blessed and important truths from the atonement of Christ. Several, however, are of particular importance to the Taiwanese. First is the fact of moral guilt. If the true nature of God has been perceived, the animist will begin to become aware of God's concern for mankind. He will also have a growing awareness of his own moral imperfection: "The goodness of God leads . . . to repentance" (Rom. 2:4). When, moreover, the corporate responsibility of man for the death of God's Son dawns upon his consciousness, a personal awareness of guilt before God beomes a possibility. This is supremely important. Unless a sense of sin is engendered by the Holy Spirit, repentance, confession, and decision will not be forthcoming.

The animist must also be confronted with the fact that Christ, in rising from the dead, has disarmed the powers and triumphed over them (Col. 2:15). He has entered the strong man's house and dealt Satan the decisive blow. As a result, all who are indwelt by the Spirit of the mighty Christ are under the protection of God. No created power in heaven, earth, or under the earth is able, henceforth, to separate those who are "in Christ" from the love of God (Rom. 8:39; Jn. 10:28).

As the fear of spirits is replaced by the experience of liberation and blessing, the redeemed Taiwanese becomes aware of the dynamic possibilities of his new orientation to all of reality (2 Cor. 5:17). His new relationship with God means the possibility of entirely new approaches to his neighbors, Taiwanese culture, the state—in short, to all of life.

VICTORY APPLIED

My treatment of animism would be incomplete if we stopped short of an application for all who would proclaim Christ in Taiwan, both foreign and national, whether as individuals or as corporate groups, mission societies or national churches. I take my cue from Paul. First, he was careful to instruct his converts in the nature and art of spiritual warfare. Paul helped the early churches to think in terms of both defensive and offensive strategies. But the apostle also made clear the means by which the power for spiritual warfare was to be appropriated. Finally, Paul in his proclamation of the Gospel to the Athenians (Acts 17) has given the Church a model of how Jesus Christ may be preached to a people whose religion is a mixture of polytheism and animism.

Instruction in Spiritual Warfare

Paul was always careful to expose and take the measure of those forces that opposed the Gospel. He called Christians-in-mission to assume a deliberate stance of resistance to them. This was premised upon his full recognition of the enemy and implemented by the utilization of certain forms of "armor" made ready by the Spirit. Recall Ephesians 6:11,12: "Put on the whole armor of God that you may be able to stand against the wiles of the devil. For we are not contending against flesh and blood, but against principalities, against powers, against the world rulers of this present darkness, against the spiritual hosts of wickedness in the heavenly places."

This exposure is followed by a description of the weaponry God has provided to overcome these demonic intelligences: truth, righteousness, the Gospel of peace, faith, salvation, and the Word of God. Since demonic spirit force can only be overcome through the use of "spiritual weapons," we need to realize that these elements of armor are not forms of magic hocus-pocus which Christians manipulate at will. We are not fighting against something abstract in a remote magical world. Rather, we are contending against the whole kingdom of darkness with all of its powers which are being used to suppress the love of God and the peace Christ promises and provides in the Gospel. This is the warfare of faith. It involves a courageous obedience to the commandments of Scripture and the rejection of all the means men normally use to advance their causes—alliances, diplomatic maneuvers, psychological or social pressure, revolutionary violence, and war. It is the determination to bring God into each issue and labor that His resurrection victory might be manifested. It is the deliberate use of what Ellul calls "the violence of love," the complete antithesis of the devil's game of using evil means to overcome evil. The writings of the Apostle Paul are filled with precepts and illustrations of this "excellent way" (1 Cor. 12:31). In his epistles he stresses again and again that the Christian is in Christ. He can therefore appropriate the "powers of the age to come" for his spiritual warfare. Indeed, he is the temple of the Holy Spirit. He can believe that God is present with him in power.

Furthermore, in the Apostle Paul's teaching, when the powers are resisted in this way, several things happen. Their true nature is unmasked. They are seen for what they really are—self-vaunting intelligences desirous of being gods, not servants, and determined on a mission of deceiving men and keeping them in alienation from God (Col. 2:20,21; Rom. 8:35).

The illusory nature of the powers is also brought to light. In exalting themselves and desiring to be like God, they have created the impression of greatness and unlimited power. When encountered and resisted in the mighty name of Jesus Christ, all their semblance of greatness fades away. They are revealed for what they are, powers having sharp limitations. Although they appear as supernatural in size and influence, they cannot go beyond limits set by God (Acts 4:28). The Christian who walks in the Spirit can overcome them.

This brings me to one active dimension found in Paul's instruction to the Church. The individual Christian and the collective body have an offensive as well as a defensive strategy. The believer's prerogative is to speak the word of faith. The "preaching of the cross" is the "power of God" unto salvation (1 Cor. 1:18). Thus when Christ is "lifted up," the powers scatter, for the cross has disarmed them. As they have once been led in His victory procession, paraded as conquered beings by the Son of God who came back from the dead (Rom. 1:4, Col. 2:15), so God's children clad in the armor of God and indwelt by His spirit can by their testimony and His blood overcome them (Rev. 12:11).

In Ephesians 3:10, we find Paul alluding to the collective action of the Church that brings the powers to subjection, "[so] that through the church the manifold wisdom of God might now be made known to the principalities and powers in the heavenly places."

What is this wisdom of which Paul speaks? Why does it cause the powers to flee? The focus of Paul's thought in this passage is the Christ-event. It is Christ who penetrated the enemy's camp and made possible the wholly unexpected— that Jews and Gentiles, who once lived under the *stoicheia* powers of this world, may now live together in Christ's fellowship. This is the greatest mystery of the ages. God offers salvation to all who repent and incorporates them into a new people, the Church which is His body. This reality is God's sign, His token, His proclamation to the powers that their bondage over men has come to an end.

In a sense, the very presence of the Church, each congregation of worshipping, witnessing, suffering, and serving believers, is a sign that the powers are doomed. The powers of God's kingdom have invaded this age and the *parousia* of the King is near.

Appropriation of Power

But the life and witness of the Church must always be carried from the place of worship into the market place, where men are. How important then that those provisions for laying hold of divine power be regularly appropriated by the individual Christian and the local congregation.

We can yet learn something from those who pursued this pilgrimage before us, those who wrestled with Apollyon and faced the lions on either side of the narrow way. Listen to the prayer of St. Patrick, the great missionary to the Irish in the fifth century. He believed with all of his being that he needed power over the evil one. He was also deeply persuaded that God was able and willing to supply this power. So he prayed (Patrick 1953:70-71):

I arise today
    THROUGH   God's strength to pilot me:
                    God's might to uphold me,
                    God's wisdom to guide me,
                    God's eye to look before me,
                    God's ear to hear me,
                    God's word to speak for me,
                    God's hand to guard me,
                    God's way to lie before me,
                    God's shield to protect me,
                    God's host to secure me—
    AGAINST   snares of devils,
    AGAINST   temptations of vices,
    AGAINST   inclinations of nature,
    AGAINST   everyone who shall wish me ill,
                    Afar and anear,
                    Alone and in a crowd.

I summon today
    ALL THESE POWERS
                    between me and these evils—
    AGAINST   every cruel and merciless power
                    that may oppose my body and my soul,
    AGAINST   incantations of false prophets,
    AGAINST   black laws of heathenry,
    AGAINST   craft of idolatry,
    AGAINST   spells of women and smiths and wizards,
    AGAINST   every knowledge that endangers man's body
                        and soul.

Christ to protect me today
    AGAINST   poison,
    AGAINST   burning,
    AGAINST   drowning,
    AGAINST   wounding,
                    So that there may come abundance of
                    reward.

Christ with me,
Christ before me,
Christ behind me,

Christ in me,
Christ beneath me,
Christ above me,
Christ on my right,
Christ on my left,
Christ where I lie, Christ where I sit, Christ where I arise,
Christ in the heart of every man who thinks of me,
Christ in the mouth of every man who speaks of me,
Christ in every ear that hears me,
Christ in every eye that sees me.

I arise today
        a mighty strength,
                the invocation of the Trinity,
                        belief in the Threeness.

Confrontation: Paul on the Mars' Hill of Taiwan

We are now ready to proclaim the Christian *kerygma* to the animist. Let us imagine that our advocate is Paul, the missionary, and that the locus of his service is Taiwan. How would Paul preach to the Taiwanese today?*

On the basis of all that has already been discussed in this study I assume his message would approximate what he preached on Mars' Hill in the city of Athens (Acts 17). He would have mastered the religious orientation of the people and the wisdom of the great sages whose proverbs are known even to the common man. Quite probably his message would also reflect the felt needs of his audience as an ethnic group. We assume that he would address the masses, not the philosophers.

Allowing for a measure of sanctified imagination, let us say that Paul is passing through the island. He finds

---

*I am indebted to Arthur Glasser's article, "Mission and the Church's Message" (*The Church's World Wide Mission*, 1966); P. A. Geusens, *God the Father Loves Us* (1969); and J. B. Phillips, *The Young Church in Action* (1955), for ideas in this section.

himself in the famed city of Pei-kang, the center of the
Ma-tsu cult.   It is the twenty-third day of the third lunar
month, the birthday of "the great goddess whom all Taiwan
worships." Thousands of pilgrims are merging from all parts
of the island.   Within the city, vast crowds of Taiwanese
surge and swell as they push towards the sacred grounds of
the temple.   As they get closer a pungent sweetness of
burning incense stings the nostrils and chokes the lungs.
Everywhere is heard the staccato of bursting fire crackers.
Excitement is at fever pitch.   It seems as if some strange
power has captured the minds and hearts of the people and
filled them with but one desire—to stand in the presence
of their protector, the goddess Ma-tsu. Many of these pilgrims
come with a real measure of spiritual hunger. Nearly all bring
a specific need. Central to their thought is the hope that the
famed Goddess of the Sea will answer their prayers—the
healing of a sick child, peace for a troubled heart, help in
a difficult decision, success in a courtship, or guidance in a
business venture. Their prayers are legion.

The Apostle Paul now comes on the scene. He has found
a widening in the street. The people have become aware of
his "foreign" presence in their midst.   All eyes are fixed on
him as he mounts a flat monument located in the center of
the square. He then faces the throng and raises his hand to
gain attention.   They sense that he is about to speak and
draw near to listen.*

"Men and women of Taiwan, I perceive that you are a
most religious people.   Traveling throughout your beautiful
island, I have been impressed that religion lies at the center
of your life.   I have seen on every hand evidence of your
fear of the spirits and concern for the gods. I have visited

---

*I interrupt Paul's "message" at crucial points to explain his
particular emphases and also to suggest possible reactions on the part
of the people.

and admired your many beautiful temples built in their
honor.   Moreover, the sincerity of your faith is evidenced
by the zeal which has brought you to this place and this
moment in your religious pilgrimage. Many have come from
afar.   Many have spent weary hours walking along Taiwan's
hot, dangerous highways. Old and young alike have braved
the scorching sun and slept under open skies to come to this
city and its famous temple. You have thereby displayed your
concern to please Ma-tsu and gain her favor.

"One thing has impressed me during my visit to your
country. I find this of greatest interest. In some temples
whether Buddhist, Taoist, or Confucian, I have found lighted
lamps, inscriptions, and other signs pointing to your knowledge of the God of Heaven. You call him T'ien Kung, Yü-
huang Shang-ti, and Tao. Moreover, in some temples, I found
your chief deity to be without a name. Apparently, He is unknown to those who worship him!* It is this God, the Father
in Heaven, whom you worship in ignorance, that I today
proclaim unto you."

In his introduction, Paul reaches out to make contact
with what is nearest the inner citadel of the people's hearts.
He demonstrates both a knowledge and an appreciation of
their religious practices and beliefs. He assumes their participation in the universal religious quest of man. But now he
proceeds directly to the theme of God.   He wants the
Taiwanese to know who He is, His concern for His creatures,
and His work on their behalf.

"This unknown and mysterious God, whom you often
call T'ien Kung, ought not to be unknown to you. He has
disclosed His eternal power and deity to you in and through
His creation.   Indeed, the heavens above and the world
around us are His handiwork. Everything reflects His wisdom

*This is documented by Thompson in his study, "Notes on
Religious Trends in Taiwan." He found twenty-one such temples.

and greatness. Have not your sages said, 'All things are derived from Heaven'? I do not have to prove to you His existence; you already know that He exists! Deep within your hearts you know there is a God who is infinitely greater than all of the gods of the temples. These gods are enclosed in shrines made by human hands. But the true God cannot be shut up in any temple or shrine. He is Lord of Heaven and earth. He fills all the universe.

"God is not to be compared with the emperor of ancient China who surrounded himself with a court and many servants and refused to be approached by ordinary men except through intermediaries he had appointed. Neither is God like a man in that we must give Him food and drink, as you do to your gods. God does not need our gifts! Indeed, the cattle on a thousand hills are His. It is rather that we need His gifts. In fact, we are already enjoying many of His good things: life, health, food, shelter, and clothing. All these are His gracious provisions for men.

"Moreover, God delights in the work of His hands. This means that you men, women, and children are the crown of His creation. The whole human race has come from Him and has filled the earth. He is not the God of one people alone, in west or east. He is the God of all mankind. And what does He desire? Just what your sages deeply longed for: 'Within the four seas, all men should be brothers.' The true God loves us all. His love is like a father's love for his children. Because of His love, He has commanded that we should seek God. Indeed, all men do seek God, especially you Taiwanese. Your great ancestors sought Him in the mysterious *tao*; others in the beauty of art; and still others in philosophical ideas of heaven. How you seek Him still— now this way, now that—through your religious experts, and even before the altars in your own homes.

"But in all of this you have gone too far. Furthermore, you keep going to the wrong places. The true and living God is not far from any of us. Indeed, our very lives are bound up in His existence. Since He is our Creator, it may be said that we live and move and have our being in Him. So you see, He is not far away. He is near us and at hand to help us. Surely, if we are made in His likeness, He must be willing that we should know Him. To live one's whole life without knowing Him would be to miss the Way of Heaven. To be indifferent to Him and seek to worship other gods—this would be folly. Your own ancient writings say, 'How tragic to abandon the Way of Heaven!'"

Up to this point, Paul has held the attention of the majority. Some have become restless as they have pondered his implication that they are worshipping idols and not real gods and that they have thereby completely missed the true God. But most are willing to hear more. So Paul continues. Now he moves quickly to his core of the message—Jesus Christ, the divine provision of redemption through His atoning death; Jesus Christ, God's gracious response to the religious quest of man. Paul pours heart and soul into his presentation. He is determined by God's grace to liberate men from their bondage to sin and the powers.

"My friends, if we are indeed God's creation, then we ought not to think of deity as some man-made image, some idol of silver or gold or stone! Surely the Creator is greater than the creature! The creature should not seek to represent Him with any human form and carry Him about in sedan chairs as though He were impotent and lifeless! This is what you and your ancestors have been doing for ages, albeit in ignorance. Think of how angry this must have made the true and living God! And yet, He has said that His mercy has constrained Him to withhold His wrath. But now that the times of your ignorance are passed, there is but one fitting attitude for all who have offended Him—repentance! As you have fled from evil spirits in the past, now you must forsake the worship of idols and flee from your sins! Turn away from all wrong attitudes toward God. You came to this festival today fully prepared in your hearts to confess your failure to Ma-tsu. Rather, I call on you to confess your sinfulness to God. But do this in the name of the one whom He has sent, Jesus Christ the Lord.

"You may ask, who is this Jesus Christ? And why should I call upon Him? My answer is direct and to the point. Prophets and seers of old spoke of Him. Your own sage, Confucius, was not far from Him when he sought for the *tao*. And now, in these latter days, God has sent Him to us. He is God's Son, the radiance of the Father's glory, the perfect expression of the nature of God, incarnated in human flesh and personality. How important it is for you to know Him. Through Him we know the Father, the one true God. Through faith in Him, we receive forgiveness—yes, even reconciliation with God.

"Perhaps you ask, why should I call upon Him? How can we know that this man is truly what He claimed to be? What merit or power does He have? How is it that He alone can save me? Your questions are reasonable. I will tell you quite simply. Two thousand years ago, the time of the great Han period, He came into this world. He was born of a virgin and lived humbly among men. 'God anointed this Jesus with the Holy Spirit and with power; he went about doing good and healing all that were oppressed by the devil, for God was with him' (Acts 10:38). Then it was that men of the Asian world plotted against that Man. Their dark deeds and evil hearts could not bear His light, and in their furious desire to quench His witness to the truth, they put Him to death, the death of a common criminal.

"But that is not the end of the story. On the third day, God raised that Man from the dead, and He is alive today. Today, He invites you to come to Him. He will be your mediator. He understands your heart for He once lived upon this earth. He understands the difficult times in which you live, for He struggled with all the trials and temptations known to men. He wrestled with all the demonic powers which plague your lives. Seeing no other way to save us, He gave His own life as a ransom when He died for us.

"Do you question the truth of all this? So would I, if I had not met Jesus, risen from the dead. Yes, risen from the grave! And in His resurrection triumph He set me free. Yes, free from my sins and free from my fears of others and of the demons. This is best of all: He demonstrated His superior power over all the powers of Satan's kingdom. He has set me free, and now I share this good news with you. He lives to forgive you for worshipping dead idols. He lives to rid you of every fear of spirit powers and evil forces. I call you this day in His name to repent! For the God of Heaven has fixed a day of judgment when He will judge you by His standards of righteousness. There will be no bribing this God on that terrible day. He cannot be bribed as your gods are. And He is merciful and will forgive you all your sins, if you repent. Turn from your sin. Worship at His feet."

Paul has spoken the fatal word. He has made his appeal for the hearts of men. Some by now are complaining bitterly. Others are accusing him of blasphemy against their gods. They are vehemently denying ever having committed anything worthy of being called "sin against Heaven." Their responses are as varied as the numbers present. Knowing Paul and the power of God, however, we are confident that some are responding in faith. How many, we will never know, but the temptation will always be to return to that place in Taiwan, to preach Paul's message, and to see for ourselves what God does whenever Christ encounters the Taiwanese.

8

Conclusion

LOOKING BACK OVER the ground covered, I find a
number of insights and recommendations which need
to be restated and underscored by way of a challenge to all
involved in missions among animists.

First, concerning animism itself, one could wish that
this study had succeeded in giving a comprehensive description and analysis of what exactly constitutes the component
parts of Chinese-Taiwanese animism. Instead, my data only
confirms what others have already observed: namely, that
animism is most difficult to isolate and describe. In any
Asian country its precise form varies from village to village,
from country to country. The reader may have sensed this
already in the author's struggle for a consistent usage of
terms. At times "animism" and "folk religion" have been
used almost interchangeably. On occasion the phenomenon under discussion could be technically described as
"animism" or "animistic." Very often, however, I found
myself examining aspects of animism which could be better

"felt" than rationally explained. And yet there is also a hard core of reality to the phenomena of animism which should be identified in large measure with "the powers" of Pauline theology. Objectifying the elements of animism in this way has a two-fold value. First, it enables us to relate the Christian view of the spirit world with that of the animist. We are not "agnostic" when we ponder the spirit forces with which he struggles. We believe that he is in touch with real intelligences who have invaded his world via its folk religion and who have "possessed" many of the impersonal elements of his cultural web. When we look at his animism in this fashion we are provided with a biblical-theological base from which to launch a spiritual, kerygmatic offensive against it.

Second, our objectifying of the elements of Taiwanese animism enables us to utilize strategic considerations in bringing it under the Lordship of Christ. It is too massive and powerful an entrenchment to be taken by any blind "general assault." Admittedly, we still lack a precise definition for Taiwanese animism, and yet we can nonetheless single out those aspects of Taiwanese religion which are the peculiar domain of animism in its most indigenous forms. Recall the ancestor cult, shamanism, temple worship, divination, and the festival. These are the main pillars upon which the animistic *corpus* rests. This *corpus* could be represented as combining two realities which Tylor has identified as the "souls of the individual creatures capable of continued existence after the death or destruction of the body" (especially the ancestor) and "all other spirits, upward to the rank of powerful deities." On the basis of our study, however, we would have to add the clarifying clause that Taiwanese "deities," whether major or minor, are conceptualized in the form of visible idols. However, the worship of such idols is no less animistic than the worship of invisible ancestors. It all adds up to the fact that any definition of

animism as it is found in Taiwanese folk religion must include
the polytheistic dimension. There are many spirits and many
gods.

We also found that in our review of four periods in the
history of China and Taiwan that animistic folk religion more
or less functioned as the center of life and the common
factor which integrated the variegated aspects of peasant life
into a coherent whole. We questioned this function when we
examined the recent period of Taiwan's semi-industrialization.
We felt we should give close and serious attention to the
impact of current social change upon that which historically
has given cohesion to life in China and Taiwan. We began to
wonder whether, in the providence of God, Taiwan is
approaching a period in its history when social dislocation
together with the threat of nuclear warfare and over-
population are converging to condition large segments of the
people to turn in groups to Jesus Christ.

We would err, however, in looking for the imminent
collapse of animistic practices in Taiwan. That which has
arisen out of the depths of Chinese antiquity is not about to
be eclipsed in a few short years. Indeed, the two hundred
or more "animistic" non-Christian religious groups currently
mushrooming in southern California's "secular cities" make
us feel that animism is a growing world-wide phenomenon,
particularly in those parts of the world more industrialized
than Taiwan.

Finally, we note with some chagrin that at this late hour
in the history of the Church's world-wide mission, missionary
strategists have yet to develop a serious theology and strategy
for bringing about effective encounter between "the powers"
in animism and the power of Christ. We have examined a
possible solution and feel that it has real merit.

We regret exceedingly that during the one hundred or
more years of mission history in Taiwan, little significant
encounter has taken place between the Lordship of Christ

and "the powers." The *kerygma* of much missionary preaching has been suited more to secular man of the West than to the animist, locked into the spirit-filled cosmos of the East. I suggest that the nature of our gospel proclamation should move more in the direction of the pattern left for us by the Apostle Paul in the book of the Acts. To be sure, the atonement of Christ must always be the kernel of the *kerygma*. Nevertheless, the Christian advocate will make little impression on the Taiwanese world view until he takes seriously the reality of the powers which have taken them captive. In terms of emphasis, we need do no more than did Paul. But this was a great deal! But if we do as much, the triumph of Christ in disarming the powers will ring loud and clear in every message we preach, and this "Good News" will be heard throughout the length and breadth of Taiwan.

It seems to me our study has underscored the importance of the Old Testament in winning the people of Taiwan to Jesus Christ. This confirms the thesis of Rowley, Wright, Warneck, and others: "One of the functions of the Old Testament has always been its role as a bulwark against paganism" (Wright 1952:19). The missionary to Taiwan should not be so limited in vision that he regards his task solely in terms of the New Testament. Again we quote Wright: "When a Christian seriously seeks to explain and expound his faith over against another religion, his initial and basic arguments are drawn from the Old Testament for it is the latter which has been a chief bulwark—against paganism" (p. 29).

Much more work needs to be done on the role of the Old Testament in the strategy of missionary proclamation. For example, consider the concept of "recital" so vital to the periodic reviving and refreshing of spiritual life among the people of Israel. Here is a ready-made concept that can be utilized in Taiwan where street corner operas are forever reciting the great events of ancient China. Surely the time has come for the recital of the mighty acts of God in ways that the animist will understand and by which he will be enabled to see new significance in these historical events.

The limited focus of our study has naturally only peripheral consideration of many related subjects. The anthropological dimensions of social change could have been given greater prominence because of their great importance for today's mission. When a people turn from one way of life to another, the responsibilities of the Christian advocate must not be limited to meeting spiritual needs only, but should extend to social reintegration. The matter of functional substitutes is but one of many related questions which warrants further study. The problem of syncretism is also closely related to our subject. It can be so destructive to the ongoing of God's purpose that the Scriptures devote considerable space to exposing its negative dimensions. W. A. Visser't Hooft's significant work, *No Other Name* (1963), has alerted the Church in our day to its importance.

The role which spiritual awakenings play in challenging animism is also a vast and important subject. One informant says that the 1907 revival in Korea "burnt the roots of shamanistic animism out of the Korean Church" and made possible the continuation of her amazing growth in the decade that followed.* Surely this has something to say to the Church in Taiwan as well. Its members are not yet fully freed from animistic tendencies, and this quite possibly contributes to its sluggish growth pattern.

Hopefully, our study has helped us to see the folly of directing evangelistic strategy towards the Confucianists and their philosophical concepts. True, these have influenced the visible structures of Taiwanese society. But when we realize that at least eighty-five percent of the people live,

---

*Another informant says revival burnt out sin. However we would recognize that these are not mutually exclusive.

move, and believe within the "Little Tradition" of animism, we do well to orient ourselves accordingly. It may be that Christians have fished too long on the wrong side of the boat in the shallows of the sea. Now they should cast their nets on the right side and reach down into the animistic deeps where the fish are plentiful.

In conclusion, permit the recording of an experience from my first term of missionary service in Taiwan. It is shared not because of its deep personal meaning to my own heart, which it had, but because it demonstrates what has been said in this dissertation about encounter.

The story concerns the life of a freshman student, a newly converted Christian who confronted the powers binding a large number of Taiwanese students.* This event took place some years ago at Christ's College in northern Taiwan.

Tom Chang was from a poor farming family in southern Taiwan, raised by his parents in the strict Buddhist tradition. He was a lad of many talents, friendly to all and full of life. His brief months of life and study at the college were suddenly interrupted by the cruel discovery that he had fallen victim to the dread disease—lymphoblastic leukemia. He immediately withdrew from campus life and entered a nearby hospital. Nevertheless, a steady stream of concerned classmates visited him, day after day. In no time at all, Tom was at death's door. But God! How strange are His ways. One morning, Tom awoke conscious that he felt stronger. The disease had been abruptly, though temporarily, arrested. New strength returned in a matter of days. As a result, Tom approached his doctor with a strange request. He wanted to pay a farewell visit to his classmates at the college on the

*The students involved obviously were not peasants, though many were from rural farm backgrounds.

following Sunday. He felt deeply constrained to share with his classmates what had happened in his own life.

Tom's visit proved memorable. Rumor of his coming had spread throughout the student body. Many gathered for Sunday evening worship with a quickened sense of anticipation. What would happen? Finally, the moment arrived; the sound of a car, a hushed silence, and then Tom appeared, as one returned from the dead.

Making his way to the front, he stood before them, pale and weak, the shadow of a smile on his gaunt face. The next few moments are difficult to describe. It seemed to me that the very powers of darkness were about to be routed. Simply and quietly, he spoke, quoting a verse of Scripture: "So, we do not lose heart, . . . though our outer nature is wasting away, our inner nature is being renewed every day." Then came his witness to a personal confrontation with eternity.

"A few weeks ago, I was like many of you are tonight: healthy, carefree, my heart filled with ambitions and little thought for God. Suddenly, leukemia—only a few weeks to live! I was terrified! But in my despair, Jesus came! He found me, overcame my fears, and saved me. You all know that I face death, but now I am no longer fearful. I live my life a day at a time, each day for Him.

"I will not be with you much longer. Oh, how my heart cries out to tell you all, yes, to warn you all. Do not say that tomorrow you will heed Jesus' words. Tonight, I plead with you."

Tom said little more than this. There was no need. God's Spirit had begun to work. And the fruits of that evening of encounter and revival have endured to this very day. Among those who forsook the ancient ways of belief and practice to follow Christ were Tom's sister and brother-in-law. A large part of the student body also encountered Jesus Christ, believed, and made decisions which later resulted in their entering the formal service of the Church.

Here, then, is evidence that Christ has conquered the powers and that He lives today to "take captivity captive," finding men and women where they are and liberating them by His grace. Those whom He calls are delivered from all their fears, particularly of "the powers" who had tyrannized them in the past. But more, in His name and victory, they can now themselves enter into enemy territory and participate in His liberation of their families, friends, and fellow citizens in the nation Christ Himself would disciple.

EPILOGUE

One is reminded of an incident in *Pilgrim's Progress*. Christian is on his pilgrimage to the Celestial City. Suddenly, upon entering a narrow passage, he is confronted with "two lions in the way." Fearful and of a mind to turn back, Christian is suddenly reminded:

> Fear not the lions for they are chained and are placed here for the trial of faith . . . and for the discovery of those that have none: keep in the midst of the path and no hurt shall come unto thee (Bunyan n. d.: 50).

> War arose in heaven, Michael and his angels fighting against the dragon; and the dragon and his angels fought, but they were defeated. . . . The great dragon was thrown down, . . . and his angels were thrown down with him. And I heard a loud voice in heaven, saying, 'Now the salvation and the power and the kingdom of our God and the authority of his Christ have come, . . . and they have conquered him by the blood of the Lamb and by the word of their testimony, for they loved not their lives unto death" (Rev. 12:7-11).

Bibliography

Addison, James T. 1925. *Chinese Ancestor Worship: A Study of its Meaning and its Relations with Christianity.* The Church Literature Committee of the Chung Hua Sheng Hui.

____. 1938. "The Changing Attitude Toward Non-Christian Religions." *International Review of Missions* 27:110-21

Albrecht, Ardon. 1965. *A Guidebook for Christians on Taiwanese Customs and Superstitions.* Translated by Ardon Albrecht and Go Sin-gi. Taipei, Taiwan: China Evangelical Lutheran Church.

Band, Edward. 1926. *Japan Mission Yearbook.* Tokyo: Christian Literature Society, 1921-1931.

____. 1948. *Working His Purpose Out: The History of the English Presbyterian Mission.* London: Publishing Office of the Presbyterian Church.

247

Bavnick, J. H. 1964. *An Introduction to the Science of Missions*. Philadelphia: Presbyterian and Reformed Publishing Company.

Berkhof, H. 1962. *Christ and the Powers*. Translated by John Howard Yoder. Scottdale, Pennsylvania: Herald Press.

Beyerhaus, Peter. 1966. "The Christian Approach to Ancestor Worship." *Ministry* 6.4:137-45.

Bruce, F. F. 1954. *Commentary on the Book of the Acts*. London and Edinburgh: Marshall Morgan & Scott.

Burkhardt, V. R. 1958. *Chinese Creeds and Customs*. Taipei: Hua Sheng Publishing Co. Vol. 3.

Campbell, Joseph. 1962. *The Masks of God: Oriental Mythology*. New York: Viking Press.

Chang, Kwang-chih. 1963. *The Archelogy of Ancient China*. New Haven and London: Yale University Press.

Chen, Chi-lu. 1968. *Material Culture of the Formosan Aborigines*. Taipei: The Taiwan Museum.

Chen, Chung-min. 1967. "Ancestor Worship and Clan Organization in a Rural Village of Taiwan." Academia Sinica, *Bulletin of the Institute of Ethnology*, 23:21-24.

Ch'iu, Ming-chung. 1970. "Two Types of Folk Piety: A Comparative Study of Two Folk Religions of Formosa." Ph.D. dissertation, University of Chicago.

Ch'ü, T'ung-tsu. 1957. "Chinese Class Structure and its Ideology." In *Chinese Thought and Institutions*.

Edited by J. K. Fairbank. Chicago: University of Chicago Press.

Creel, H. G. 1937. *The Birth of China.* New York: Frederick Ungar.

———. 1938. *Studies in Early Chinese Culture.* Baltimore: Waverly Press.

Cullmann, O. 1955. *The State in the New Testament.* London: SCM Press.

Day, Clarence Burton. 1969. *Chinese Peasant Cults.* Taipei: Ch'eng-wen Publishing Co.

De Groot, J. J. M. 1892-1910. *The Religious System of China.* Leiden: E. J. Brill. Vol. 6.

Denney, James. 1902. *The Death of Christ.* London: Hodder and Stoughton.

Diamond, Norma. 1966. "K'un Shen: A Taiwanese Fishing Village." Ph.D. dissertation, Cornell University.

Doré, Henri. 1914-1938. *Researches Into Chinese Superstitions.* 13 vols. Shanghai: Tusewei Press.

Eberhard, Wolfram. 1937. *Early Chinese Cultures and Their Development: A New Working-Hypothesis.* Translated by C. W. Bishop. Washington: Smithsonian Institute.

———. 1959. *Chinese Festivals.* New York: Henry Schuman.

———. *The Local Cultures of South and East Asia.* Translated by Aide Eberhard. Leiden: E. J. Brill.

Eliade, Mircea. 1964 *Shamanism: Archaic Techniques of Ecstasy.* Translated by Willard R. Trask. New York:

Bollingen Foundation.

Elliott, Alan J. 1955. *Chinese Spirit-Medium Cults in Singapore*. Monographs on Social Anthropology, series 14. London, London School of Economics and Political Science, Department of Anthropology.

Ellul, Jacques. 1969. *Violence*. Translated by Cecelia Gaul Kings. New York: The Seabury Press.

_____. *The Meaning of the City*. 1970. Translated by Dennis Pardee. Grand Rapids, Michigan: William B. Eerdmans.

Freytag, Justus. 1969. *The Church in Villages of Taiwan*. Tainan, Taiwan: Theological College Research Center.

Freytag, Walter. 1957. *The Gospel and the Religions*. Translated by B. S. Cozens. London: SCM Press.

Gallin, Bernard. 1966. *Hsin Hsing, Taiwan: A Chinese Village in Change*. Berkeley: University of California Press.

Gates, Alan F. 1966. "Church Growth in Taiwan." M.A. thesis, Fuller Theological Seminary, Pasadena, Calif.

Geusens, P. A. 1969. *God the Father Loves Us*. Taipei: Hua Ming Press.

Godet, F. L. 1893. *Commentary on the Gospel of John*. Grand Rapids, Michigan: Zondervan Publishing House. Vol. 2.

Goforth, Rosalind. 1937. *Goforth of China*. Grand Rapids, Michigan: Zondervan Publishing House.

Granet, Marcel. 1932. *Festivals and Songs of Ancient China*. Translated by E. D. Edwards. London: George

Routledge and Sons.

_____. 1958. *Chinese Civilization*. Translated by Kathleen
E. Innes and Mabel R. Brailsford. New York: Meridian
Books.

Grichting, Wolfgang L. 1971. *The Value System of Taiwan
1970*. Taipei.

Grundmann, W. 1932. "Der Begriff der Kraft in der Neutes-
tamentlichen Gedankenwelt." In G. Kittel.

Hackett, William. 1969. "Christian Approach to Animistic
Peoples," *The South-East Asia Journal of Theology*,
Vol. 10, No. 2, 3:48-83.

Harris, W. T., and Parrinder, E. G. 1960. *The Christian
Approach to the Animist*. London: Edinburgh House
Press.

Harvey, Edwin D. 1933. *The Mind of China*. London:
Oxford University Press.

Hodous, L. 1929. *Folkways in China*. London: A. Probs-
thain.

Horner, Norman A., ed. 1968. *Protestant Cross Currents in
Mission*. Nashville and New York: Abington Press.

Hsieh, Chiao-min. 1964. *Taiwan—ilha Formosa.* Washington:
Butterworths.

Hsü, Hsin-yi. 1968. "A Multivariate Approach to the Anal-
ysis of the Cultural-Geographical Factors of the Chinese
Folk Religion." Ph.D. dissertation, University of
California at Los Angeles.

Hsü, Ti-shan. 1971. *Fu-chi mi-hsin ti yen-chiu* 扶箕迷信

的研究. Taipei: Commercial Press.

Hu, Chang-tu. 1960. *Religion in China*. London: Hutchins' University Library.

Hwang, C. H. 1968. *Joint Action for Mission in Formosa*. New York: World Council of Churches Friendship Press.

Jordan, David K. 1972. *Gods, Ghosts, and Ancestors*, Berkeley: University of California Press.

Kallas, James. 1966. *The Satanward View*. Philadelphia: The Westminster Press.

Keesing, Felix M. 1958. *Cultural Anthropology: The Science of Custom*. New York: Holt, Rinehart and Winston.

Kitagawa, Joseph M. 1960. *Religions of the East*. Philadelphia: The Westminster Press.

Kittel, Gerhard, ed. 1964. *Theological Dictionary of the New Testament*. Translated by Geoffrey Bromiley. Grand Rapids, Mich.: Wm. B. Eerdmans. Vol. 2.

Kraemers, R. P. 1961. "Changing Chinese Identity: From Cultural Totality to Nation Among Nations." *The South-East Asia Journal of Theology*. 2.4:31-43.

Kuo, Ho-lieh. 1970a. *Taiwan min-chien tsung-chiao (Folk Religions in Taiwan)*. Taipei.

_____ 1970b. Letter to author, October 3.

Kulp, Daniel Harrison. 1925. *Country Life in South China: The Sociology of Familism*. New York: Teachers'

College, Columbia University. Vol. 1.

Ladd, George E. 1964. *Jesus and the Kingdom*. New York, Evanston, and London: Harper and Row.

Lin, Shao-yang. 1911. *A Chinese Appeal to Christendom*. New York and London: G. P. Putnam's Sons.

MacGregor, G. H. 1955. "Principalities and Powers: The Cosmic Background of Paul's Thought." In *New Testament Studies*. Cambridge: University Press. 1:17-28.

Mackay, George Leslie. 1895. *From Far Formosa*. New York: Fleming H. Revell Co.

Malinowski, Bronislaw. 1954. *Magic, Science and Religion*. New York: Doubleday & Co.

Middleton, John. 1967. *Myth and Cosmos*. Garden City: Natural History Press.

Moody, Cambell H. 1907. *The Heathen Heart*. Edinburgh and London: Oliphant, Anderson and Ferrier.

_____. 1921. "Gentiles Who Never Aimed at Righteousness." *International Review of Missions* 10:364-75.

Madel, S. F. 1951. *The Foundations of Social Anthropology*. London: Cohen and West.

Needham, J. and Wang Ling. 1956. *Science and Civilization in China*. Cambridge: Cambridge University Press. Vol. 2.

Nida, Eugene A. 1960. *Message and Mission*. New York: Harper and Brothers.

Nida, Eugene A., and William A. Smalley. 1959. *Introduc-*

ing Animism. New York: Friendship Press.

Parker, Edward Harper. 1905. *China and Religion*. London: John Murray.

Patrick, Saint. 1953. *The Works of St. Patrick*. Westminster, Md.: Newman Press.

Plopper, Clifford H. 1969. *Chinese Religion Seen Through the Proverb*. Glencoe: The Free Press.

Powell, Cyril H. 1963. *The Biblical Concept of Power*. London: The Epworth Press.

Radcliffe-Brown, A. R. 1952. *Structure and Function in Primitive Society*. Glencoe: The Free Press.

Redfield, Margaret P., ed. 1962. *Human Nature and the Study of Society: The Papers of Robert Redfield*. Chicago and London: The University of Chicago Press.

Redfield, Robert. 1960. *The Little Community and Peasant Society and Culture*. Chicago: The University of Chicago Press.

Reichelt, Karl L. 1951. *Religion in a Chinese Garment*. Translated by Joseph Tetlie. London: Lutterworth Press.

Saso, Michael R. n.d. *Taiwan Feasts and Customs*. Hsinchu, Taiwan: Chabanel Language Institute.

Schoeps, Hans-Joachim. 1968. *The Religions of Mankind*. Translated by Richard and Clara Winston. Garden City: Doubleday & Co.

Schoonhoven, Calvin R. 1966. *The Wrath of Heaven*. Grand Rapids: Wm. B. Eerdmans.

Shearer, Roy E. 1968. "Animism and the Church in Korea." M.A. thesis, Fuller Theological Seminary, Pasadena, Calif.

Smith, Howard D. 1968. *Chinese Religions.* London: Weidenfeld and Nichols.

Song, Choan-seng. 1970. "Whither Protestantism in Asia Today." *The South-East Asia Journal of Theology* 1:66-76.

Thelin, Mark. 1963. "Religion in Two Taiwanese Villages." *Journal of the China Society* 3:44-57.

Thompson, Laurence G. 1964. "Notes on Religious Trends in Taiwan," *Monumenta Serica* 23:319-49.

_____. 1969. *Chinese Religion: An Introduction.* California: Dickenson Publishing Co.

_____. 1970. "Notes on Taiwanese Religion in Early Ch'ing." Mimeographed paper presented at ASPAC, El Colegio de México, June 24-27.

_____. 1970. "Yu Ying Kung: The Cult of Bereaved Spirits in Taiwan." Mimeographed paper presented at Western Conference of AAS, Montana State University, October 16-17.

Thornberry, Mike. 1968. "The Encounter of Christianity and Confucianism: How Modern Confucianism Views the Encounter." *The South-East Asia Journal of Theology* 10.1:47-62.

Tippett, Alan. 1969. *Verdict Theology in Missionary Theory.* Lincoln, Illinois: Lincoln Christian College Press.

Tylor, Sir Edward B. 1958. *Primitive Culture*. New York: Harper.

Varg, Paul A. 1958. *Missionaries, Chinese and Diplomats: The American Protestant Missionary Movement in China, 1890-1952*. Princeton: Princeton University Press.

Visser't Hooft, W.A. 1963. *No Other Name*. London: SCM Press.

Wales, H. G. Quaritch. 1957. *Prehistory and Religion in South-East Asia*. London: Bernard Quaritch.

Wallace, Anthony F. C. 1966. *Religion: An Anthropological View*. New York: Random House.

Warneck, J. 1954. *The Living Christ and Dying Heathenism*. Grand Rapids: Baker Book House.

Welch, Holmes. 1957. *Taoism: The Parting of the Way*. Boston: Beacon Press.

Wright, G. E. 1950. *The Old Testament Against Its Environment*. Chicago: Henry Regenery Co.

———. 1952. *God Who Acts*. London: SCM Press.

Yang, C. K. 1957. "The Functional Relationship Between Confucian Thought and Chinese Religion." In *Chinese Thought and Institutions*. Edited by J. K. Fairbank. Chicago: University of Chicago Press.

———. 1961. *Religion in Chinese Society: A Study of Contemporary Social Functions of Religion and Some of Their Historic Factors*. Berkeley: University of California Press.

Index

Addison, J., 7, 169, 170-72
A-r, 193
Agape, 203
Albrecht, A., 167-68
Albright, 221
Analects, 48
Ancestor cult, 27, 28, 19, 30, 36-38, 52, 113-20, 145, 192-93
  Classical period, 43-45
  origin of, 27
  personator, 43
  Shang, 28-30
  tablet, 99
  Taiwan, 118-20
Ancestor worship, 3, 28, 30, 60, 118-19, 192, 193, 221
Aneloi, 187
Angels, 182-83, 190
Animism, 1-2, 14, 17, 28
  barrier to church growth, 2
  definition of, 6-7, 240-41
  formation of, 25-26
  source material of, 23, 25-26, 28
An-yang, 28
Apekdusamenos, 200

Archai, 182, 187, 194
Archeology, 13, 20-21, 23-24, 27
Astral worship, 188, 195
Attitudes
  faulty, 18
  missionary, 155
  to non-Christian religions, 169-173

Band, E., 155, 163
Barth, K., 171
Batak, 2
Berkhof, H., 173-74
Beyerhaus, P., 193
Bruce, F. F., 190-91
Buddhism, 2, 17, 39, 72-80, 90-91, 103, 111-12, 123
  Bodhisattva, 75, 104
  Buddha, 74-75, 111, 138
  Greater Vehicle, 75
  Karma, 76, 78
  Lesser Vehicle, 75
  persecutions of, 76-77, 91
Bultmann, R., 161, 174
Bunyan, John, 246
Burkhardt, V., 117

257

CHINESE MATERIALS AND RESEARCH AIDS
SERVICE CENTER

OCCASIONAL SERIES

Robert L. Irick, General Editor

1. *An Annotated Guide to Taiwan Periodical Literature, 1966,* edited by Robert L. Irick (1966). Out of print. (See No. 15 below.)
2. *A Ming Directory — 1968,* compiled by Ronald Dimberg, Edward L. Farmer, and Robert L. Irick (1968). Out of print.
3. Wan, Grace, *A Guide to* Gwoyeu Tsyrdean (1969). Paperbound, 43pp. ISBN 0-89644-134-2.
4. *"Nothing Concealed": Essays in Honor of Liu Yü-yün,* edited by Frederick Wakeman, Jr. (1970), xv, 221pp. ISBN 0-89644-198-9.
5. Eberhard, Wolfram, *Sternkunde und Weltbid in Alten China: Gesammelte Aufsätze* (1971), 417pp. ISBN 0-89644-203-9.
6. Eberhard, Wolfram, *Moral and Social Values of the Chinese: Collected Essays* (1972), xiv, 506pp. ISBN 0-89644-356-6.
7. Chan, David B., *The Usurpation of the Prince of Yen, 1403-1424* (1976), xi, 173pp. ISBN 0-89644-457-0.
8. *An Author-Title Index to* Ch'üan Han San-kuo Chin Nan Pei-ch'ao Shih 全漢三國晉南北朝詩篇名目錄 , compiled by Mei-lan Marney (1973), 160pp. ISBN 0-89644-530-5.
9. *Modern Chinese Authors: A List of Pseudonyms,* compiled by Austin C. W. Shu, 2nd revised and enlarged edition (1973). ISBN 0-89644-531-3.

10. *An Annotated Guide to Current Chinese Periodicals in Hong Kong,* compiled by Paul P. W. Cheng (1973), xii, 71pp. ISBN 0-89644-358-2.

11. Day, Clarence Burton, *Career in Cathay* (1975), 185pp. ISBN 0-89644-420-1.

12. *Vietnamese, Cambodian, and Laotian Newspapers: An International Union List,* compiled by G. Raymond Nunn and Do Van Anh (1973), xiii, 104pp. ISBN 0-89644-532-1.

13. *Burmese and Thai Newspapers: An International Union List,* compiled by G. Raymond Nunn (1973), xii, 44pp. ISBN 0-89644-533-X.

14. *Indonesian Newspapers: An International Union List,* compiled by G. Raymond Nunn (1973), xv, 131pp. ISBN 0-89644-534-8.

15. *An Annotated Guide to Taiwan Periodical Literature, 1972,* edited by Robert L. Irick (1973), ix, 174pp. ISBN 0-89644-359-0.

16. Yu, Chang-kyun, *Sa-seong Thong-ko* or *Ssu-sheng T'ung-k'ao (A Comprehensive Study of Four Tones)* (1973), xxiv, 286pp. ISBN 0-89644-535-6.

17. Yu, Chang-kyun, *Meng-ku Yün-lüeh (Abbreviated Chinese Rimes in the Mongolian Script)* (1974), xxxiii, 290pp. ISBN 0-89644-536-4.

18. *An Index to Stories of the Supernatural in the* Fa Yüan Chu Lin法苑珠林志怪小說引得 , compiled by Jordan D. Paper (1973). Paperbound, ix, 29pp. ISBN 0-89644-537-2.

19. *Translation and Permanence in Chinese History and Culture: A Festschrift in Honor of Dr. Hsiao Kung-ch'üan,* edited by David C. Buxbaum and Frederick W. Mote (1973), xxvi, 433pp. ISBN 0-89644-357-4.

20. *An Index to the* Ch'ao-yeh lei-yao 朝野類要引得, compiled by Stephen Hsing-tao Yü (1974), x, 28pp. Paperbound. ISBN 0-89644-538-0.

21. *Neglected Formosa: A Translation from the Dutch of*

Frederic Coyett's 't Verwaerloosde Formosa, edited by Inez de Beauclair (1975), xviii, 207pp. ISBN 0-89644-416-3.

22. Day, Clarence Burton, *Peasant Cults in India* (1975), xviii, 126pp. ISBN 0-89644-421-X.

23. Biggerstaff, Knight, *Some Early Chinese Steps Toward Modernization* (1975), vii, 107pp. ISBN 0-89644-417-1.

24. Taylor, Romeyn, *Basic Annals of Ming T'ai-tsu* (1975), vi, 212pp. ISBN 0-89644-433-3.

25. Wang, Sing-wu, *The Organization of Chinese Emigration, 1848-1888* (1978), xviii, 436pp. ISBN 0-89644-480-5.

26. Chiang, Kuei, *The Whirlwind,* translated by Timothy A. Ross (1977), frontis., x, 558pp. ISBN 0-89644-493-7.

27. Ch'en, Ku-ying 陳鼓應, *Lao Tzu: Text, Notes, and Comments,* translated and adapted by Rhett Y.W. Young 楊有維 and Roger T. Ames (1977), viii, 341pp. ISBN 0-89644-520-8.

28. *A Catalog of Kuang-tung Land Records in the Taiwan Branch of the National Central Library,* compiled by Taiwan Branch of the National Central Library, with an introduction by Roy Hofheinze, Jr. (1975), xxvii, 77pp. ISBN 0-89644-439-2.

29. *Studia Asiatica: Essays in Asian Studies in Felicitation of the Seventy-fifth Anniversary of Professor Ch'en Shou-yi,* edited by Laurence G. Thompson (1975), xxvii, 485pp. ISBN 0-89644-476-7.

30. Day, Clarence Burton, *Popular Religion in Pre-Communist China* (1975), viii, 102pp. ISBN 0-89644-422-8.

31. Cohen, Alvin P., *Grammar Notes for Introductory Classical Chinese* (1975), 58pp. ISBN 0-89644-419-8.

32. *A Union List of Chinese Periodicals in Universities and Colleges in Taiwan* 中華民國台灣地區大專院校中期刊聯合目錄 , compiled by William Ju 諸家畯 (1976), xvii, 580pp. ISBN 0-89644-539-9.

33. *Papers in Honor of Professor Woodbridge Bingham: A*

Festschrift for his Seventy-fifth Birthday, edited by James B. Parsons (1976), xvi, 286pp. ISBN 0-89644-466-X.

34. *Concordances and Indexes to Chinese Texts,* compiled by D. L. McMullen (1975), x, 204pp. ISBN 0-89644-427-9.

35. Shih, Shu-ch'ing, *The Barren Years and Other Short Stories and Plays* (1976), vii, 255pp. ISBN 0-89644-473-2.

36. Day, Clarence Burton, *The Indian Interlude* (1977), x, 151pp. 16 pages of photos. ISBN 0-89644-500-3.

37. Day, Clarence Burton, *The Birth Pangs of Pakistan* (1977), viii, 141pp. ISBN 0-89644-498-8.

38. Donner, Frederick W., Jr., comp., *A Preliminary Glossary of Chinese Linguistic Terminology* (1977), x, 117pp. ISBN 0-89644-521-6.

39. Reinecke, John E., *Feigned Necessity: Hawaii's Attempt to Obtain Chinese Contract Labor, 1921-1923* (1979), xviii, 697pp. ISBN 0-89644-572-0

40. Gates, Alan Frederick, *Christianity and Animism in Taiwan* (1979), X, 262pp., 4 photos., 3 fig. ISBN 0-89644-573-9

CHINESE MATERIALS AND RESEARCH AIDS
SERVICE CENTER

RESEARCH AIDS SERIES

Robert L. Irick, General Editor

1. *A Classified Index to Articles on Fiscal Policy (1945-65)* 財政論文分類索引, compiled by Frank K. S. Yüan 袁坤祥 and Ma Ching-hsien 馬景賢 (1967), xxxvi, 303pp. ISBN 0-89644-540-2.
2. *A Classified Index to Articles on Economics (1945-65)* 經濟論文分類索引, compiled by Frank K. S. Yüan 袁坤祥 and Ma Ching-hsien 馬景賢 (1967), 2 vols., ciii, (1), 1-792pp. + iii, (1), 793-1,742pp. ISBN 0-89644-541-0.
3. *A Classified Index to Articles on Money and Banking (1945-65)* 貨幣金融論文分類索引, compiled by Frank K. S. Yüan 袁坤祥 and Ma Ching-hsien 馬景賢 (1967), xliii, 329pp. ISBN 0-89644-542-9.
4. *A Concordance to the Poems of Li Ho (790-816)* 李賀詩引得, compiled by Robert L. Irick 艾文博 (1969), xlii, 217pp. ISBN 0-89644-543-7.
5. *A Chinese-Mongolian Dictionary* 漢蒙字典, compiled by Harnod Hakanchulu 哈勘楚倫 (1969), lxxviii, 1,536pp. ISBN 0-89644-544-5.
6. *A Typeset Edition of the Diary of Weng T'ung-ho with Index* 翁同龢日記排印本附索引, edited by Chao Chung-fu 趙中孚 (1970). Text in 5 vols., 5, 1-524pp. + 525-993pp. + 995-1,522pp. + 1,523-2,002pp. + 2,003-2,448pp. Index to be announced. ISBN 0-89644-545-3.

7. *Title and Author Index to* Ts'ung-shu *in Taiwan Libraries* 臺灣各圖書館現存叢書子目索引, compiled by Wang Pao-hsien 王寶先. Part I: Title Index, 2 vols. (1976), xxi, 868pp. + ii, 740pp. Part II: Author Index (1977), xii, 190pp. ISBN 0-89644-546-1.

8. *A Typeset Edition of the* Tu-li ts'un-i 讀例存疑重刊本, edited by Huang Tsing-chia 黃靜嘉 (1970), 5 vols., 1-262pp. + 4, 1-372pp. + 2, 373-699pp. + 2, 701-1,025pp. + 2, 1,027-1,357pp. ISBN 0-89644-547-X.

9. *A Concordance to the* Kuan-tzu 管子引得, compiled by Wallace Johnson 莊爲斯 (1970), lxxviii, 1,188pp. ISBN 0-89644-548-8.

10. *Index to the Ho Collection of Twenty-Eight* Shih-hua 索引本何氏歷代詩話, compiled by Helmut Martin 馬漢茂 (1973), 2 vols.: vol. 1, xviii, 533pp.; vol. 2, 1, 860pp. ISBN 0-89644-549-6.

11. *A Concordance to the* Kuo-yü 國語引得, compiled by Wolfgang Bauer 包吾剛 (1973), 2 vols.: vol. 1, xlii, 808pp.; vol. 2, iv, 486pp. ISBN 0-89644-550-X.

12. *A Concordance to the* Jen-wu Chih *with a Text* 人物志引得, compiled by Wolfgang Bauer 包吾剛 (1974), xvi, 240pp. ISBN 0-89644-551-8.

13. *A Concordance to* Han-fei Tzu 韓非子引得, compiled by Wallace Johnson 莊爲斯 (1975), xxxix, 978pp. ISBN 0-89644-552-6.

14. *A Concordance to the Poems of Wei Ying-wu* 韋應物詩注引得, compiled by Thomas P. Nielson (1976), lxxii, 220pp. ISBN 0-89644-553-4.

15. *An Index to Sung Dynasty Titles Extant in* Ts'ung-shu 叢書示引宋文子目, compiled by Brian E. McKnight (1977), xii, 373pp. ISBN 0-89644-554-2.

16. *An Annotated Guide to Documents on Sino-Japanese-Korean Relations in the Late Ch'ing Dynasty* 清季中日韓關係資料卅種綜合分類目錄, compiled by Li Yü-shu 李毓澍 (1977),

2 vols., xxxii, 1-699pp. + xxxii, 701-1,169pp. ISBN 0-89644-555-0.

17. *Modern Japanese Authors in Area Studies: A Namelist,* compiled by Austin C. W. Shu (1978), xii, 151pp. ISBN 0-89644-517-8.

IN PREPARATION

"A Index to Diplomatic Documents of the Late Ch'ing Dynasty (1875-1911) 清季外交史料引得," compiled by Robert L. Irick 艾文博.

"Index to Chinese Terms in the English Translations of Henry Doré, *Researches into Chinese Superstitions,* vols. 1-10 and 13," compiled by Anne S. Goodrich.

"Chinese Names of Foreigners in China," edited by Robert L. Irick 艾文博 and Linda Marks.

"Taiwan Publications, 1964-1974: An Index by Subject, Author, and Title to New Works and Reprints appearing in CMRASC Booklists," edited by Robert L. Irick.

**CHINESE MATERIALS AND RESEARCH AIDS
SERVICE CENTER**

BIBLIOGRAPHICAL AIDS SERIES

Robert L. Irick, General Editor

1. *A Checklist of Reference Works in Teng and Biggerstaff Now Available in Taiwan* (1970), 2, 33pp. Paperbound. ISBN 0-89644-199-7.
2. Lei Shu: *Old Chinese Reference Works and a Checklist of Cited Titles Available in Taiwan,* compiled by Austin C. W. Shu (1973), xvii, 37pp. Paperbound. ISBN 0-89644-527-5.
3. *A Descriptive Catalog of the Ming Editions in the Far Eastern Library of the University of Washington,* compiled Chikfong Lee (1975), xvii, 53pp. Paperbound. ISBN 0-89644-425-2.
4. *Chinese Folk Narratives: A Bibliographical Guide,* compiled by Nai-tung Ting and Lee-hsia Hsü Ting (1975), xiii, 68pp. Paperbound. ISBN 0-89644-434-1.

SERIES COMPLETED

CHINESE MATERIALS CENTER

REPRINT SERIES

1. Lewis, Ida Belle, *The Education of Girls in China* (San Francisco: CMC, 1974; Repr. of New York: Teachers College, Columbia University, 1919), (xii), 92pp., 1 folding map.
2. Beal, Samuel, intro. and tr., *The Life of Hiuen-Tsiang by the Shaman Hwui Li* (San Francisco: CMC, 1974; Repr. of London: Kegan, Paul, Trench, Trübner & Co., 1911), (ii), xlviii, 218pp.
3. Giles, Herbert A., tr., *Strange Stories from a Chinese Studio* (San Francisco: CMC, 1974; Repr. of London: T. Werner Laurie, 1916), (ii), xxiv, 488pp.
4. Morse, H.B., *In the Days of the Taipings* (San Francisco: CMC, 1974; Repr. of Salem: The Essex Institute, 1927), frontis., (iv), xiv, 434pp.
5. Howard, Harvey J., *Ten Weeks with Chinese Bandits* (San Francisco: CMC, 1974; Repr. of New York: Dodd, Mead and Company, 1927), frontis., (ii), xxxiv, 399pp., 1 folding map.
6. Hall, W.H. & W.D. Bernard, *The Nemesis in China* (San Francisco: CMC, 1974; Repr. of London: Henry Colburn, 1847), (iv), xvi, 272pp.
7. Thomson, John, *Through China with a Camera* (San Francisco: CMC, 1974; Repr. of Westminister: A. Constable & Co., 1898), (ii), xiv, 284pp.
8. Duyvendak, J.J.L., tr. and ed., *The Book of Lord Shang* (San Francisco: CMC, 1974; Repr. of London: Arthur Probstain, 1928), (ii), xvi, 346pp.
9. Kerr, John Glasgow, *A Guide to the City and Suburbs of Canton* (San Francisco: CMC, 1974; Repr. of Hong Kong: Kelly and Walsh, 1918), viii, 103pp. 1 folding map.

10. Grey, John Henry, *Walks in the City of Canton* (San Francisco: CMC, 1974; Repr. of Hong Kong: De Souza & Co., 1875), (vi), vi, 695, lxipp.

11. des Rotours, Robert, *Traité des fonctionnaires et Traité de l'Armée* (San Francisco: CMC, 1974; Repr. of 2nd ed.— revised and corrected [Leiden: E.J. Brill, 1948]), cxx, 499 + (iv), 594 (ii)pp., 9 folding maps, 1 folding chart, 2 v.

12. Burns, Islay, *Memoir of the Reverend William C. Burns, M. A., Missionary to China from the English Presbyterian Church* (San Francisco: CMC, 1975; Repr. of New York: Robert Carter and Brothers, 1870), (viii), viii, 595pp.

13. *Report of the Advisory Committee Together with Other Documents Respecting the Chinese Indemnity* (San Francisco: CMC, 1975; Repr. of London: Her Majesty's Stationery Office, 1926), (ii), 197pp.

14. *Report of the Commission of Extraterritoriality in China* (San Francisco: CMC, 1975; Repr. of London: His Majesty's Stationery Office, 1926), (ii), 130pp.

15. Beale, Louis & G. Clinton, *Trade and Economic Conditions in China, 1931-1933, Together with an Annex on Trading Conditions in Manchuria* (San Francisco: CMC, 1975; Repr. of London: His Majesty's Stationery Office, 1933), (ii), 174pp., 1 folding map.

16. *Report on the Trade of Central and Southern China* (San Francisco: CMC, 1975; Repr. of London: His Majesty's Stationery Office, 1898), (ii), 99pp.

17. *Papers Relating to the Riot in Canton in July 1846 and to the Proceedings Against Mr. Compton, a British Subject, for His Participation in That Riot* (San Francisco: CMC, 1975; Repr. of London: T.R. Harrison, 1847), (ii), vi, 130pp.

18. *Correspondence Respecting Insults in China* (San Francisco: CMC, 1975; Repr. of London: Harrison and Sons, 1857), (ii), viii, 228pp.

19. *Correspondence Respecting Anti-foreign Riots in China,*

1891-1892 (San Francisco: CMC, 1975; Repr. of London: Her Majesty's Stationery Office, 1891), (iv), 176pp.

20. *Correspondence Respecting the Attack on British Protestant Missionaries at Yang-chow-foo, August 1868* (San Francisco: CMC, 1975; Repr. of London: Harrison and Sons, 1869), (ii), iv, 78, (4) 18pp.

21. *Correspondence Respecting the Attack on the Indian Expedition to Western China, and the Murder of Mr. Margary* (San Francisco: CMC, 1975; Repr. of London: Harrison and Sons, 1876, 1877), (ii), iv, 148pp.

22. *Papers Relating to the Rebellion in China and Trade in the Yang-tze-kiang River* (San Francisco: CMC, 1975; Repr. of London: Harrison and Sons, 1862), (ii), iv, 158pp. 1 folding map.

23. *Further Papers Relating to the Rebellion in China* (San Francisco: CMC, 1975; Repr. of London: Harrison and Sons, 1863), (iv), 196pp.

24. Hamberg, Theodore, *The Visions of Hung-siu-tshuen and Origin of the Kwang-si Insurrection* (San Francisco: CMC, 1975; Repr. of Hong Kong: China Mail Office, 1854), (iv), vi, 63, (i), xiipp.

25. *Foreign Relations of the United States, 1901: Affairs in China. Report of William W. Rockhill, Late Commissioner to China, with Accompanying Documents* (San Francisco: CMC, 1975; Repr. of China reprint edition, 1941), (ii), 391pp.

26. *Correspondence Respecting the Revision of the Treaty of Tien-tsin* (San Francisco: CMC, 1975; Repr. of London: Harrison and Sons, 1871), (ii), viii, 467pp.

27. Allman, Norwood F., *Handbook on the Protection of Trade-marks, Patents, Copyrights, and Trade-names in China* (San Francisco: CMC, 1975; Repr. of Shanghai: Kelly & Walsh, 1924), (vi), iv, 207, 5pp.

28. Hsia, Ching-lin, *Studies in Chinese Diplomatic History* (San

Francisco: CMC, 1975; Repr. of Shanghai: Commercial Press, 1925), (ii) xii, 266, 4pp.

29. Song Ong Siang, *One Hundred Years' History of the Chinese in Singapore; Being a Chronological Record of the Contribution by the Chinese Community to the Development, Progress and Prosperity of Singapore; of Events and Incidents Concerning the Whole or Sections of That Community and of the Lives, Pursuits and Public Service of Individual Members Thereof from the Foundation of Singapore on 6th February 1919* (San Francisco: CMC, 1975; Repr. of London: John Murray, 1923), (iv), xxii, 602pp.

30. Sargent, A.J., *Anglo-Chinese Commerce and Diplomacy (Mainly in the Nineteenth Century)* (San Francisco: CMC, 1975; Repr. of Oxford: Clarendon Press, 1907), frontis., xii, 332pp.

31. Rasmussen, O.D., *What's Right with China: An Answer to Foreign Criticisms* (San Francisco: CMC, 1975; Repr. of Shanghai: Commercial Press, 1927), (ii), xx, 255pp.

32. Soothill, W.E., *China and the West: A Sketch of Their Intercourse* (San Francisco: CMC, 1975; Repr. of London: Humphrey Milford, 1925), frontis., (iv), viii, 216pp.

33. Arnold, Jolean, et al., *Commercial Handbook of China* (San Francisco: CMC, 1975; Repr. of US Dept. of Commerce, Bureau of Foreign and Domestic Commerce, Miscellaneous Series No. 84 [Washington: Government Printing Office, 1919]), frontis., (ii), 630pp., 2 folding maps. + frontis., (ii) 470pp. 2v.

34. *Further Correspondence Respecting the Disturbances in China,* China No. 1, 5 & 6 (San Francisco: CMC, 1975; Repr. of London: His Majesty's Stationery Office, 1901), (ii), xxiv, 200 + (ii), xvi, 162 + xiv, 175pp. For the first volume of documents on this subject, see no. 90.

35. *Correspondence Relative to the Earl of Elgin's Special Missions to China and Japan, 1857-1859* (San Francisco: CMC, 1975; Repr. of London: Harrison and Sons, 1859), (ii),

xii, 488pp.

36. Legge, James, tr., *A Record of Buddhistic Kingdoms: Being an Account by the Chinese Monk Fa-Hien of His Travels in India and Ceylon (A.D. 399-414) in Search of the Buddhist Books of Discipline* (San Francisco: CMC, 1975; Repr. of Oxford: Clarendon Press, 1886), (iv), vx, (i), 123, (45)pp., 1 folding map.

37. Tucci, G., *On Some Aspects of the Doctrines of Maitreya [Nātha] and Asaṅga (Being a Course of Five Lectures Delivered at the University of Calcutta)* (San Francisco: CMC, 1975; Repr. of Calcutta: Univ. of Calcutta, 1930), (viii), 82, 2pp.

38. Watters, Thomas, *On Yuan Chwang's Travels in India, 629-645 A.D.* (San Francisco: CMC, 1975; Repr. of London: Royal Asiatic Society, 1904), (ii), xvi, 401 + vi, 357pp., 2 folding maps. 2v.

39. Nanjio, Bunyiu, *A Catalogue of the Chinese Buddhist Tripitaka: the Sacred Canon of the Buddhists in China and Japan* (San Francisco: CMC, 1975; Repr. of Oxford: Clarendon Press, 1893), xxxvi, 480 columns.

40. Beal, Samuel, *Si-yu-ki: Buddhist Records of the Western World; Translated from the Chinese of Hiuen Tsiang (A.D. 629)* (San Francisco: CMC, 1976; Repr. of London: Kegan Paul, Trench, Trübner & Co., n.d.), (ii), cxii, 242 + viii, 369pp. 2v. in 1.

41. Rockhill, W. Woodville, tr., *The Life of the Buddha and the Early History of His Order; Derived from Tibetan Works in the* Bkah-Hgyur *and* Bstan-Hgyur; *Followed by Notices on the Early History of Tibet and Khoten* (San Francisco: CMC, 1976; Repr. of London: Kegan Paul, Trench, Trübner & Co., Introduction dated June 1884), xii, 273pp.

42. Edkins, Joseph, *Chinese Buddhism: A Volume of Sketches, Historical, Descriptive, and Critical* (San Francisco: CMC, 1976; Repr. of Trübner's Oriental Series, 2nd rev. ed.

[London: Kegan Paul, Trench, Trübner, & Co., 1893]), (ii), xxxiv, 453pp.

43. Grousset, Réné, *In the Footsteps of the Buddha,* tr. from the French by Mariette Leon (San Francisco: CMC, 1976; Repr. of London: George Routledge & Sons, 1932), (ii), xii, 352pp., 2 folding maps.

44. Mateer, A.H., *Siege Days: Personal Experiences of American Women and Children During the Peking Siege* (San Francisco: CMC, 1976; Repr. of New York: Fleming H. Revell Co., 1903), (ii), 411pp.

45. Eitel, Ernest J., *Hand-book of Chinese Buddhism; Being a Sanskrit-Chinese Dictionary with Vocabularies of Buddhist Terms in Pali, Singhalese, Siamese, Burmese, Tibetan, Mongolian and Japanese* (San Francisco: CMC, 1976; Repr. of 2nd rev. and enl. ed. [Tokyo: Sanshusha, 1904]), (x), 324pp.

46. Suzuki, Teitaro, *Acvaghosha's Discourse on the Awakening of Faith in the Mathâyâna* 大乘起信論 (San Francisco: CMC, 1976; Repr. of Chicago: Open Court Publishing Co., 1900), (ii), xviii, 160pp.

47. Taam, Cheuk-Woon 譚卓垣, *The Development of Chinese Libraries under the Ch'ing Dynasty, 1644-1911* 清代圖書館 發展史 (San Francisco: CMC, 1977· Repr. of Shanghai, 1935), ix, 107pp.

48. Johnston, Reginald Fleming, *Buddhist China* (San Francisco: CMC, 1976; Repr. of London: John Murray, 1913), (vi), xviii, 403pp.

49. des Rotours, Robert, *Le Traité des Examens, Traduit de la Nouvelle Histoire des T'ang (Chap. XLIV, XLV)* (San Francisco: CMC, 1976; Repr. of 2nd ed.—revised and corrected [Paris: Librairie Ernest Leroux, 1932]), (ii), xii, 417pp.

50. Tucci, Giuseppe, *Pre-Dinnāga Buddhist Texts on Logic from Chinese Sources* (San Francisco: CMC, 1976; Repr. of

Gaekwad's Oriental Series No. XLIX [Baroda: Oriental Institute, 1929]), (viii), xxx, 338pp.

51. Tucci, Giuseppe, *The Nyāyamukha of Dignāga, the Oldest Buddhist Text on Logic, After Chinese and Tibetan Materials* (San Francisco: CMC, 1976; Repr. of Heidelberg: O. Harrassowitz, 1930), (vi), 72pp.

52. Rosenberg, Otto, *Die Probleme der Buddhistischen Philosophie*, tr. by E. Rosenberg (San Francisco: CMC, 1976; Repr. of Heidelberg: O. Harrassowitz, 1924), (ii) xvi, 287pp.

53. Kitayama, Junyu, *Metaphysik des Buddhismus, Versuch Einer Philosophischen Interpretation der Lehre Vasubandhus und Seiner Schule* (San Francisco: CMÇ, 1976; Repr. of Stuttgart, Berlin: Verlag Von W. Kohlhammer, 1934), (ii), xvi, 268pp.

54. Waldschmidt, Ernst, *Gandhara Kutscha Turfan, Eine Einführung in die Frühmittelalterliche Kunst Zentralasiens* (San Francisco: CMC, 1976; Repr. of Leipzig: Klinkhardt & Biermann, 1925), (ii), 116pp., 66 pages of photos.

55. Sōgen, Yamakami, *Systems of Buddhistic Thought* (San Francisco: CMC, 1976; Repr. of Calcutta: University of Calcutta, 1912), (ii), xx, 316, xxxvipp.

56. von Zach, E., tr., *Yang Hsiung's* Fa-yen *(Worte Strenger Ermahnung) ein Philosophischer Traktat aus dem Beginn der Christlichen Zeitrechnung* (San Francisco: CMC, 1976; Repr. of Sinologische Beiträge IV [Batavia: Drukkerij Lux, 1939]), (viii), 74pp.

57. Pfister, Louis, *Notices Biographiques et Bibliographiques sur les Jesuites de l'Ancienne Mission de Chine, 1552-1773* (San Francisco: CMC, 1976; Repr. of Variétés Sinologiques Nos. 59 & 60 [Shanghai: Imprimerie de la Mission Catholique, 1932, 1934]), (vi), xxvi, 561, 6 + (vi), x, 547, 38pp. 2v. in 1.

58. Beal, Samuel, tr., *Texts from the Buddhist Canon, Commonly Known as Dhammapada, with Accompanying Nar-*

ratives (San Francisco: CMC, 1977; Repr. of Boston: Houghton, Osgood & Co., 1878), (iv), viii, 176pp.

59. Nyanatiloka, *Buddhist Dictionary: Manual of Buddhist Terms and Doctrines* (San Francisco: CMC, 1977; Repr. of Island Hermitage Publication No. 1 [Colombo: Frewin & Co., 1950]), (vi), vi, 190pp., 1 folding diagram.

60. McGovern, William Montgomery, *A Manual of Buddhist Philosophy, Vol. I Cosmology* (San Francisco: CMC, 1977; Repr. of London: Kegan Paul, Trench, Trübner & Co., New York: E.P. Dutton & Co., 1923), (x), 205pp.

61. Soothill, W.E. *The Lotus of the Wonderful Law or the Lotus Gospel: Saddharma Pundarika Sūtra, Miao-fa Lien Hua Ching* (San Francisco: CMC, 1977; Repr. of Oxford: Clarendon Press: 1930), frontis., (ii), xii, 275pp.

62. Herrmann, Albert, *Die Alten Seidenstraßen Zwischen China und Syrien: Beiträge zur Alten Geographie Asiens, I. Abteilung, Einleitung, die Chinesischen Quellen, Zentralasien nach Ssě-ma Ts^cien und den Annalen der Han-Dynastie* (San Francisco: CMC, 1977; Repr. of Berlin: Weidmannsche Buchhandlung: 1910), (ii), viii, 130pp., 1 folding map.

63. Wilson, Andrew, *The "Even-Victorious Army": A History of the Chinese Campaign under Lt.-Col. G. G. Gordon, C. B. R. E., and of the Suppression of the Tai-Ping Rebellion. A Reprint Edition with Marginal Notes by Capt. John Holland* (San Francisco: CMC, 1977; Repr. of Edinburgh & London: William Blackwood and Sons: 1868), (vi), xxxii, 396 + 397-410pp., 1 folding map.

64. Ui, H., *The Vaiśesika Philosophy According to the Daśapa-dārtha-Sāstra: Chinese Text, with Introduction, Translation, and Notes,* ed. by F. W. Thomas (San Francisco: CMC, 1977; Repr. of Oriental Translation Fund, New Series Vol. xxiv [London: Royal Asiatic Society: 1917]), (iv), xii, 265pp.

65. Waddell, L. Austine, *The Buddhism of Tibet or Lamaism,*

with Its Mystic Cults, Symbolism and Mythology, and in Its Relation to Indian Buddhism (San Francisco: CMC, 1977; Repr. of London: W.H. Allen & Co., 1895), frontis., (ii), xx, 598pp.

66. Medhurst, W.H., *The Foreigner in Far Cathay* (San Francisco: CMC, 1977; Repr. of London: Edward Stanford, 1872), (xii), 192pp., 1 map.

67. Dennys, N.B., ed., *The Treaty Ports of China and Japan: A Complete Guide to the Open Ports of Those Countries, Together with Peking, Yedo, Hongkong, and Macao, Forming a Guide Books & Vade Mecum for Travellers, Merchants, and Residents in General* (San Francisco: CMC, 1977; Repr. of London: Trübner and Co., 1867), (iv), viii, (2), 668pp., x1, 26 appendixes, 24 folding maps, 4 maps, 1 diagram.

68. Der Ling, Princess, *Two Years in the Forbidden City* (San Francisco: CMC, 1977; Repr. of New York: Moffat, Yard & Co., 1912), frontis., (ii), ix, (5) 383pp., 17 pl.

69. Broomhall, Marshall, *The Bible in China* (San Francisco: CMC, 1977; Repr. of London: The Religious Tract Society, 1934), (vi), xvi, 190, (2)pp.

70. Bryson, Mary F., *John Kenneth Mackenzie, Medical Missionary to China* (San Francisco: CMC, 1977; Repr. of London: Hodder & Stoughton, 1891), frontis., (iv), xv, (1), 404pp.

71. Stauffer, Milton T., *The Christian Occupation of China: A General Survey of the Numerical Strength and Geographical Distributon[sic] of the Christian Forces in China, Made by the Special Committee on Survey and Occupation, China Continuation Committee, 1918-1921* (San Francisco: CMC, 1977; Repr. of Shanghai: China Continuation Committee, 1922), (vi), 14, 469, cxiipp.

72. MacGillivray, D., *A Century of Protestant Missions in China (1807-1907), Being the Centenary Conference Historical Volume* (San Francisco: CMC, 1977; Repr. of Shanghai:

American Presbyterian Mission Press, 1907), (iv), viii, 678, xl, 52pp., 1 map.

73. *Musings of a Chinese Mystic: Selections from the Philosophy of Chuang Tzu,* with an Introduction by Lionel Giles (San Francisco: CMC, 1977; Repr. of the Wisdom of the East Series [London: John Murray, n.d.]), (ii), 112pp.

74. Mullie, Jos., *The Structural Principles of the Chinese Language, An Introduction to the Spoken Language (Northern Pekingese Dialect),* tr. by A. Omer Versichel (San Francisco: CMC, 1977; Repr. of Peiping: the Bureau of Engraving & Printing, 1932), (viii), xxxiv, 566, (2)pp., 1 chart. + (viii), 691, (2) pp. 2v.

75. Guinness, M. Geraldine, *The Story of the China Inland Mission* (San Francisco: CMC, 1977; Repr. of London: Morgan & Scott, 1897, 1900), frontis., (iv), xviii, 476pp., 1 folding map. + (iv), xii, 512pp., 1 folding map. 2v.

76. Broomhall, Marshall, *The Jubilee Story of the China Inland Mission, with Portraits, Illustrations & Map* (San Francisco: CMC, 1977; Repr. of London: Morgan & Scott, 1915), frontis., (iv), xvi, 386pp., 1 folding map.

77. De Groot, J.J.M., *Les Fêtes Annuellement Célébrées à Émoui (Amoy), Étude Concernant la Religion Populaire des Chinois,* tr. by C. G. Chavannes, Annales du Musée Guimet Tome Douzième, with a new Introduction by Inez de Beauclair and Harvey Molé (San Francisco: CMC, 1977; Repr. of Paris: Ernest Leroux, Editeur, 1886), frontis., xxiv, xxvi, 400pp. + frontis., (iv), vi, 401-832pp., 24 illus. 2v.

78. Hedin, Sven, *Across the Gobi Desert,* tr. H. J. Cant (San Francisco: CMC, 1977; Repr. of New York: E. P. Dutton & Company, 1932), frontis., (iv), 402pp., 114 illus., 1 map, 2 folding maps.

79. Johnson, Samuel, *Oriental Religions and Their Relation to Universal Religion: China* (San Francisco: CMC, 1978; Repr. of Boston: James R. Osgood & Co., 1877), (iv), xxiv, 975pp.

80. Sirr, Henry Charles, *China and the Chinese: Their Religion, Character, Customs, and Manufactures: The Evils Arising from the Opium Trade: with A Glance at Our Religious, Moral, Political, and Commercial Intercourse with the Country* (San Francisco: CMC, 1978; Repr. of London: Wm. S. Orr & Co., 1849), frontis., (iv), xvi, 448pp. + frontis., (iv), viii, 443pp. 2v.

81. *List of the Higher Metropolitan and Provincial Authorities of China, Corrected to December 31st 1885* (San Francisco: CMC, 1978; Repr. of Peking: Pei-t'ang Press, 1886), (iv), 20pp.

82. Mayers, S.F., *List of the Higher Metropolitan and Provincial Authorities of China (with Generalogical Table of the Imperial Family), Compiled by the Chinese Secretaries, H.B.M. Legation, Peking, Corrected to June 1st, 1907* (San Francisco: CMC, 1978; Repr. of Shanghai: Kelly and Walsh, 1907), folding chart, (x), 50pp.

83. *Who's Who of American Returned Students* 遊美同學錄 (San Francisco: CMC, 1978; Repr. of Peking: Tsing Hua College, 1917), (vii), v, viii, vi, 215, iv, ivpp.

84. Mackie, J. Milton, *Life of Tai-ping-wang, Chief of the Chinese Insurrection* (San Francisco: CMC, 1978; Repr. of New York: Dix, Edwares & Co., 1857), frontis., (ii), xii, 371pp.

85. Gillis, I.V. and Yü Ping-yüeh, comp., *Supplementary Index to Giles' "Chinese Biographical Dictionary"* (San Francisco: CMC, 1978; Repr. of Peiping: 1936), (viii), 86pp.

86. Löwenthal, Rudolf, *The Religious Periodical Press in China*, with 7 maps and 16 charts. (San Francisco: CMC, 1978; Repr. of Sinological Series No. 57 [Peking: The Synodal Commission in China, 1940]), (viii), vi, 294pp.

87. *Who's Who in the Far East, 1906-7 June* (San Francisco: CMC, 1979; Repr. of London: Japan Press), (viii), 352, (56)pp.

88. *Who's Who in the Far East, 1907-8 June* (San Francisco: CMC, 1979; Repr. of Hong Kong: China Mail), (xxxviii), 352, (24) pp.

89. Cordier, M. Henri, *L'Imprimerie Sino-Européenne en Chine, Bibliographie des Ouvrages Publiés en Chine par les Européens Au XVIIE et au XVIIIE Siècle* (San Francisco: CMC, 1979; Repr. of Paris: Imprimerie Nationale, 1901), (iv), x, 76, 32, (24)pp. 3 foldings.

90. *Correspondence Respecting the Insurrectionary Movement in China, Presented to Both Houses of Parliament by Command of Her Majesty, July 1900,* China No. 3 (San Francisco: CMC, 1979; Repr. of London: Her Majesty's Stationery Office, 1900), (iv), xvi, 115pp. For the second, third, and fourth volumes of documents on this subject, see no. 34.

CHINESE MATERIALS CENTER

ASIAN LIBRARY SERIES

Robert L. Irick, General Editor

1. *Translations from Po Chü-i's Collected Works: III, Regulated and Patterned Poems of Middle Age (822-832)*, translated and described by Howard S. Levy, rendered by Henry W. Wells (1976), xxxiv, 215pp. ISBN 0-89644-463-5.
2. *Translations from Po Chü-i's Collected Works: IV, The Later Years (833-846)*, translated and described by Howard S. Levy, rendered by Henry W. Wells (1978), li, 711pp. ISBN 0-89644-518-6.
3. Marney, John, *A Handbook of Modern Chinese Grammar* (1977), 78pp. Paperbound. ISBN 0-89644-464-3.
4. Wells, Henry W., tr., *Diary of a Pilgrim to Ise,* attributed to Saka Jūbutsu, with illustrations by Ch'eng Hsi (1977), xii, 135pp. Paperbound. ISBN 0-89644-501-1.
5. Teng Shou-hsin, *A Basic Course in Chinese Grammar: A Graded Approach through* Conversational Chinese (1977), xii, 135pp. Paperbound. ISBN 0-89644-502-X.
6. Carrington, George Williams, *Foreigners in Formosa, 1841-1874* (1977), frontis., map, index, xiv, 308pp. ISBN 0-89644-506-2.
7. Lee, Orlan, *Legal and Moral Systems in Asian Customary Law: The Legacy of the Buddhist Social Ethic and Buddhist Law* (1978), map, index, xxiv, 456pp. ISBN 0-89644-524-0.
8. Miao, Ronald C., ed., *Chinese Poetry and Poetics, Vol. 1* (1978), xiv, 375pp. ISBN 0-89644-525-9.

9. Sailey, Jay, *The Master Who Embraces Simplicity: A Study of the Chinese Philosopher, Ko Hung, A.D. 283-343* (1978), index, xxvi, 658pp. ISBN 0-89644-522-4.

10. Pruitt, Ida, *A China Childhood* (1978), xi, 205pp. ISBN 0-89644-523-2.

11. Kracke, Edward A., Jr., *Translations of Sung Civil Service Titles, Classification Terms, and Governmental Organ Names,* rev. ed. (1978), xiii, 35pp. ISBN 0-89644-526-7.

12. Lee, Yu-hwa, *The Last Rite and Other Stories* (1979), xviii, 303pp. ISBN 0-89644-574-7

IN PREPARATION

Shan-yüan Hsieh, "The Life and Thought of Li Kou, 1009-1059."

Robert L. Irick, "Ch'ing Policy Toward the Coolie Trade, 1847-1878."

Edward Gerald Martinique, "Chinese Traditional Book-binding: A Study of its Evolution and Techniques."

Arnold J. Meagher, "Introduction of Chinese Laborers to Latin America: The 'Coolie Trade,' 1847-1874."

Ronald C. Miao, "The Life and Lyric Poetry of Wang Ts'an, 177-217."

Constance Miller, "Technical and Cultural Prerequisites for the Invention of Printing in China and the West."

Shiow-jyu Lu Shaw, "The Imperial Printing of Early Ch'ing China, 1644-1805."

Paul Vander Meer, "Farm-plot Dispersal: Lu-liao Village, Taiwan, 1967."

CHINESE MATERIALS CENTER

RESEARCH AIDS SERIES

Robert L. Irick, General Editor

1. *Research Guide to the* Chiao-hui hsin-pao ("The Church News"), *1868-1874* 教會新報目錄導要 , compiled by Adrian A. Bennett (1975), xviii, 342pp.   ISBN 0-89644-528-3.
2. *Research Guide to the* Wan-kuo kung-pao ("The Globe Magazine"), *1874-1883* 萬國公報目錄導要 , compiled by Adrian A. Bennett (1976), xvi, 519pp.   ISBN 0-89644-529-1.